FRANK MOORES
THE TIME OF HIS LIFE

FRANK
THE TIME OF HIS LIFE
MOORES

JANICE WELLS

KEY PORTER BOOKS

Library and Archives Canada Cataloguing in Publication

Wells, Janice, 1948–
    Frank Moores : the time of his life / Janice Wells.

ISBN 978-1-55263-786-9

    1. Moores, Frank D. (Frank Duff), 1933-2005. 2. Prime ministers—Newfoundland and Labrador—Biography. 3. Progressive Conservative Party of Newfoundland and Labrador—Biography. 4. Progressive Conservative Party of Canada—Biography. 5. Lobbyists—Canada—Biography. 6. Newfoundland and Labrador—Biography. I. Title.

FC2176.1.M66W44 2008   971.8'04092   C2008-902213-0

ONTARIO ARTS COUNCIL
CONSEIL DES ARTS DE L'ONTARIO

The publisher gratefully acknowledges the support of the Canada Council for the Arts and the Ontario Arts Council for its publishing program. We acknowledge the support of the Government of Ontario through the Ontario Media Development Corporation's Ontario Book Initiative.

We acknowledge the financial support of the Government of Canada through the Book Publishing Industry Development Program (BPIDP) for our publishing activities.

Key Porter Books Limited
Six Adelaide Street East, Tenth Floor
Toronto, Ontario
Canada M5C 1H6

www.keyporter.com

Text design: Marijke Friesen
Electronic formatting: Alison Carr
All photographs courtesy of the Moores family unless otherwise indicated.

Printed and bound in Canada

08 09 10 11 12 5 4 3 2 1

To Bill with love and gratitude

Contents

PREFACE

IN THE SPRING OF 2000 I was given a ticket to a Tory fundraising dinner. Frank Moores was the guest speaker. As I sat listening to the introductions outlining the accomplishments of his government, I kept thinking, I didn't know that, or I'd forgotten that, and it struck me that there had never been a book written about Frank Moores and his government. As a CBC television host in the seventies and as the wife of a Tory organizer, I'd known Frank Moores perhaps better than the average person, but I was taken aback to realize that I probably remembered him like most people: as a playboy first and a premier second.

I had no idea how to contact him, so I wrote to him in care of Craig Dobbin, expressing my feeling that a book should be written and that I'd like to do it, with Moores's cooperation, adding that I thought he knew he could rely on me to be fair. One day the phone rang. The caller was Frank, saying he'd be honoured to have me do it, but he wanted it to be a complete biography. With the exception of his second wife, Janis Johnson, I have enjoyed access to his family, friends, and colleagues, and I am the one who has been honoured with his and their trust.

I joined CBC television in Corner Brook as the host of a daily half-hour talk show a few weeks before Moores was first elected premier in October, 1971. My name then was Janice Jackson, and I was frequently confused with Janis Johnson. To cite only one instance, in late December, 1971, when the news leaked out that Moores and Janis Johnson were enjoying the Caribbean together, irate viewers called CBC station manager Dick O'Brien, demanding that the brazen hussy who was breaking up a family with seven children be taken off the air. O'Brien took pleasure in pointing out that, because I was actually on the air and it was a live show, they obviously had the wrong woman. Even so, I feel that the connection of my name with Frank Moores never did go away in many people's minds. As I hope will become clear in the course of this book, I never had any romantic link with him.

This project began as an authorized biography. For a number of health and personal reasons on both sides, four years passed before we really got started, and by that time, Frank was battling cancer. When it became impossible to complete the work with him, I relied on the observations and reflections of his peers for a significant perspective in presenting an authentic representation of both the man and the politician.

Frank Moores was a renaissance bayman, and my goal became to paint a portrait of who this extraordinary Newfoundlander was, not just what he did publicly. Still, much of interest in his life has been left out of this book, and many people who could have contributed were not contacted. Because this is a biography, the political years have not received the detailed attention I had first intended to give them. I leave to the political scientists, the economists, and the sociologists the pleasure of compiling a comprehensive inventory and analysis of reforms, policies, successes, and failures of the Moores government, and I fervently hope someone takes up the task.

I met with Frank Moores in December of 2004 when he was doing well with his cancer treatments and was optimistic about his prognosis. At that time I allowed him to tell his story without much challenge from my part because I wanted to go over his statements and compare them with my own research before engaging in further discussion. Due to unexpected circumstances I was unable to get back to him as soon as I'd planned. His prognosis changed in the spring, his condition worsened quickly and he died a week before our second session was to take place. I have presented his version of events as he told them.

Much of the material for this book came from personal interviews and newspaper records. Many thanks to everyone who graciously gave me their time, recollections, and opinions: Beth Moores, Dodie Lalor, Megan Nutbeem, Debbie Moores Stark, Tom Farrell, John Crosbie, Alex Hickman, Bill Marshall, Vic Young, Brian Peckford, John Lundrigan, Fred Stagg, Leo Barry, Charlie White, Eric Dawe, Ed Roberts, Craig Dobbin, George Hutchings, Ed Poole, Tom Marshall, Roy McMurtry, Bill Somers, Chris Wansbrough, Terry Malone, and Greg Alford. My apologies go to those who could have added richly to this book and did not get the opportunity.

It was a privilege to work with Frank Moores and to get to know his gracious wife and family. Special thanks go to Beth Moores and Vic Young for reviewing the early manuscript and sections of this book.

I am grateful to the late Dorothy Moores for saving every newspaper clipping and magazine article that concerned her son, mostly from the St. John's *Evening Telegram* and *Daily News* but also from the *Toronto Telegram*, *The Globe and Mail*, the *Ottawa Citizen*, the *Toronto Star*, the *National Post*, and *Maclean's*; as well, she saved invitations, letters, original documents, and copies. I owe thanks to Beth Moores, Stu Moores, Dodie Lalor, and Bill Marshall for photographs, to Charlie White for the loan of recording equipment and for photographs, and to Nancy Hitchens and Donna Pinhorn for the transcription of what were sometimes poor quality tapes. *The Globe and Mail* and the *Toronto Star* on-line provided comprehensive timelines for the Airbus affair. www.heritage.nf.ca is a valuable resource for information and links on Newfoundland and Labrador history, as is the Centre for Newfoundland

Studies at Memorial University in St. John's, the Newfoundland section of the A.C. Hunter Library, and the Newfoundland and Labrador Legislative Library.

I am extremely thankful to Memorial University economist Wade Locke for his efforts to calculate the value of the unconsummated deal with René Lévesque and to the J.R. Smallwood Foundation for the assistance of a research grant.

I am blessed with two wonderful and supportive sisters, Jocelyn Greene in St. John's and Karin Brown in Toronto. I am especially grateful to Karin for accompanying me to St. Andrew's College for Frank Moores's memorial service and for her unfailing hospitality.

My greatest debts are to Anna Porter, for her encouragement and friendship, and to my partner in life, Bill MacDonald. Without his confidence and support I would not be able to devote myself full-time to writing. I thank him for the title for this book and the intelligent and sharp objectivity that gave me the courage to follow my instincts on theories that, while unproven, are no more unproven than theories that have been presented as fact by elements of the Canadian press.

CHAPTER 1

July 14, 2005

THIRTY YEARS AFTER THE FACT, Frank Duff Moores, former premier, millionaire playboy, high-powered lobbyist, and subject of scandal, is now being called the 'father of democracy' by many in Newfoundland and Labrador. He was indeed all of those things, but in the end he was simply a passionate Newfoundlander who made a contribution and then did what countless thousands of other Newfoundlanders have done: left home to make a living, stayed where most of his children and grandchildren lived, and then returned home for his funeral. He would have felt he was in good company.

Cochrane Street United Church in old downtown St. John's is full. From my vantage point in the front row of the balcony, I turn over my own memories of Frank Moores, gaze down on the crowded pews, and wonder what others are thinking.

I look at Beth, his widow and third wife, trim and straight in a meticulously tailored black suit, hatless, paying rapt attention to every word. I wonder if she's thinking of the day, over twenty-five years ago, when Frank followed her to the airport in St. John's and stood tapping on the security glass, oblivious to his constituents staring at him, trying to convince her that she wouldn't be just another notch on his bedpost. Is she feeling a sense of relief that the strain of the past eighteen months of illness is over, feeling guilty about feeling relieved? Or have her thoughts already gone ahead, back to the empty house on the point in Chaffey's Lock, Ontario, without the life force that was Frank Moores, the husband to whom she was always "my girl."

I can't see Senator Janis Johnson, his tall, blonde second wife, but I know she's here. I wonder how she feels, excluded from sitting with the family while her son eulogizes his father. Maybe Janis is thinking of what she described to me as a "wild ride" and of the countless journals she kept about the man and his political life. Or is she, whom some have called the 'ice maiden,' thinking of the passion that was Frank Moores and regretting that she ever tried to tame him.

I look for Dodie, his first wife, the mother of seven of his children. Can she possibly be that tiny, delicate-looking woman leaning ever so slightly on one of his six daughters? Is she thinking of the eighteen-year-old with the flashing smile who lured her away from the University of Toronto to a small fishing town in Newfoundland? Perhaps she's reliving the golden years before politics, when Frank ran the family fish business and she raised the children, when money and friends were plentiful and she grew to love Newfoundland. And is she thinking how different her life might have been if her husband had never entered politics?

I wonder how many other women are here, like me, with personal memories of the famous smile and charm, and how many have more intimate memories than mine.

I see former Nova Scotia premier Gerry Regan. Is he thinking of Frank Moores's contributions at premiers' conferences? Perhaps he is recalling his own troubles with the opposite sex and musing that Frank was lucky not to get caught. I wonder if he understands that Frank Moores was too much a gentleman to harass anybody, that he was the pursued almost as often as the pursuer.

Is Danny Williams comparing the job he took on as Newfoundland's seventh premier to the one Moores took on as its second premier? Will Williams's victory over the federal government, giving Newfoundlanders and Labradorians the right to more benefits from their offshore resources, compare in history and importance to Moores's victory over Joey Smallwood, giving Newfoundlanders and Labradorians the right to dissent without fear? Is he thinking of all the legislation, taken for granted today, that brought about massive reform under Frank Moores? His wife and mother are next to him. I smile, wondering if the current Tory premier's mother is remembering how she danced on the first Tory premier's desk thirty-four years ago, the night he vanquished Joey Smallwood.

John Crosbie is looking a little frail. I wonder if he's thinking that, if not for Frank Moores, he might have been premier of Newfoundland. Is he remembering the clashes of will in and out of cabinet, or his frustration with Moores's laid-back approach to everything Crosbie approached intensely? Or has hindsight given him a different perspective on the man he described as lazy?

I recognize some union leaders and many civil servants. Do they know that the first strike in the history of the Newfoundland Association of Public Employees, which took place in 1973, could occur only because Frank Moores gave them the freedom to strike?

There's former premier and current Chief Justice Clyde Wells, an old political foe. Is he giving Moores any credit for all his sweeping legal reforms? Is he reflecting on the blame that was heaped on his administration for severely degrading the Moores administration's public tendering and public service commission advancements?

I look around for the three Brians. Brian Tobin is here, seated near the front. I wonder if he's comparing his political sense and timing with that of Frank Moores and feeling like an amateur. Brian Mulroney is not here, nor is Brian Peckford. Mulroney is recovering from a serious illness. I wonder if he would have come; does he regret cutting off Frank cold for so many years because of a perceived disloyalty? Peckford, I suspect, might not feel welcome at the funeral of the man he once served as executive assistant and minister to, succeeded as premier, and then disparaged. I wonder if his own less-than-distinguished exit from the premier's chair altered his perspective on Moores.

Frank's only sister Megan, looking very smart at almost eighty years old, has been assisted into the church, using a walker. Her mind must be full of memories of the little brother who called her Memo and could do no wrong in his mother's eyes. Megan is what Newfoundlanders call 'a character,' with her constant cigarette, ritual before-lunch martini, and slightly bawdy remarks. I reflect that a lust for life must have run in the Moores family.

Seated more or less together, more or less by political stripe, are past and present politicians, some of them in diapers during the crazy 1971-1972 election standoff. Can any of them imagine being offered a $50,000 bribe to change parties, or being whisked off to Panama on a private jet, or being set up in a Montreal whorehouse, or avoiding a plot to have him committed to a mental hospital? In their ignorance or innocence, are they remembering Frank's legend as a lady-killer without realizing that Frank Moores was also a giant-killer?

Premier Danny Williams speaks of how Moores's government policies and initiatives strengthened Newfoundland and Labrador. Close friends speak of his school years and the early years in Harbour Grace and in politics, and two of his children speak passionately about their father. It is the solemn, respectful stuff that funerals are made of, but the irreverent tales of Mike Ballentine, his roommate from St. Andrew's College, evokes Frank the legend, an early master at getting the girls. The greater the challenge the more masterful he became, promising much and prompting one wag to remind him that he couldn't marry them all. The chuckles from around the church seem like breaths being let out in relief that Frank Moores was being eulogized in death as he embraced life: with respect but with candour and humour.

Interspersed with the tributes are two songs perhaps unusual for the occasion, "Saltwater Joys" and "Song of Newfoundland." I think of the stirring sound of the bagpipes that began the service and the spiritual message of "Hear Me," sung by Frank's son-in-law Chris Hutton, and I muse about how there is no oddity in this combination. From the first haunting note of his beloved bagpipes, the air in the church has seemed saturated with the enigma of Frank Moores. I think of a recent remark by St. John's lawyer Charlie White, his old friend and one of his eulogizers: "Frank was remarkably misunderstood and understood, and all by the same people." I think about the family's amazement at the number of people at the wake who spoke of all the things Frank had done quietly for them and others. As I stand outside the church later, after the piped strains of "Amazing Grace" have faded, listening to the conversations of time-worn fishermen, retired hockey players, judges, and civil servants, I think that he probably *was* both misunderstood and understood, but with affection and by people from all walks of life.

The wives form distant points of a triangle in the crush outside the church. At the private Government House reception afterwards, I speak to Janis, who is standing alone, looking strained and shaky. Janis has crashed the invitation-only reception and is telling people that she is there representing the Senate. I see her tap Dodie on the shoulder and watch Dodie turn and call her Beth by mistake. I'm told it's the first time Dodie has spoken to Janis in over thirty years.

I make my way out to where the smokers have gathered on the veranda to speak to Beth. Beth, composed and dignified at the funeral home and church, is agitated now by Janis's presence in the inside room. Beth wants her purse, but getting it involves passing Janis, and Beth refuses to deal with Janis today. I offer to retrieve the purse. As I climb the stairs I think about my days with Frank and Beth when they each smoked in front of me and asked me not to tell the other. I think about my personal memories of Frank, his offering me a job, making the inevitable pass, and accepting rejection gracefully, and the liking that developed between us. I reflect on how I had instantly liked Beth when we first met almost twenty-five years ago, and how I was right when I thought they seemed really good together.

Then I realize that my favourite memory of this extraordinary man, who had hosted kings and con men, is a recent one, from when I stayed with them, beginning the process for this book. On the first night, Beth cooked a pork roast, surprising me by asking directions from Frank, who I didn't know was a gourmet cook, and we ate at the dining room table. On the second night I asked, "Where would you be eating if I wasn't here?" and she replied they'd be watching *Jeopardy*, eating from TV trays. And so we curled up in comfortable chairs in the living room with glasses of red wine and Frank's favourite dinner, shepherd's pie, and we matched wits along with *Jeopardy*. I do very well in *Jeopardy*, but Frank did better.

Beth told me about Frank's wish for a simple service in the little church in Elgin, Ontario, and about how Brian Tobin, in a phone call just a week before Frank died, had expressed his strong feeling that Frank should have a state funeral. When she brought it up to Frank, he was reluctant, saying "What if nobody comes? What if only fifty people show up?" And she laughed and said, "Frank, there are fifty of us."

I think about the extraordinary modesty of an outport Newfoundland boy who changed the course of history in his beloved province, who came to be called one of the most powerful men in Canada and to be considered by some as one of the most corrupt, who dined with queens and presidents but said Jack Joe Molloy from St. Shott's was the most interesting person he'd ever met, and I marvel at the man who was always liked by the women he discarded and the men he defeated. The man the old timers called a laddio and Joey Smallwood called Frankie Baby. Frank the giant-killer.

CHAPTER 2

There is No Peace

IN 2007, more than two years after he died, Frank Moores was in the news again. A German-Canadian businessman, Karlheinz Schreiber, whose name was well known to Canadians for his role in what was called the Airbus affair, was running out of time and options in his fight to avoid extradition to Germany to face criminal charges. His appeal having been denied, he had only a few weeks left before being put on a plane to Germany, where, he believed, he might well spend the rest of his life in jail. Schreiber needed to buy time, and being the star witness against a former prime minister in a probe by the House of Commons Ethics Committee and in a public inquiry commissioned by the Canadian government would give it to him.

Frank Moores and others whom he would include as central to his story were dead. Dead men can't testify, and in death Frank Moores was more important than ever to Karlheinz Schreiber. Later in this book, Frank Moores talks about his relationship with Karlheinz Schreiber and what is known as the Airbus affair. His version isn't sensational, but it may well be more accurate than anyone else's so far, and it is his only public explanation. Karlheinz Schreiber did not respond to several requests from me for an interview.

Since 2004, when the Ontario Superior Court ruled that Schreiber could be extradited to Germany and Liberal Justice Minister Irwin Cotler ordered his deportation, Karlheinz Schreiber had continued to fail in a series of bids to remain in Canada. At one point he was actually on a plane bound for Germany and was taken off at the last minute.

In January 2007 Karlheinz Schreiber's $1.3-million bail bond expired, and he was taken into custody by Canadian authorities. In February another appeal against extradition was rejected. With his freedom gone and his options running out, Schreiber sought a judicial review of the extradition order, based on comments made by a German judge. In March 2007 the Ontario court once again ordered Schreiber deported. Schreiber countered by launching a lawsuit against former prime minister Brian Mulroney for failing to provide any services for the $300,000 Schreiber claimed to have paid him after he left office. Schreiber's original contention was that he gave Mulroney the money because Mulroney needed it and Schreiber was a nice guy. Now he was claiming that Mulroney was to have helped him establish a factory to build light armoured vehicles for a European company, Thyssen AG, and to have promoted Schreiber's pasta business.

In May Schreiber wrote to the former prime minister threatening, among other things, to say that Mulroney had received money from Frank Moores's lobbying company, Government Consultants International, from Moores himself, from his partner Gary Ouellet and from Gerald Doucet, and that he had supported fraud related to the Thyssen project. That he named four potential sources of illicit payments, used the word fraud with no supporting context, and included the phrases "this is my last warning" and "my patience comes to an end" indicated the lengths to which Schreiber was prepared to go.

In June the Federal Court of Canada rejected Schreiber's bid for a judicial review of the extradition order, and in August Schreiber was ordered to pay Mulroney's $64,000 legal bill for the unsuccessful lawsuit. In October the Supreme Court denied Schreiber a second leave to appeal extradition.

On October 31 the CBC TV program *the fifth estate* aired a show about what may have been Brian Mulroney's only offence, trying to cover up his relationship with Schreiber and the $300,000 he accepted from him after he left office. It starred Karlheinz Schreiber. The public was offered the testimony of a man wanted in his native country for tax evasion, fraud, forgery, bribery, and breach of trust; Frank Moores, now deceased, made a convenient middleman. The show aired an amateur video of Moores in a German beer garden, singing and obviously feeling no pain, celebrating, according to Schreiber, the payment of the $20 million he was to share with Mulroney. Although the sight of Frank Moores half-cut and having a good time was hardly proof of anything, nothing Schreiber said was challenged by the host, Lynden MacIntyre.

Then on November 13, 2007 MacIntyre told CBC radio's *The Current* that the Airbus scandal was a "non-scandal," that Brian Mulroney couldn't be connected to it in any way, but that people close to Mulroney, "such as lobbyists," were involved. MacIntyre said that Frank Moores and GCI were the people handling the Airbus deal, but he offered no evidence. Even though he and other journalists had spent years and millions trying to prove the truth of what had turned out to be a non-scandal, he also said that Karlheinz Schreiber "knows what he knows," that everything the self-proclaimed master of *schmiergelder* (grease money) had ever told him "all kind of added up," and that Schreiber "has never lied to us or misled us." MacIntyre's ability to ignore his own role in the perpetuating of the non-story was almost as striking as his willingness to give Karlheinz Schreiber a stage from which to orchestrate his fight against extradition.

A 1998 letter on GCI letterhead from Frank Moores to Franz Josef Straus surfaced, and the CBC jumped on it as "irrefutable proof" that, despite his denials, Frank Moores had indeed been involved with lobbying Air Canada on behalf of Airbus. Actually, the letter is ambiguous and its context is complicated. It references an earlier letter of 1986 regarding the sale of Airbus aircraft to Wardair, which was a client of GCI. Franz Josef Strauss was the premier of Bavaria. In Germany sitting politicians commonly rotate as heads of merged companies; Straus was chairman of Aerospatiale, the company that produced Airbus, and also chairman of the separate company Messerschmidt-Bölkow-Blohm, MBB, a client of GCI that was also a shareholder in Airbus.

The letter to Straus could have been written by Moores to alert a valued client, Messerschmidt-Bölkow-Blohm, of a situation affecting both that client and another GCI client, Wardair. It has also been suggested by someone very close to Moores and GCI that Frank Moores may not have written the letter at all. The salutation is formal, to "Dr. Strauss," but the letter is signed "Frank." Moores, a stickler for protocol and procedure, always signed "F.D. Moores" to letters to people with whom he was not on a first-name basis. The source pointed out that Karlheinz Schreiber, who sometimes used an office at GCI and had easy access to GCI letterhead, and who had much to gain from implicating Frank Moores and Brian Mulroney, was also wanted for forgery in Germany. Typical of people to whom I spoke about Karlheinz Schreiber, this person was adamant about not being identified because "you don't know what he might say or do next."

One thing Schreiber did next was file an affidavit with Ontario's Superior Court of Justice, claiming this time that Mulroney had in fact still been prime minister when they sealed the deal for lobbying services and that they negotiated the terms at the prime minister's Harrington Lake retreat in Quebec on June 23, 1993, two days before Mulroney stepped down from office. Schreiber also claimed that Mulroney promised to discuss his situation with Prime Minister Stephen Harper at a forthcoming visit to Harrington Lake.

Throwing Stephen Harper's name into the mix did the trick. Harper announced a review of Mulroney's dealings with Schreiber, and Karlheinz Schreiber won his reprieve. Brian Mulroney responded by issuing a statement urging government to call a full public inquiry into the Airbus affair. Under pressure in the Commons, Harper announced that University of Waterloo president David Johnston had been engaged to look into an inquiry and to lay out the terms. On November 15, 2007, the Ontario Court of Appeals rejected Schreiber's final bid to stay in the country. Schreiber warned that he would not cooperate with the public inquiry if he was extradited.

During the last week in November, the House of Commons Ethics Committee began hearings formally titled "Study of the Mulroney Airbus Settlement." The hearings were televised across the nation. It was the best forum yet for Karlheinz Schreiber. Even the trappings of prison—appearing in shackles on the first day, having his pants fall down in front of the TV cameras because his belt had been taken away—did nothing to lessen Schreiber's enthusiasm for the role of a somewhat jolly but naive and wronged businessman. One veteran female national journalist gurgled in a television panel that he was so endearing, like a teddy bear.

The night before his first appearance before the commons ethics committee, Schreiber told CBC radio's *As It Happens*, "I have documents and very important information placed at safe places, so if something would really happen to me, then it would all be disclosed." At one point he said his revelations "would be like Christmas," but despite requests to produce this information, the committee's stocking remained basically empty.

Some members of the ethics committee were embarrassingly ill prepared, and they all appeared more interested in scoring political points and having their opinions validated than in challenging Schreiber's often blatant inconsistencies. In the November affidavit that precipitated the ethics committee probe and the call for a public inquiry, Schreiber does not include any of the allegations relating to the May letter, making instead a vague reference to "statements made by Frank Moores." At one point he said that Frank Moores was furious with Brain Mulroney for cancelling the Bear Head light armoured vehicle project in 1990, but then he also said that he himself didn't know the project had been cancelled until 1995, offering no explanation as to how this was possible, particularly when in 1992 his friend Elmer MacKay had made a public statement about the government's having chosen General Motors to build the vehicles. In another part of his testimony he mentioned a circumstance that was common knowledge among insiders for years: during the period when Frank Moores and Brian Mulroney were supposedly in collusion, they were not even on speaking terms.

On December 11 Schreiber stated that he had transferred some $5 million from his "success fees" to Government Consultants International. When he stated in January 2008 that the entire amount of Airbus commissions, $20 million, had gone into the GCI account, no one mentioned his previous testimony that the sum was $5 million. No one questioned why it would all have gone to GCI or how it was paid. No one noted that nothing irregular was found on GCI's books when the RCMP raided its offices and that of its accountant, or that the RCMP was in possession of all of Frank Moores's bank records and had found nothing to confirm Schreiber's allegations or to warrant charges of any kind. No one said, "Surely, Mr. Schreiber, the $20 million wasn't also handed over in envelopes of cash," or referenced his recent statement to CBC's Peter Mansbridge that he had never given cash to any politician or former politican other than Brian Mulroney. No one asked what proof Mr. Schreiber had that he hadn't pocketed the $20 million himself and masterminded the whole Mulroney-Moores Airbus conspiracy to cover the fact that the Airbus contract was awarded on merit, without any help from him or any high-level Canadians, and he had taken the success fee fraudulently. No one asked Schreiber to explain why he said that Mulroney surrounded himself with unsavoury lobbyists. When they did ask pertinent questions, they didn't insist on getting answers or even coherency. This exchange between Liberal Ralph Goodale and Schreiber illustrates this peculiar situation.

Goodale: Did Airbus authorize any payments to be made to facilitate the contract? If so, to whom were those payments to be made, when were they made, how much were they, and were these amounts deductible as expenses on the Airbus side?

Schreiber: It is quite different, sir. It is not money you spend or do with money based on the success, it was the commission. Do you understand? No business, no commission. In other words, the official agreement which was made with Airbus through a company, IAL, which is the trust company in Liechtenstein, which, by the way, doesn't belong to me, this is another one, and it is not even necessary, because you could have been there and be the trustee for Airbus, or GCI. Now, when the success is there and you get your commission on the business, and this was stated, by the way, from the RCMP at the beginning as well, GCI, if they want to get paid in Switzerland, it's not illegal. As long as they declare the tax in Canada whenever they take money out or whatever the tax was, it's the end of the story, they can decide whatever they want—and that was my job. When you speak about these helpful donations, which was a very, very big world in all these years, it was always a discussion from the industry and the government, 'Look, there are many other countries, they do this all over the place.' That's true, it's absolutely true. I mean, I witnessed this everywhere. You have to get the possibility to deduct these, no?

Goodale did not pursue his questions.

In his last appearance before the committee, Mr. Schreiber was asked directly by the chair, Paul Szabo, whether "to the best of your knowledge and belief you have brought to the attention of this committee all material matters related to the motion before us." In classic Schreiber style, he replied, "Yes," confirming that he had brought all material matters to the committee, but then he insured his importance to the future inquiry by adding, "I think I can add more."

That inquiry will surely involve Frank Moores, whose reputation has been considered expendable by everyone involved in trying to prove the existence of an Airbus affair. Moores left an estate valued at well over $3 million, mainly comprised of his Birch Point property at Chaffey's Lock, and investments he had acquired through the sale of his Canadian Helicopter Corporation options. It was a lot of money but a far cry from the multi-millions he was supposed to have made from Airbus and reasonable, considering that he had become a millionaire before he turned forty. Frank Moores accepted and appreciated the good life as his birthright before he ever met Karlheinz Schreiber.

CHAPTER 3

Charm School

EVEN AT FRANK MOORES'S christening there was controversy and a love triangle. His mother wanted to call him Gordon Duff, combining her family name with that of the boyfriend she had met and wanted to marry while she was away in Canada, studying music at Acadia University in Wolfville, Nova Scotia. Silas Moores may or may not have known about Gordon, but he knew he wasn't about to have a son called G.D. Moores, so when the minister asked the name, he quickly said, "Frank Duff."

Dorothy Duff Moores came from a prominent mercantile family in Carbonear, Newfoundland, which, in her youth, was still an autonomous Dominion in the British Empire. Steeped in the British class system introduced by the West Country English merchants who made fortunes in Newfoundland, outport families around the turn of the twentieth century were as conscious of pedigree as the old St. John's aristocracy or the New York One Hundred. Dorothy Duff's mother had been a Greaves, a niece of Lord Stanley of Stanley Cup fame and a great-niece of Lord Stanley of Stanley cup fame and of the Earl of Derby. Her paternal grandfather, William Duff, of the same family as the famous Scottish missionary Dr. Alexander Duff, immigrated to Harbour Grace, a town very close to Carbonear, in the mid-eighteen hundreds; he became a successful businessman, the governor of the Savings Bank of Newfoundland, and an elected member of the colonial legislature in 1889 and again in 1903.

Dorothy's mother, Frank's beloved Nana Duff, was somewhat of a celebrity in her own right. Using Mary Stanley, her grand-mother's name, as a pseudonym, she wrote a weekly cooking column called "The Scrapbook," and she was a contributor to *Maclean's* magazine. In the tradition of the times, because there were no hotels in Carbonear, important visitors to the community were house guests of the Duffs, and Dorothy was imbued from an early age with the importance of etiquette, entertaining, and doing things in the proper manner. While they indulged their only child in many ways, such as allowing her the first car ever owned in Carbonear, Dorothy's parents wouldn't tolerate her marrying some unknown fellow from Canada; when she was eighteen, her university career at Acadia came to halt.

Silas Moores, literally the boy next door, awaited Dorothy in Carbonear. While he belonged to a newly risen merchant family, Silas was definitely not of Dorothy's station. The Moores family traced its Newfoundland roots back to mid-seventeenth-century fishermen from Devon. Si's father and uncle had been fishermen who started a small dry goods business in Freshwater, which later moved to Carbonear and became W.J. Moores Ltd. Si Moores began his business career at fifteen, getting transport to Portugal with a small load of fish and bringing back a load of salt. The fishermen in the area supported him, and he eventually owned one of the biggest salt fish operations in Newfoundland, North Eastern Fish-eries. Even so, he was not quite what the Duffs had in mind as a suitor for their only daughter, but nineteen-year-old Dorothy was not about to be deterred again, even when Si Moores, late for his wedding at the house next door, jumped over the fence between the two properties and showed up with the seat of his morning suit ripped right down the middle.

Si quickly became a leading businessman in the community, and when the Moores entertained visitors from Japan and Europe, they gave many people in the area their first glimpse of people of a different race. Dorothy always wore makeup, and her nails were manicured and polished; she dressed impeccably, with hats and gloves for every occasion and every outfit. In her house she always had fresh flowers, which she arranged herself. She and Si had frequent overnight guests, and it was nothing for Dorothy to give a dinner party for twenty-four people. She was very involved in the menus and how things were to be done, but she had maids and cooks to carry out her instructions. Even when there were no guests, she set a beautiful table: her everyday dishes were blue and white Wedgwood china, her cutlery was silver, and her napkins and tablecloths were always linen.

The importance of etiquette and doing things correctly was a natural part of the upbringing of her two children, Megan and Frank, the younger by five years, born in 1933. She doted on the little strawberry blonde boy, dressed him in proper little sailor suits, and raised him—as he would be described many times in later life—as to the manor born, accustomed to famous people from a very early age. One of his earliest memories was of "this Rickenbacker guy lifting me aboard a big two-engine airplane." He was three years old.

Child psychologists might say that Frank Moores was a classic confirmation that growing up with unconditional love and acceptance creates a loving and confident person. He spent his formative years surrounded by adoring women: his mother and his Nana Duff, the maids and cooks, and his big sister, although naturally she was often less enchanted than the others. The young fellow's eclectic leisure activities foreshadowed the man he was to become. He was a top junior tennis player in the Dominion of Newfoundland, winning many cups before he went off to Canada and boarding school. He also embraced all the more common pastimes of the typical outport boy. He began a lifelong love affair with the streams and rivers of Newfoundland when he was very young, and his appreciation for adventure began at the same time.

"I learned to trout when I was about three. When I was ten or eleven, four of us went out on the line by Carbonear, about a five-mile walk out in the woods, and built ourselves a camp, wasn't bad either, had four bunks in it, and it kept the rain off. We'd go for a week or two. You had some flour and you got some fish, snared some rabbits or whatever, brought in some other grub. Nowadays if some eleven-year-old went off for two weeks in the woods, the search parties would be giving up, never mind starting, but it was a natural thing to do where I was.

I had one very close call. Robert Duff and myself rowed over to the squid jigging grounds on the south side of Carbonear. The squid never struck, and all of the fishermen went in, and we decided we should go in, too, but the wind had come up from the southwest and we couldn't row against it. So here we were, floating out the harbour. We cleared Carbonear Island, next stop Ireland. As we cleared the island we saw another boat, Captain John Blackwood from Wesleyville. They pulled alongside and hauled us aboard. When we got back in to W.J. Moores's wharf, it was getting pretty dark. Dad was on the wharf with about two hundred fishermen and all the boats, setting up grids for how to search the bay for the best chance of finding us. I can hear him now: 'Skipper Jack, did you see any boys out in the bay?' 'Yes, Skipper Si, I got 'em on board.'

There was a big cheer from everyone on the wharf...the prodigal son was home. I came over the side of the wharf and Dad's belt was coming off at the same time, and I got a real licking, bent over right on the wharf. Not too long after that he took two of my buddies and me up to St. Pierre for the trip in a schooner. Rough as hell—nothing like a bedbug to make you sit up all night; the bed was full of them—but we got to St. Pierre, and that was quite an experience for a young fellow."

CHAPTER 4

Rising to the Top

THE SONS OF WEALTHY St. John's merchants such as the Crosbies were sent off to boarding school in the manner of their English forefathers, not just to be educated but to make contacts that would open doors for the rest of their lives. Frank's sister Megan went to Havergal College in Toronto. Up until grade six Frank attended a four-room school in Carbonear, with one teacher for three grades. Then he left for St. Andrew's College, a boarding school in Aurora, Ontario, north of Toronto, most of whose alumni occupied the upper echelons of corporate, legal, and political power. The quality of the early education he had received in Carbonear was such that he skipped a grade when he started at St. Andrew's, a fact that he repeated often and with great pleasure when describing the calibre of teaching in Newfoundland at the time.

Many families sent their children to school in England. Canada was a foreign country, and Newfoundland was tied very strongly to Britain. However, Si Moores had established a branch of North Eastern Fisheries in Gloucester, Massachusetts, and he and Dorothy spent a portion of their winters in Boston. This meant that they could easily travel to Ontario to visit their children.

Getting to Canada from Newfoundland in the 1940s was an arduous trip for anyone, but for the son of Silas and Dorothy

Moores, it was considerably less arduous. To take Frank to school the family took the train to the port town of Botwood, on the central Newfoundland coast, where they boarded a Pan American Flying Boat. They settled into big plush easy chairs in the plane's living room setting and took off for Shediac, New Brunswick, where they went ashore and had lunch. After lunch, they boarded the Flying Boat again, and that night they had dinner at the Starlight Room at the top of the Waldorf Astoria in New York. Even for a wealthy man's son, from Carbonear to the Waldorf Astoria was, as Frank described it, "one hell of a leap."

Twelve years old and six feet two inches tall, Frank Moores danced that night with the wife of a friend of his father's. He stood on the balcony looking at the stars and the lights of New York City and felt that he was on top of the world. The next day he gave his sister the slip and hopped on a bus offering a half-day tour of the city. Megan was sobbing, his mother distraught, and his father giving a missing persons report to a New York City policeman when Frank finally showed up at the hotel hours later. It was time to head for Toronto and St. Andrew's.

Frank was taller than all the other boys, thin as a rake, and didn't speak like anyone else at St. Andrew's. He arrived dragging a trunk by a rope and was sent to the dormitory to unpack. When he came back downstairs to the reception welcoming the new boys, he approached the headmaster and said, "Excuse me, sir, but I got no place to put me trunk." The master looked at his wife, raised his eyebrows, and shook his head in dismay, admitting later that he didn't expect Frank Moores to last long.

In fact he did extremely well at St. Andrew's. He had a good academic record, even achieving a first prize in scripture, and he took part in most sports, including four years on the football team. The scripture prize, coupled with his request that his parents purchase a painting of the chapel, the centrepiece of the school, caused great alarm to his father, who feared his son might become a minister instead of the doctor he and Dorothy envisioned.

On March 31, 1949, when the Dominion of Newfoundland officially became a Canadian province, upperclassman John Crosbie and Frank Moores were made to stand up on a table at St. Andrew's and sing O Canada. Instead they gave a resounding rendition of Ode to Newfoundland, which was resoundingly booed. The following year Moores wrote an article for the school magazine; entitled Newfoundland, it argued that the world at large was just becoming aware of the potential of Newfoundland. A year after that he was editor of the magazine.

Frank became head prefect, and he served as commanding officer of the cadet corps for two years in a row, a significant honour because it very rarely happened. The corps had won Best Cadet Corps in Ontario for seventeen out of twenty-one years; the first year Frank commanded, his second-last year at St. Andrew's, was only the fifth time they didn't win the award, which caused him considerable distress. The next year, the St. Andrew's corps under Major Moores won, achieving the highest marks ever given to a cadet corps in Canada. During his command, he introduced a twenty-man pipe band with full dress uniform, including feather bonnets, and, because it was a Highland regiment, he himself wore a kilt.

While Frank was commander, Si went to see his son at the school for the first time. Frank didn't understand why his father had never come to visit, especially during the winters when he lived in Boston; he didn't find out until years later that Si Moores was afraid that he might embarrass his son by not wearing the right clothes or saying the right things. When I asked him what he considered his greatest accomplishment, he said, "To come from Carbonear Elementary School and go to St. Andrew's and be head prefect and commanding officer of the cadet corps. In everything else, I had a lot of people helping me. That one I did on my own." That led to the proudest moment in his life.

"We had a church parade in Toronto, and we formed up at Rosedale Park to march to St. Paul's. As Commanding

Officer I was shouting out, doing all the stuff you had to do, and I saw Dad and Megan and Mom over by the fence. I walked over and saluted Dad, kissed Megan and Mom, and said, 'I'll see you after the church service.' So we started off. It was a good parade, the pipes were playing, and I looked over and here was Dad, keeping right in step, marching up the sidewalk beside me, and I felt pretty good about that. He kept striding along with the rest of us, and all of a sudden, I looked over—we'd gotten pretty near the church—and there was no sign of him. I thought he must be tired or he gave up on this. I got in the church and the boys started to file in in double file, and I walked over to Mom and Megan and I said, 'Where's Dad? Has he lost all interest in this?' Mom said, 'No indeed, he couldn't come any further because he couldn't see.' I said, 'What do you mean, he couldn't see?' She said, 'Well, the tears were coming out of his eyes because he was so proud of you.' Jesus, I had to go in then and read the lesson in the church, and I was like someone smacked me in the guts. The fact that my dad, whom I worshipped, felt that way about me was a big moment in my life, the biggest ever."

Frank probably first demonstrated his ability to charm the press around this time. He and two of his friends were unable to get tickets for a Grey Cup game in Toronto. The ever-resourceful Frank fabricated a story about how three boys wanted to see the game so badly that they had hitched a ride on a fishing boat all the way from Newfoundland to Boston and then hitchhiked to Toronto, and now they couldn't get tickets. Somehow he got the tale to the press. The story and a picture of the threesome landed on the front page of *The Globe and Mail*, and the lads who had come from no farther away than Aurora, a few miles north on Yonge Street, ended up with box seats.

Frank's gift for smooth talk made him bit of a legend around St. Andrew's. Another escapade involved a trip to Appleby College,

Oakville, to play football. After the game Frank felt like going in to Toronto for a bit of fun, but the boys were all supposed to go back to St. Andrew's on the bus. Frank made up a story about having run into Sir Leonard Outerbridge, the lieutenant-governor of Newfoundland. He explained to the coach that Sir Leonard, a friend of his family, had invited him and some of his friends to the Royal York Hotel for dinner, and he thought that the boys shouldn't miss the opportunity to meet the lieutenant-governor. The coach agreed, and off four of them went to party in Toronto, getting a cab back to school late that night. The next day Frank, who was the head prefect at the time, explained it all again to the headmaster, who had to agree with the coach: it would have been bad form to turn down the lieutenant-governor.

Most of the boys at St. Andrew's came from families wealthier than the Moores, but Frank always seemed to have more money than his friends. He didn't throw it around, but he was generous, and lack of money never stood in the way of anyone's having a good time. The St. Andrew's boys liked Frank's sense of humour, too, and they were somewhat fascinated with his success with girls, especially older ones. On Sundays the boys assembled in the chapel for morning services and then had free time between lunch and dinner. Next to the school was a big apple orchard, and after lunch on any fine Sunday, Frank could be seen heading over there with a blanket over his shoulder and his transistor radio, meeting some girl from the area.

Bill Somers, a classmate, was only a few days younger than Frank, but he describes Frank as well ahead of the crowd at an early age and "quite mature when it came to the ladies." Years later, an older woman whom Frank had pursued when he was a teenager told Somers that Frank Moores had more sex appeal in his little finger than most men had in their entire bodies.

Frank's best friend, future stockbroker Terry Malone, wasn't as successful with girls as Frank was, so Frank and Bill Somers took him to a house of ill repute in Toronto that Frank knew about. The seventeen-year-old Frank led the trio in and took control of making sure everyone was well looked after. The awkward Malone took his galoshes off on the front steps; he ended up making an embarrassed exit with his shirt on inside out and refused to go back for his galoshes, but a fellow couldn't be Frank Moores's best friend and remain shy around women.

Frank's reputation as a lover was capped by his affair with a school nurse. He got hurt playing football and had a lot of headaches. The regular nurse was away for some reason, and her replacement was an attractive younger nurse. Frank got home late one night from Toronto and crept into his room to find that the senior house master had fallen asleep on his bed, waiting for him. Frank backed out of the room, went up to the infirmary, and stayed all night. When the master checked, the nurse confirmed his story about spending the night in the sick bay. He began spending more nights there. The headaches seemed to be getting worse.

Then another student became ill in the middle of the night, went to the infirmary, and caught Frank coming out of the nurse's bedroom. "From then on, the boys were pretty well in awe of him," says Somers. "It also seemed as though he'd get little scoldings for things that we'd expect big trouble from, and some of us decided from early on that if we were going to get into any deviltry, we wanted Frank Moores along."

Going back and forth to Newfoundland for Christmas or short holidays was usually out of the question. Frank was a popular guest with his friends' families, and a few of his schoolmates would spend the summer with the Moores family in Newfoundland. Frank's parents made the boys from St. Andrew's very welcome. Life was good; Dorothy Moores's red convertible was at their service, the cook fed them and baked cakes every day, and the maids picked up after them. Frank and the boys from the mainland cut quite a swath among the girls at the dances in Harbour Grace or at the old CLB Armoury in Bay Roberts. Retired Liberal MHA Eric Dawe remembers him as "having star quality even in those days, a big shiner among the girls, but very genuine, never small, never cheap, and never overbearing."

Terry Malone spent several summers in Harbour Grace. Once when Frank had booked two dates at the same time, he asked Terry to fill in, assuring him he'd have a good time. Malone suspected the woman was married because Frank told him to pull up in a dark driveway and flash his lights. When the woman came out, got into the dark car, and started talking about how she hadn't seen him for so long, Malone realized she thought he was Frank. He also realized quickly that she wasn't really interested in talking, so into the back seat they climbed. He never did tell her he wasn't Frank. When Frank found out, his main concern was that Malone might not have lived up to his prowess.

On one occasion Frank's ability to shine at dances took a while to take effect. At the Cadet Corps dance in Frank's last year at St. Andrew's, Terry Malone had a blind date. Torontonian Dodie Pain had been persuaded by a friend to go with Malone even though he was a couple of years her junior. As soon as he saw Dodie Pain, Frank lost interest in his own date. Malone dated Dodie a few times, and after each date Frank would subtly inquire if he was going to take her out again; finally he confessed that as soon as Dodie and Malone stopped dating, he was going to ask her out. According to Terry Malone, "he was in love with her from day one. He knew exactly what he wanted."

It was fortunate that Frank was in his final year because his focus on school immediately diminished. He thought Dodie Pain was the most beautiful woman he had ever seen. The fact that she was a bit older and not eager for his advances raised his interest so much that he started skipping school to go see her. He'd make his way to Toronto and spend hours on her front porch, "rubbing around in puppy love," sometimes running for a cab when it was almost dawn to get back to school on time—an expensive habit, not to mention highly inappropriate for the head prefect.

On one particular morning there were three cars pulled up at the gate going into the school; the first was the janitor going in for the day, the second was the duty master going in for the day, and the third was a cab carrying the head prefect, sneaking in after the night. Frank instructed the cab driver to drive down the quadrangle as fast as he could when the other two cars went around to the back so Frank could go in the front door. He was just inside when up the back stairs came the master on duty. Frank immediately picked up the bell to waken everyone, even though it was about five minutes early, causing the master to compliment him on being so prompt.

Dodie Pain was a challenge to a charmer used to getting what he wanted. He convinced another girlfriend who was a telephone operator to put through free calls to Dodie, unconcerned that she might listen in. He wrote to Dodie constantly and talked about her all the time. His friends used to say that she was the only one who wouldn't go to bed with him, so he had to marry her to get her, but when he actually did get married before he turned nineteen, most of them felt a sense of total unreality.

CHAPTER 5

Destiny

IT IS IMPORTANT to understand the history and political climate that shaped Frank Moores. Moores grew up in a Newfoundland that had equal status with Canada as a dominion of the British Empire. Newfoundland was richer in natural resources than any single province in Canada, but to Britain it was a cash cow, or more accurately a cash fish. Discovered in 1497 and officially claimed by Sir Humphrey Gilbert in 1583 as England's first overseas colony, Newfoundland nevertheless lagged behind other colonies. Settlement was not encouraged or supported; in fact, settlement was outlawed until 1610 because British merchants wanted complete control over, and use of, the wealth from Newfoundland's fishing grounds.

For over a hundred years, fishing families were brought out in the spring and taken back in the fall. Life was much more primitive and harsher than in supported colonies in other parts of the New World, and justice, such as it was, depended on the whim of the fishing admiral, an office awarded to the captain of whichever boat was the first to arrive in a harbour in the spring. Women came with their husbands to 'make the fish,' and in spite of the hardships, many families preferred the relative freedom in the new-found land to the conditions they endured back home. The earliest of Newfoundland's permanent settlers were fishermen and their families who stole away to isolated coves and hid when it was time to go back to England in the fall. Only fiercely determined and tough, independent spirits would face the uncertainty of winter with few provisions and little shelter in such bleak locations, and it was from these beginnings that the Newfoundland race developed.

The Newfoundland economy suffered from the worst kind of British colonialism. All the decisions made by England in relation to Newfoundland were calculated to increase the profits taken back to England and not to benefit the colony. Nevertheless Newfoundland rejected Confederation with Canada in 1869 and remained a colony until 1907, when it acquired full dominion status. The independent country then successfully negotiated a trade agreement with the United States, only to have it blocked by the British government after objections from Canada. In the First World War, almost an entire generation of future leaders of the small nation was wiped out fighting for Britain. In 1934 staggering under the debt incurred by its tremendous support of Britain in the war and close to bankruptcy due to neglect and corruption, the Dominion of Newfoundland gave up its self-governing status, and a Commission of Government appointed by Britain took over.

In 1946 the Newfoundland National Convention voted to hold a referendum to decide between continuing the Commission of Government and restoring Responsible Government. A well-known radio broadcaster who had tried business and dabbled in socialism, one Joey Smallwood, emerged as the leader of a group proposing Confederation with Canada, and he started a move to have that option included in the referendum.

Newfoundland had developed a strong relationship with the United States during the Second World War. Newfoundland's location was so strategic to the defence of North America that the Pentagon called it their "clenched fist, daring the Germans to come any closer." Newfoundland became so heavily fortified with American military bases that Field Marshall Goering told Hitler in a memo that the island of Newfoundland was "like a giant aircraft carrier and must be destroyed." In the post-war climate of the Confederation debate, American influences were much stronger in Newfoundland than any Canadian presence.

This circumstance, coupled with the fact that Newfoundlanders had traditionally traded with and emigrated to the Boston states, suggested that economic union with the US would be natural. However, economic union with the United States was not offered as an option in the referendum, and historians have uncovered documents indicating a conspiracy between Britain and Canada to determine the outcome of the vote. Others argue the claim, but there is no denying a determination in Canada to complete the federation from sea to sea, to gain control of trading, airspace, and the minerals secretly discovered in Labrador in 1945, and to keep Newfoundland from strengthening its ties with the United States.

The Confederation debate in Newfoundland was passionate and bitter enough to divide families. After a second referendum, on July 22, 1948, the Dominion of Newfoundland voted 52% in favour of becoming a province of the Dominion of Canada and Joey Smallwood was the leader elect.

As 'the Father of Confederation,' Joey Smallwood felt omnipotent. Si Moores was pro-Confederation, but unlike most confederates he was never pro-Smallwood. Smallwood invited him into the first cabinet following Confederation, but Si wasn't interested in diverting his attention away from the fish business; from the beginning of Smallwood's rise to power, Si had decided to keep his distance.

In 1951 Frank graduated from St. Andrew's and enrolled in Boston University on a quasi-athletic scholarship. It was a more natural choice than a Canadian university because of his father's close connection to the Boston fish markets, and he could stay in the apartment his father maintained there. His parents thought he should study medicine, but Frank's university career ended abruptly before two months were up when he took exception to the views of a history professor who had no use for the British or

Canadians. The fact that Frank was from Newfoundland, a British dominion that had chosen to become a Canadian province, seemed to incense him, and he was continually shaking his finger in Frank's face while lecturing on the shortfalls of his heritage. After one particularly rancorous session, Frank hit him, and he was kicked out of school. An investigation determined that he had been extraordinarily provoked, but although both the dean and the football coach asked him to return, Frank really had no interest in a medical career or indeed in continuing at university, and he went to work on the Boston fish pier.

His parents, however, thought he was still going to university. In January, when they arrived in Boston for the winter, Frank would get up at three o'clock in the morning to go to work and arrive home again mid-morning, and his father quickly figured out that something was fishy in more ways than one. Frank confessed, saying that he wanted to work in the business with his father. His mother was quite upset, but a part of Si was delighted, and it was agreed that Frank would return home in the fall and join his father at North Eastern Fisheries.

There was one problem. From Boston, Frank could get back and forth to Toronto occasionally to see Dodie, but from Newfoundland it would be a different story. So he proposed. Twenty-one-year-old Dodie was finishing her second year studying physiotherapy at the University of Toronto, and she wasn't enthusiastic about giving up her prospective career to move to a small town in Newfoundland with an eighteen-year-old. All the same, within months they were engaged and planning a September wedding. Dodie was working at a resort for the summer, and Frank took a job pumping gas there to be close to her. Terry Malone was to be the best man, but he quickly realized that not much had changed.

Malone believed that Frank couldn't help himself, that he could fall in love with five women at a time, but only if they were older than he was. He was quite serious with most of them, and when the inevitable happened and one girl thought she was pregnant, he intended to marry her. When it turned out she wasn't pregnant, the scare slowed him down, but not for long. With the fiancée that he was madly in love with right there in town, Frank started a torrid affair with another older girl who was a regular customer at the gas station. For a brief time he thought he was in love with both women, and it was only a month before the wedding to Dodie that he came to his senses. The wedding went ahead as planned, and eighteen-year-old Frank Moores returned to Newfoundland with a wife.

CHAPTER 6

The Idyllic Years

CANADIAN SCHOOLS WEREN'T TEACHING anything at all about Newfoundland, and the new Mrs. Moores had little idea of what she was getting into. After a two-week honeymoon in Bermuda, Frank took his city bride back to a small rented house by the shore in Carbonear. The wind whistled through ill-fitting windows, one unfinished room had a dirt floor, and a coal stove in the hall provided heat. Splits had to be cleaved every morning for kindling and wood brought in to keep the fire going in the kitchen wood stove. Within a few months Dodie was pregnant with Susan, the first of their seven children.

Dodie's arms usually had a burn or two, as did the baby, once she started to walk and fall against one stove or another. It was hard work, but harder to be from upalong and far away from her mother. The high heels she wore on the sidewalks of Toronto didn't suit the rough dirt roads of her new home. It didn't matter. People were friendly and nice, her husband was very affectionate and always called her darling, and she was in love.

When the house they built nearby in Harbour Grace was ready, life became much easier. The house stood on a beautiful piece of land overlooking the bay, and it had lots of room and all the conveniences for entertaining. Both Frank and Dodie always remembered it as a happy home where they had lots of fun. They hosted dinner parties and bridge games, bowled, rarely missed a hockey game, and Frank played poker. The dinner parties were a favourite with Frank. He appreciated good food and wine even then, but although he was to become a remarkable chef in later life, Dodie Pain had to learn to cook. She was pleased that Frank always made a point of thanking her for preparing dinner parties, even though she had hired help.

Dodie remembers it as "a nice life, a good life, very, very social and very proper." With Dorothy Moores and Nana Duff as her models, it was also a little daunting. While her mother-in-law welcomed her into the family and was good to her, there was always a right way and a wrong way to do things, and she was expected to do them the right way. Dodie discovered that while Frank was very relaxed with everybody and didn't care where people came from or their status in life, he was "rather proper" in a lot of ways, particularly when it came to the manners of gracious living.

Frank's sister Megan had married an Englishman, Bob Nutbeem, and they were also living in the area, raising a family and becoming world-class breeders of Newfoundland dogs. The two families would gather every week around Dorothy Moores's table for a meal or perhaps afternoon tea, always formally served with silver and china regardless of the ages of the children and often accompanied by a singalong around the piano while Dorothy played. At their grandmother's table, Frank's children began to receive the kind of social training their father had also gotten at a very young age.

Frank's hero-worship for his father continued in business, and Si gave him his head. When Frank came on board North Eastern Fisheries had one plant and 120 employees. Within a few years it grew into a plant that employed over a thousand people. Soon the father and son team built three more plants at nearby Port de Grave, Old Perlican, in Trinity Bay, and Fermeuse, farther away on the Southern Shore. North Eastern became the largest fish processor in North America; its modern new plants employed two thousand people, 850 in Harbour Grace alone, and they provided a market for more than three thousand fishermen.

The personal touch that would become Moores's strength in politics became evident early in his business career. To keep in touch with his fishermen, he liked to be there when a boat came in, and at some time every day he could be found on a wharf somewhere on the coast. Juggling the plant and the wharf may not always have been the best strategy, especially for a man who liked to play as much as he liked to work, but the sentiment expressed by one of his suppliers was a common one: there was no one better to deal with— "he was honest and straightforward and his word was his bond."

The only falling out between Frank and Si occurred when Frank faced his first big challenge. One morning before a long weekend, they were very short of fish, and Frank called all their suppliers. Then the fish seemed to strike everywhere at the same time; full trucks appeared from as far away as the Cape Shore and Trinity Bay, and boats arrived loaded to the gunnels. By the end of the day, with a million pounds of fish in the holding room, thirty-seven trucks remained lined up on the road. Frank remembered it well. "Dad came into the plant and said, 'I think you've ruined us.' I said, 'I think I may have, but I'll do the best I can with it.' He said, 'Well, I'm not going to stay around to watch; I'm very disappointed in you.' With that, he went out the door."

Moores explained the situation to the Harbour Grace plant workers and asked them to work through the long weekend; only three declined. By working day and night, taking ten-minute lunch breaks and no coffee breaks, they processed all the fish by Tuesday morning. Then, as Frank recalled, Si arrived, wearing the fur hat that he pulled further down over his eyes the madder he was. "He said, 'Well, how much did you have to dump?' I told him to take his fine business and big concrete buildings that he was so proud of and stick them all up his arse. I turned around and walked out the door, went home, and went to bed."

A few hours later, amazed at what his son had achieved, Si

woke him to apologize, and the two got out the Scotch. By the time Dorothy, Megan, and Dodie arrived to see what they could do to repair this rift, Frank and Si were hammered and telling each other uproarious stories.

Moores's organizational ability began to show itself in the community. To some extent his mother may have inspired his commitment to public service. Dorothy was a tireless volunteer, particularly in helping people get access to medical care and other basic services, and she did a lot of things for people in the community that no one ever knew about. "I was born into a very privileged family, which was no credit to me," Moores said. "I was just very, very lucky. But I remember the poverty around me when I was growing up and even later." A generous man, he quietly helped people who didn't have very much, putting in water systems for some and giving land to others. He was the youngest president in the history of the Kiwanis Club, and he and the other club members would distribute Christmas gifts to needy families. He remembered going to one house in particular. "There was no one home. I walked in the kitchen, and there was a baby without a stitch of clothes on in the sink, and I could see my car, which was parked on the other side of the house, through the walls; the openings were maybe half an inch wide. So you did something about it, like buying clothes for the baby, and all this sort of thing. Anyone would have done it, but that was one example that I experienced."

Between community involvement and business, he was always busy, doing so many things that he didn't have a lot of time to be home with his rapidly increasing family. To a degree, that was the way it was in the 1950s, when men supported the family and women worked at home, but a beautiful wife and young family wasn't enough to keep Frank Moores in Newfoundland, let alone Harbour Grace.

Constantly caring for a child in diapers, Dodie wasn't keen on travel, except for the occasional trip to visit her family in Toronto. At the same time, Moores's love of partridge hunting and salmon fishing was almost matched by his love of the theatre and fine dining. The fish business necessitated regular trips abroad, and he made the most of them. While wealthy Newfoundlanders were discovering Florida, Frank Moores was discovering the Aegean Sea; eventually, he bought a yacht there—a converted war cruiser whose staff included King Constantine's former cook—which he rented out when he wasn't using it.

In 1959 he landed the Birds Eye arm of the British conglomerate Unilever as customers for cod fillets. By 1960-1961 North Eastern Fisheries was selling virtually 90 per cent of their production to Birds Eye, and Birds Eye was depending on them in turn for 90 per cent of the fish dinners they produced. Frank went back and forth once a month, often for two weeks at a time, one week to sell fish and then a week to "look around." "There was nothing to do at home in the winter and spring," he explained, "so I got to know London and other places very well."

Even though the times were very different, the irony of a man with a wife and several little children saying there was nothing to do at home in the winter and spring didn't seem to occur to him. While Dodie kept the home fires burning, her husband fell in love with Europe. After meetings with Birds Eye, he'd trace his roots in West Country England; he got to know Norway while seeking new fishing boats; he explored Germany while looking for new markets. He loved the centuries-old taverns, where he'd have lunch and admire the old woods and fixtures, and he credited the experience of soaking up history in Europe with teaching him to respect and be more appreciative of the bigger scheme of things, rather than "just our own narrow lifestyle."

Jaunts to Europe aside, the Newfoundland winter still stretched out. In the late fifties, contemplating the seasonal nature of the fishing industry, Frank decided that the work force needed a major winter diversion and that hockey should provide it. There was no arena? Not a problem—North Eastern Fisheries supplied all the building material except the steel. To make the ice surface, ammonia lines were run across the road from the plant. Plant workers contributed through payroll deductions, and area residents bought bonds. The Conception Bay Cee Bees, a senior team that would become legendary in Newfoundland hockey history, was about to be born.

Senior hockey in Newfoundland was very big in those days. Fans travelled by train all over the island, following their teams, and from the first year it entered the league, Frank Moores's Cee Bees was the team to beat. Harbour Grace lawyer Doug Moores, a former member of the team, observed in his eulogy at Moores's funeral that Frank didn't want just a hockey team, he wanted a winning team, and he created the Cee Bees largely in his own image, recruiting George and Alex Faulkner to be the foundation on which the team was built. Alex later became the first Newfoundlander to play in the NHL, and George was a star for Team Canada in the world championships.

The team was a big part of Frank's life and the lives of everyone within travelling distance to the arena. Home games were always packed, and there's no doubt that his role in creating the team and his continuing involvement in it contributed to his popularity and his initial success in politics. Moores was eventually inducted as a builder into the Newfoundland and Labrador Hockey Hall of Fame.

In July 1962 Si Moores died suddenly of a heart attack. Chairmen of banks and businessmen from far and wide came to pay their last respects to a man who had built an empire from a load of imported salt. During the traditional home wake, fishermen and their wives who had gathered outside the house joined those inside when they began singing the mariners' hymn "Eternal Father, Strong to Save," with its heartrending refrain, "Oh, hear us when we cry to Thee / For those in peril on the sea." Moores recalled walking out on the front veranda to see "hundreds of people spread right down, right across the lawns, down on the street, fishermen all who normally should have been fishing, all singing," and being too choked up to speak.

Not quite twenty-nine, Frank Moores found himself running a multi-million dollar business. With some excellent advisors, he carried on for a few years, but he and the business missed Skipper Si's hand on the helm. Frank decided to pursue a vision he had of turning the seasonal fishery into the year-round operation that he was convinced was necessary in order to stay competitive in the European market. He planned to work toward the establishment of a European-style super port and auction system, and to do this he decided he had to get a partner with money to come on board.

He had been selling fish to Unilever-Birds Eye Foods in the UK for a few years by that time, and he liked dealing with the Englishmen. Even though it was cheaper to sell his product in the US, with the English he was confident that if he had a handshake, he had a deal, and it would be honoured every time. In his experience with the Americans, orders could be cancelled or fish sent back because the market dropped, or the prices could be haggled over on nonexistent problems.

At that stage, North Eastern was supplying every cod that Birds Eye used in the UK. Moores convinced Birds Eye management that North Eastern could not continue to supply them competitively by depending on the inshore fishery; the company needed a big infusion of capital to purchase deep sea ships. The Unilever board agreed to supply the money in return for 51 per cent of North Eastern, which was fine with Moores. He came under severe criticism for this deal, but he never stopped defending it. He was always rankled by suggestions that he was too much of a playboy to give the business the attention it needed without his father's firm hand, or that he had made a mistake in bringing in Birds Eye.

"I genuinely thought that 49 per cent of a huge year-round operation was a hell of a lot better than 100 per cent of a business that was struggling every damn winter. Almost everyone originally thought it was a great idea. They came in with a lot of money and built four ships over two years;

thirty-three ships was the objective in the business plan. They had a sister company in Germany called Nordsee, who were brilliant fishermen. They invented the factory ship, much to our chagrin today, but it was a great idea at the time. None of us knew the cod stocks were about to disappear. They came over and trained our crews, and I was hired to manage the place for three years, with an option to renew.

All of a sudden they started to bring in their own people, which was fine if they had brought in a few, but God, there were dozens of fairly high-priced people on the payroll year-round, before there were any fish caught to pay for it. It made no sense. You get the fish first, then you get the people after, or together, if you're lucky. We started to lose money because of the huge overhead the place was carrying."

Moores's sister Megan was a vice-president of the business. While their father was alive this involved nothing much more than visiting the office occasionally; Si would often open the safe and hand her a bundle of cash, saying she might as well have it as the tax department. Megan remembers Si saying, on more than one occasion, "If this ever gets too heavy, sell it." It soon got too heavy for Frank, but he had some regrets. "When the falling out finally came, and there was a falling out, I resigned and they accepted my resignation. I would have loved to have stayed, it was never my plan to leave early. Those were our happy years at home, incredibly happy years."

Birds Eye had paid Moores almost $2 million for his shares, a sizable fortune in the early 1960s. After he left, the operation floundered. Within three years Birds Eye was closing plants and pulling out of Newfoundland, and eventually the company sold its $12 million worth of assets to the Newfoundland government for under $2 million.

The year was 1966. Thirty-three–year–old Frank Moores had been married for fourteen years, had seven children, and well over a million dollars to work—or play—with.

CHAPTER 7

Giving Back

IN THE SPRING OF 1967, the federal Liberals had just chosen a new leader, Pierre Elliot Trudeau. Canadians were about to come under the spell of Trudeaumania, and Newfoundlanders were becoming ready to break the spell of Joey Smallwood, who had been premier since Confederation with Canada in 1949.

Joey was synonymous in mainland Canada with Newfoundland politics. In his own mind he was no less than the saviour of Newfoundland. He was fond of saying that the Almighty God had raised him up so he could bring Newfoundlanders into Confederation. His political power had never been questioned, let alone challenged.

Joey told people how to vote in both provincial and federal elections, and Joey chose the candidates. Whether you wanted to or not, when Joey anointed you to run, you ran; few refused. It's not surprising that Smallwood sought out the Moores family; not only were they prominent, they came from good Liberal stock in a land where people traditionally voted the way their fathers had.

He experienced rare opposition from family members. First Si Moores had turned him down, and Megan Nutbeem did the same. Joey had decided that Megan Moores Nutbeem should be his first lady cabinet minister and offered her any post she wanted. He'd arrive at the Nutbeems' house in Harbour Grace and polish off a bottle of port wine while extolling the virtues of elected office to Megan. Megan wouldn't run until her children were older. When her little brother became leader of the Tories, Megan says that she gave up on any thoughts of politics for herself because she believed that charges of nepotism would keep Frank from appointing her to cabinet, and the tourism position she wanted.

Moores, described in the press of the time as "socially prominent," had been keeping busy with directorships and volunteer positions. By now he was a Mason, a Kiwanis past president, and past governor of the Fisheries College, and he had served as director of the Fisheries Council of Canada, the Atlantic Provinces Economic Council, and the Frozen Fish Trades Association. He held director positions on the boards of prominent business firms in and outside Newfoundland and served as commissioner on the Newfoundland Fisheries Commission, the International Commission for the North Atlantic Fisheries, and on Joey Smallwood's Royal Commission on the Economic Prospects of Newfoundland.

The Economic Prospects Commission report was critical of just about everything Smallwood was doing. Moores was only one member, but he had personally gone beyond critical to being "extremely opposed to Joey Smallwood's dictatorship." Moores believed Smallwood's method of governing was immoral. As he became more convinced of this, he lost any respect he had once had for Joey Smallwood. He described Joey as a failure in just about everything he did until the convention for the National Assembly about Confederation with Canada. Years later, towards the end of his own premiership, Moores had some interesting visits with Smallwood. Although he realized that both he and Joey had learned a lot from the experiences they went through as premiers, he still thought Joey Smallwood was "in essence a colossally stupid man."

Moores recalled Smallwood as "an incredibly arrogant and power-consumed demagogue who thought the fishery was the arse end of mankind." He knew from serving on fisheries commissions that trying to convince Joey of the importance of the fishery and its potential was useless. Giving examples of successful fisheries in other countries meant nothing because to Smallwood, fishing was a last resort for an impoverished, uneducated people. Moores believed that it was the backbone of Newfoundland's economy and that Smallwood was totally wrong in his fixation on emulating industrialized nations with economies based largely on manufacturing. His biggest objection to what he called "Smallwood's harebrained schemes," was not that they were poorly thought out and often plain ridiculous but that they ignored the resources, nature, and culture of the Newfoundland people and therefore were doubly doomed to failure. He also believed that Smallwood harboured a basic distrust of local business to develop any resources for him and that he thought the Newfoundland people were too stupid to understand his vision.

But the fear in the province bothered Moores most. "Anyone who worked for the government or for a contractor that worked for the government, who had a family member in a similar position or depended on government licensing, stood to lose their livelihood by speaking against the government. Today you'll still find arguments about this in Newfoundland, and people who say it wasn't like that, but you'll invariably find that these people were Smallwood supporters who were not in a position to experience the reality of others."

The financially independent and socially secure Frank Moores was a well-travelled monarchist who didn't suffer much from the Newfoundland colonialist inferiority complex and had nothing to fear from Joey Smallwood. He was not political by nature, and his convictions about the absence of democracy in Newfoundland steered him to the Progressive Conservatives only by chance and only because Joey was a Liberal.

Even before he sold the fish business, Moores's restlessness had taken him back and forth to Toronto almost as often as to Europe. In 1960 he started two businesses in Toronto and engaged Terry

Malone to run them. Nordefic Designs was to import Norwegian-designed furniture, and Nordepic Investments would take advantage of Malone's experience in market trading. Moores brought a young woman over from Norway to be the secretary, and Malone and his sister were enlisted to find her an apartment and furnish it, ensuring that Frank had a Norwegian companion when he visited Toronto "to check on the business." Neither company really took off, and the young Norwegian went home after a year or so.

Another of Moores's St. Andrew's College contacts was Roy McMurtry, the future Attorney General and Chief Justice of Ontario. McMurtry worked on Robert Stanfield's campaign in 1967, was leader of the Ontario Conservative party, and was a good friend of the recently deposed national leader, Dalton Camp. On one of his trips to Toronto, Moores was feeling generally bored. While having lunch with McMurtry, he wondered what he could get into next. McMurtry suggested that he start putting back into society what he'd taken out, which Moores flippantly interpreted as a suggestion that he go to work in some developing country in Africa or elsewhere. The developing country McMurtry had in mind was Newfoundland.

Moores was surprised when McMurtry said he could make a contribution because he knew nothing about politics, yet the idea of working against Joey's domination of Newfoundland appealed to him. McMurtry told him that the best way to learn a lot about politics very quickly was to go back to Newfoundland, get a nomination, and run. Moores had never even been to a political meeting and knew nothing about nominating conventions or even much about party lines. He only knew that Smallwood had to go. McMurtry persuaded Moores to stay on an extra day and meet with party leader Bob Stanfield.

Concerned that Stanfield's quiet persona wouldn't make a big impression on Frank Moores, McMurtry stressed to Stanfield the need to speak with passion and enthusiasm. The three men met in Stanfield's suite at the Royal York Hotel. Moores kept professing his political inexperience, saying that to just go back and try to get elected didn't seem like a practical idea. Stanfield, trying to take McMurtry's advice, told Moores that if he was as committed to public service and making a contribution to his province as he said he was, then it was time for him to get off the wharf and into the water.

The fishing analogy may have tipped the scales. Moores went back to Harbour Grace and gathered about twenty-five of what he called his "key guys," fish agents, friends, and community leaders, people he knew well personally, in the basement of his house. He poured everyone a drink and said, "B'ys, I'm going into politics." The assembled crew was elated, cheering and slapping him on the back, and then someone asked when he had gotten the call from Mr. Smallwood.

Joey Smallwood was as involved in federal politics as he was in provincial. He ran the show in Newfoundland, and that included running all the campaigns. The federal party, knowing not to mess with a sure thing, let him do it his way. The cheering in Moores's basement turned first to puzzlement, when Moores said Smallwood hadn't called him, and then to horror, when he announced he was running on the other side. Amid cries of "Lord Christ, Frank, you can't, have you gone clear off your head?" and "Do you want to be elected, or do you want to make a damn fool of yourself?" Moores told them he was not only going to run, he was going to win.

In actual fact, winning wasn't as unlikely as it would have been even a few years earlier. Joey had moved his chess pieces around perhaps once too often. In the fall of 1967 Jack Pickersgill, a federal Liberal Joey had imported to become Newfoundland's representative in the federal cabinet, resigned his seat in Moores's home district of Bonavista-Trinity-Conception to become chairman of the Canadian Transport Commission. A by-election was called, and Joey had Charlie Granger resign his provincial seat in the Gander district to run in the federal seat. He then called a provincial by-election to fill Granger's seat and appointed the mayor of

Gander as the candidate. The people of the district were given no choice about either the provincial or the federal candidate, and they were starting to grumble.

The Gander district election in 1967 was pivotal for the PC Party because it opened the first crack in Joey's armour. The saying was that the Tories in Newfoundland could hold their meetings in a phone booth, except of course phone booths were even scarcer than Tories in those days. The Tories usually had a struggle to find any-one to run against Smallwood's man and Jack Pickersgill had proven to be an excellent champion of Newfoundland and his dis-trict. Harold Collins, a bayman and a supervisor with Canadian National Telegraph, had had the courage to run against Joey's can-didate twice and had been defeated. The Tory hierarchy in St. John's, under new leader Gerry Ottenheimer and party president John Carter, perhaps taking a leaf from Joey's book, decided that this time they could pick a better candidate than Collins and para-chuted in their choice, John Lundrigan. Lundrigan, an associate professor at Memorial University in St. John's was from the district and had been a campaign manager for one of Collins's failed at-tempts. Collins refused to step aside for Lundrigan, and the first Progressive Conservative nomination meeting ever held in New-foundland ensued.

Tories from other parts of Newfoundland were almost as fed up with the St. John's Tory establishment as they were with Small-wood. Led by Dr. Tom Farrell, president of the Humber East PC Association, a group from Corner Brook headed for Gander to support Collins. They weren't eligible to vote, so the movement created great interest in the provincial press. Lundrigan, realizing that the party had made a mistake, withdrew just before balloting was to begin.

The Tories rallied around Collins and, with a very slim margin, won every poll but one. St. John's always had a few Tory seats, rural Newfoundland virtually none. The busy town of Gander wasn't exactly rural by Newfoundland standards, but it was the first area outside St. John's to break with the Smallwood tradition and start to loosen Smallwood's hold. This was the political stage in Newfoundland in the fall of 1967. In the spring of 1968 Frank Moores made his entrance.

CHAPTER 8

Taking on the Giant

ALTHOUGH THE IMMINENT ELECTION was in the federal district of Bonavista-Trinity-Conception, running PC federally was running against Joey. Because of Collins's victory, for the first time there were three people running for the federal Tory nod; Memorial University professor, Dr. Hubert Kitchen; federal government employee and former area resident George Bradbury and Moores. It was a huge area encompassing three bays and almost two hundred communities, and getting the nomination was far from a forgone conclusion for Moores. He could count on support from Conception Bay, which took in Carbonear, Harbour Grace, and the Moores fish plants, but he wasn't well known in Bonavista Bay and Trinity Bay. At first it was hard to find Tories to support anyone, but not for long.

Moores began the rounds, visiting places where he didn't know a soul, and soon he found out he had support just because he was willing to take on Smallwood. A well-known Tory in Bonavista, Cal Rider, pitched in to get a crowd together there and in the surrounding areas, and Moores gradually started getting names from all over the district. On route by himself to his first meeting with the group in Bonavista, Moores dropped in to the new Holiday Inn in Clarenville. He introduced himself to the only person in the bar and asked him who the Tories in the area were. Jerry Duffitt informed

Moores that there was only one that he knew of, ironically a fellow by the name of Mike Singleton, who was out of town. When Moores said he'd like to get a few sensible people together and have a talk with them, Duffitt suggested another person who might help him, a woman named Kay Mercer.

Moores went off and found Kay Mercer, who said she'd see if there were any people around who might be interested. When he arrived back in Clarenville the next night, Kay Mercer had assembled some forty people, and the mood was ebullient. Moores never considered himself a natural speaker, but in those days he felt particularly awkward because of his inexperience. He simply told them what he was doing, what he felt was at stake, and why he felt it was so important to have a strong two-party system. His reception was enthusiastic enough to encourage him to ask if they might get a few carloads or maybe even a busload from Clarenville to come out to the upcoming nominating convention.

The convention was scheduled to be held in the basement of a church in Whitbourne which could hold two hundred people. When the party association started to sense that there might be a larger crowd, the decision was made to move it some thirty miles away to the S.W. Moores Memorial Stadium in Harbour Grace. Built by Frank Moores and renamed for Si after his death, the stadium's name evoked strong sentiment in the middle of Moores's home territory. The move was protested by the other candidates and attacked by Smallwood, who was already watching carefully. In fact Smallwood must have been feeling a premonition even at that point. Just before the convention was about to begin, he went on provincial television and charged Moores with refusing to reinvest any of the money he and his family had received for the sale of North Eastern Fisheries in the business; he also accused Moores of buying off the convention.

Moores was fairly confident of the support of the people close to him and their families, but he had no idea how many votes he might need to beat the other two candidates for the nomination. He was standing outside the stadium chatting to a supporter when a big yellow school bus arrived, then another one, and another one. He counted seventeen buses from Clarenville alone. People were hanging out of the bus windows, shouting, cheering, "roarin' and bawlin'," and it was Frank Moores's first hint of what might be happening. Moores's slogan was Frank Is the Man, and the people who came to the stadium definitely had a sense that Frank Moores was the man to pull off a miracle: he polled close to 90 per cent on the first ballot. But the battle was just beginning.

Pierre Trudeau was prime minister, and the Liberal candidate was a man by the name of Jim Tucker, but there was no doubt in anyone's mind that Frank Moores was taking on Joey Smallwood. That election campaign was the most vicious Newfoundland has ever seen, much more so than the provincial one that followed. Smallwood could smell the breakthrough, and he sensed that Frank Moores was the danger.

Moores knew instinctively that the greatest hope for change lay with the province's youth, so he sought students from Memorial University to make up his key organizational team. A young fellow from St. John's named Charlie White had started the first PC Party organization on campus. White had just finished his undergraduate studies and had a job lined up in preparation for law school in the fall. Frank Moores had other plans for the young man he had never met. However, Charlie White had heard of Frank Moores. When the phone rang and Moores asked him to get on board, White didn't hesitate. The next day he was at Moores's house in Harbour Grace.

White didn't really think that Moores had a chance. Smallwood had all but three seats in the Newfoundland legislature, and the incumbent, Jim Tucker, had won the federal seat by a landslide. Moores told White that Smallwood had actually approached him to run as a Liberal, that he would have kicked Tucker out to make way for Moores. When White asked why he didn't go with Smallwood, Moores said, for the same reason White had started the PC party at MUN: there had to be a fundamental change in Newfoundland, and he was going to take a shot at it.

Initially White took the attitude that even if they didn't win they would chip away at Smallwood's feet and "irritate him to no end because he thought he could buy anybody under any circumstances." Moores made it clear that he was in it to win, that this wasn't going to be another token Tory campaign. It was April, the election had not been called, but it was coming; on that first afternoon he and Charlie White laid out the district, identified the areas where he wasn't well known, and planned their organization, effectively beginning a campaign that would last nearly two months.

The Conservatives had never won as much as 30 per cent of the vote in the district. White had worked on Stanfield's leadership campaign and had an idea about what might be needed to overcome tremendous odds. The two decided that a blitz campaign was necessary and it would cost money. Jim Tucker was said to know all the voters in the district by their first names. Like most members of Smallwood's provincial caucus, he had no political clout, but people liked him, as indeed did his opponent Frank Moores. It didn't matter. They knew they weren't running against Jim Tucker and they weren't running against Pierre Trudeau. They were tackling Joey Smallwood head on.

Moores used the slogan It won't be long now. "Ladies and gentlemen, it won't be long now" began and ended every meeting and public address. Every time he responded to a charge or statement of Smallwood's, he ended with "Mr. Smallwood, it won't be long now," and the slogan became a buzzword all over Newfoundland. Bob Nutbeem, Megan's husband, started on the signage and promotional material, but he soon realized that most local suppliers were afraid to work against Joey's man. Bumper stickers, buttons, and sailor hats had to be brought in from Montreal with their consistent message: It won't be long now.

For the first time ever, Newfoundlanders and Labradorians saw a real political campaign. The Confederation debate had been fierce but not organized according to any campaign formula. There was a little federal help—Roy McMurtry made a trip down—but for the most part the federal mainstream PCs had long since given up on Newfoundland. Despite Stanfield's initial encouragement, Frank Moores and the other six Tory federal candidates were pretty much on their own.

Moores and White recruited three more young men from Memorial and supplied them with cars with sound systems. White had a master list of where they planned to be, and they'd send an advance car out a few days before, announcing the meeting. Much of rural Newfoundland still didn't have television and many older rural voters were illiterate, so sound was the key. When people heard the announcement that Mr. Moores was going to speak, everybody showed up, including the Liberals, who usually made up most of the audience because they made up most of the population.

At that time a candidate was allowed to fund his own campaign. Moores spent about $55,000, three times what he had expected and, in today's terms, close to a quarter of a million dollars. Moores provided it all, later saying that he didn't even know you could get money from the party. Had he needed the party's help, he would have been in trouble. The Tory war chest was not overflowing and they wouldn't have wanted to waste much if any of it was in Joey Smallwood's Newfoundland.

Charlie White acted as official agent and campaign manager. He and Moores were together every day for the entire campaign. White describes it today as the most gruelling campaign he has been ever involved in. They were on the road—dirt roads—almost every day. There were few hotels, and because people were nervous, they were lucky sometimes to get even a room in a boarding house; often they had to keep driving late at night to avoid sleeping in the car. They weren't always successful. After a night spent in the car and a breakfast of canned Vienna sausages or a bag of chips, they'd start out again. Moores began to think he had developed an ulcer, so finding fresh milk was added to the list of daily musts. This was not an easy thing in outport Newfoundland in 1968 unless they could scare up a local farmer with a few cows. With both transportation and refrigeration being unreliable, canned and powdered milk were the norm, and reconstituted milk was the closest many communities got to fresh. Partway through the campaign, Frank spilled some of his precious milk under the front seat of the car, and after a few hot days another car had to be sent for.

Another reason the milk was needed was to counteract the damage caused by the scattered nights in the homes of people brave enough to stand up in an open hall and be identified as Tories. Out would come the bottle, straight dark rum, while all hands sat around the kitchen table talking late into the night and enjoying a "lunch" of homemade bread and pies, bottled moose, and jam, the best "the missus" could find to put out for Frank Moores.

The common perception is that Moores was lazy, and he sometimes said it himself, but he maintained that it was a matter of motivation. Despite the occasional late night, Charlie White describes him as "the least lazy person I have ever worked with through an intense period like that. Never for one minute did he have his eye off the ball. There was no stopping him or slacking off and drinking and not being able to get up and go the next morning."

White was fascinated by Moores's ability to fill a room. Clearly he had an aura about him, and there was no question that many women found him extremely attractive. White was present many times when Frank was openly propositioned without the slightest invitation on his part whatsoever, and he maintains that while Frank certainly showed an interest in some women, when they were on that early campaign trail he never acted on it. "We were too exhausted." Because of this, White always felt that Moores's reputation as a hard-drinking womanizer was exaggerated and that the legend was considerably greater than the facts.

Having said that, he likes to say that he is probably the only person who spent a night in bed with Frank Moores and came away untouched. One night Moores and White arrived at a small hotel in Trinity Bay called the Done Roamin' to find there was only one room left. White asked how many beds it had. The answer: one. White recalls the two of them looking at each other, too tired to drive on, and then spending the night, "each of us with our hands clutched on our respective edge, facing away from each other."

Dodie Moores was back home in Harbour Grace with their seventh and last child, Andrea, still in diapers. By this time Moores' fifteen-acre property included a ranch-style house with a dance studio for the little girls complete with mirriros and ballet bar, a swimming pool, horse stables, and a guest house, and it was valued at $150,000, a fortune in 1968. Charlie White and other campaign workers stayed there when they were in the area. On those occasions Dodie would sometimes sit in on discussions and offer opinions from a woman's perspective. Although Frank hadn't asked her opinion or discussed his decision to run for office with her, she was happy with it because she thought he had a lot to offer. She was used to Frank being away and didn't foresee a lot of change in their family life.

Joey Smallwood couldn't believe what was happening. He had never actually had to talk about issues. People would vote for whoever Joey sent around, and there were MHAS living in St. John's who rarely if ever visited their outport districts. Moores talked of the big picture, and his knowledge of the fisheries served him well. The North Eastern plants were still operating. People credited Frank's father with having built a major employer for the area and credited Frank with expanding it significantly. His involvement with the hockey team and the stadium opened doors for him in the Conception and Bonavista bay communities in which people travelled for miles to watch the Cee Bees play. Many business and opinion leaders who had supported Smallwood in the Confederation debate twenty years earlier had come to the conclusion that they had exchanged one colonial master for another. People started pinning their hopes on Frank Moores from the very beginning.

His effortless charisma was matched by what many describe as his greatest asset, his fundamental generosity of spirit. Regardless of what was said and done by Smallwood or his henchmen, Moores took it in stride and seldom got drawn into retaliating. When he did, his response was always milder than the attack, telling supporters who got upset, "What do you expect? The Smallwood animal is the Smallwood animal, and that's what he does."

Joey Smallwood knew that there was more than one way to rid himself of a thorn in his flesh. Moores and White were campaigning in Bonavista when they got word that Mr. Tucker would like to meet with Mr. Moores. Charlie White advised Moores to ignore the summons, but Moores was curious, so White went with him to the meeting in a small, dismal hotel room. Tucker was very uncomfortable with White's presence but Moores insisted he stay. After considerable weaving around, the deal came out: if Moores threw the election—not necessarily withdrew, but wound down so that Tucker had a good chance at coming back to win, and did win—Tucker had been authorized by Smallwood to say that Frank Moores would be the next senator from Newfoundland.

Moores's response was thanks but no thanks. White describes it as a flash point in the campaign, recalling that when word got around that Frank Moores was in for the long haul and couldn't be bought off by Smallwood, other Newfoundland constituencies became very interested in what was happening in Bonavista-Trinity-Conception, and their own campaigns were galvanized as a result. Joey called in Pierre Trudeau to help squash the upstart.

In those days a prime minister campaigning in a rural district in Newfoundland was virtually unheard of, but Pierre Trudeau visited Trinity-Bonavista-Conception during the 1968 campaign on three different occasions. Trudeau hadn't fully attained his own star status by that time, and certainly not in rural Newfoundland, where his urbane manner wasn't nearly as impressive as Frank Moores's down-to-earth personality. When Moores stood on the wharf talking to the boys, he didn't talk down to them, he was one of them. Rural voters were enthralled with a sophisticated and successful businessman talking to them on an equal basis about things like access to roads that would let them get inland to cut wood.

Moores's empathy with people from every station in life would stay with him forever. It was one of the qualities that everyone spoke of. John Crosbie, the man who became both his colleague and his challenger, made a comparison that would have given him a good laugh. Frank Moores as premier was an admitted source of aggravation and frustration to Crosbie, but after Frank's death, Crosbie had high praise for Frank's personality, comparing him to Pope John Paul II. "He had the Pope's people qualities," Crosbie said, "interested in meeting people and always showing a human face. Obviously he had ability—look at his record at St. Andrew's—but it's all about trust, whether people trust you and think you're really interested in helping them. He had that."

John Lundrigan was back on the faculty of MUN when he was once again persuaded by Gerry Ottenheimer to run, this time federally in Gander-Twillingate. He agreed, really just for the experience; neither Ottenheimer nor Lundrigan thought the Tories had a chance of winning the seat. The first campaign donation Lundrigan received was $500 from Frank Moores, a large amount in 1968, when Lundrigan's entire campaign cost $9,000. Lundrigan's description of the Frank Moores he knew links Moores with another time, and it would have pleased him perhaps as much as Crosbie's would have amused him. "If Frank had been born in France in the pre-revolutionary days he would have been the leader of the revolution, and the people who would have been his biggest supporters would have been the peasants. He had a pretty privileged background, but he didn't identify with the elite, he identified with the downtrodden. He was a revolutionary, without question."

CHAPTER 9

Goliath Falters

SMALLWOOD FOCUSED all of his attention on Bonavista-Trinity-Conception. The more Joey and Trudeau came to the district, the better, as far as Moores was concerned. The contrast between the past and the future was re-enforced every time Joey spoke, and nobody in the district believed that Trudeau was genuinely interested in them. The dynamics of the fight in Bonavista-Trinity-Conception carried over to the other districts more and more as the campaign progressed.

Moores was going through the campaign having a wonderful time in spite of the gruelling pace. He enjoyed the warmth of the people and their eagerness to meet him, even if only for their own entertainment. As he entered a community, a car ahead of him played the accordion music of Newfoundland son Harry Hibbs over the sound system. Moores would arrive a few minutes later, get out on the side of the road, and speak through a bullhorn. People would come out and shake hands, he'd chat a bit, make his standard remarks, and then go on to the next place. The truck behind him played bagpipe music. The atmosphere was a bit circus-like until one community brought Moores up short, making him realize how much what he was doing meant to people and what an effect it could have on their lives. This profound experience never left him.

I suppose I hadn't really thought through why I was doing this, other than I thought it was the right thing to do. I arrived at Melrose, the music blaring and no one paying any attention whatsoever—not one soul in sight, even though I was on time for a change. So I got out with my bullhorn and started talking into thin air about who I was, what I wanted to do and how Newfoundland had to change, and I can see it now as clear in my eyes as if it was yesterday. I noticed, in one house right next to me, a curtain came back, and then I saw one lady walking down the path, and the next minute I saw another woman coming from a different direction, and I saw a couple of men coming up the road. And all of a sudden they started to run, and I saw women jumping over fences, literally, and all of a sudden I was surrounded by some two hundred people. They all came down. An Irish Catholic community, they'd been voting Tory all their lives, whenever they had a candidate.

And that is why they never got anything—nothing—in the middle of a sea of Protestants, for want of a better term. When I looked at these people, without any doubt in my mind at all, it was a moment when I almost quit politics because I realized that, no matter what, even if I did more than I had hoped I'd ever be able to do, it wouldn't be a tenth of what these people had to have.

You could see the hope in their eyes, blind hope, immediate hero worship. Cheering, patting me on the back, all this stuff. I was supposed to be on my way to Catalina, but I drove up on the hill and I parked the car. Charlie came alongside and asked me what I was doing. I told him what had happened and I said, 'I'm going home for two or three days to think about if I can carry on with this or not.' He said, 'You can't do that.' I said, 'Well, I'm going to do it,' and I did. And I decided, if I don't do anything, they'll be no better off than they are now, and if I do even a little bit, they'll be a little bit better off than they are now. It's the moment where I totally committed to the people in politics. To be premier or to be a member of parliament was a nice title, but to me it never meant anything really. The only reason I ever went into politics was because of ordinary people.

Ordinary people were starting to talk about Frank Moores. Alex Hickman, Smallwood's attorney general, had never met Moores, but he had heard of Moores's ability early. On a vacation in Prince Edward Island with his wife and children, he stayed at the same place as the headmaster from St. Andrew's College. On finding out Hickman was from Newfoundland, Moores's former headmaster asked him if he knew Frank Moores and proceeded to tell the story of the gawky boy and his trunk, adding that Frank Moores had turned out to have more leadership ability than most they'd had at the prestigious school.

Partway through the election campaign, Hickman was standing outside a store in Manuels, a small community just outside St. John's. On a house next door, a couple of carpenters were working on different ends of the roof, hammering away, and every once in a while he'd hear one say It won't be long now, and the other reply, "No, b'y, it won't be long now." Hickman said to himself, it's catching on.

Shortly after the incident in Manuels, Smallwood was pontificating to his cabinet that the Liberals would take seven seats again. Hickman had doubts about St. John's East and West and decided to keep them to himself, but he spoke up and said that he thought that fellow Moores might do well around the bay. Smallwood scoffed at the suggestion that a rich merchant's son might beat Jim Tucker, but Hickman pointed out that there were a lot of Moores signs out there; he later made a bet with fellow cabinet minister Ed Roberts that the Tories would take six seats.

Joey Smallwood was less worried than irritated, and he decided to rid himself of this annoyance once and for all by attacking

Moores's reputation. Two days before the election, the district of Bonavista-Trinity-Conception was flooded with copies of a pamphlet from the Liberal Party of Newfoundland and Labrador called *The Truth about Mr. Frank Moores and North East Fisheries.* At the same time, Joey's voice, reading the pamphlet, was heard over public address systems from six vehicles dispersed throughout the district.

Referring to Moores as a millionaire candidate whose family had grown rich on the backs of Newfoundland fishermen, the pamphlet said that Moores had received $2 million when he sold North East but refused to put back one cent to keep the business going, and that the government had had to give North East $1 million to keep it operating. It said that Moores had been fired from the company, and it ended by telling voters that they should "teach this very rich young man a lesson." The tape playing didn't last very long. Five of the drivers gathered the courage to refuse to play it. The one who tried to carry on soon gave up, saying that he feared he was going to be killed if he didn't stop.

Undaunted, Smallwood held a meeting at the fish plant in Carbonear. On an improvised stand in front of a crowd of fishermen and plant workers he was even less guarded in his language, calling Moores, among other things, the son of the blood-sucking merchant who bled the people for decades.

Moores sought legal advice from St. John's Tory lawyer Bill Marshall and decided that the best response was to get a rebuttal out into the district quickly. Charlie White and Bob Nutbeem wrote the response out by hand, calling it "The Truth about the Big Lie," and over the next two days they circulated about three thousand mimeographed copies throughout the district.

Describing the attack on his dead father as vicious and terrible, Moores accused Smallwood of "gutter politics, mudslinging, and personal abuse as his only way out against a man who offers himself in service to the people." What makes this rather bland remark noteworthy is that such public criticism of Smallwood was a novelty, and the press all over the province ate it up. The momentum was building, and Moores, White, and their team were living it twenty hours a day.

While doing some last minute door-to-door campaigning, Moores crossed paths with Jim Tucker, and Tucker quietly apologized for what Smallwood was doing. After the election Tucker took the bold step of stating publicly that he had always believed in getting as high as he could by his own skill and pluck, not by tramping on his opponent; what the premier did he did on his own, and he had no part in it.

Moores recalls that people everywhere were upset about the attacks. "I went back to the garden party in Melrose the next year because that's where my life changed in politics, and they were still talking about it. Phil Donovan and Father Hawco asked me into the back room, I thought for a drink. I went back and they said, 'Look, we tried to find those sons of bitches who voted against you all year, and we can't lay our hands on one of 'em.' The very fact that there were eight or ten ... who actually voted against me had them upset for a whole year."

Helped by Frank Moores's momentum and Smallwood's extremism, the Tories made Newfoundland history by winning six of the seven federal seats, while the rest of the country was swept off its feet by Trudeaumania. The morning after the election, the stunned Liberals sitting around the caucus table were treated to a display of classic Smallwood egotism and denial. He entered the room to a long silence. Then he said that if the election were held all over again that day, the Liberals would take seven seats, that the people of Newfoundland realized that morning for the first time that they had voted against *him*, and that they would never have done it if they'd understood what they were doing. He also noted that Pierre Trudeau, being a French-Canadian, had had a negative effect on the vote.

The rich merchant's son took great pride in the fact that most of his votes had come from the families of the fishermen and plant workers who had been his employees. He gave as an example the small community of Port de Grave. Moores considered the fishermen there to be the best small boat fishermen in the world and respected them for telling him flat out that they were all Liberal. Almost to a man, they had changed their vote because of Smallwood's tape.

CHAPTER 10

Mr. Moores Goes to Ottawa

FRANK MOORES ARRIVED IN OTTAWA with high and idealistic expectations of being able to improve life for the people in his district. He describes walking into the House of Commons for the first time as an incredible moment in his life, "this huge green chamber with the Speaker's chair up there, and you look at it and you realize it's the parliament of your country and you are now, all of a sudden, part of it. That's a time when it all comes together inside of you pretty fast." In his impassioned maiden speech on fisheries, he spoke of the need to expand the three- and twelve-mile limits and stressed the need for conservation, citing concerns over the damage being done on the Hamilton and Red banks by the Germans and the Russians. Some of the concerns he articulated in 1968 are still discussed today as among the most pressing needs for the fishing industry, but having delivered the message he was most passionate about, he became an infrequent participant in House debate. He was used to being a mover and shaker. He saw that his input into the national debate as a back-bencher in opposition would be miniscule, and that wasn't what Frank Moores had expected. The excitement of the campaign and the adrenaline rush of taking on Joey were gone; after starting off with such great anticipation, he soon became very bored.

With no real political ideology, Moores was also taken aback by what he described as the national Tory nuthouse. "The internal politics between the western right-wing conservatives, died-in-the-wool redneck Tories (excluding Joe Clark), and the progressive central Canadians such as the Reverend David MacDonald and Flora MacDonald and all that crew—the Dalton Camp group—were incredibly tedious. The closer you got to Newfoundland, the less the MPs concerned themselves with party 'wings,' and the Newfoundland MPs didn't have any real leanings one way or the other." Sometimes Moores felt like climbing the walls of the 'nuthouse.'

Dodie Moores saw her husband's election as an opportunity to be close to her family in Toronto. Given that Frank was expecting to be very busy, it wasn't hard to make the decision that she and the children would live in Toronto and Frank would commute on the weekends. She had no idea of her husband's constant need for attractive female companionship. She knew that he liked affection and that he always noticed what other women wore, but he was attentive to her when he was with her, taking great interest in her clothes, choosing some of them and wanting her to buy more. He was loving and affectionate, and she didn't realize that her charming husband always needed somebody to be charming with, whether she was there or not. After a while he was not coming back to Toronto every weekend like they'd planned.

Moores had moved into an apartment building within walking distance of Parliament Hill. It was full of MPs, and his next-door neighbour was Don Jamieson, the only Liberal MP elected in Newfoundland that year. In the evenings they swapped stories over a few drinks. The new fellows learned the ropes from the older hands. Some of them didn't need to learn that, married or not, you could live a bachelor's life when you were in Ottawa. Two knocks on the wall asked, "Is there anyone there?" and three knocks back meant, "Someone is, so stay away."

At this time, the Conservatives were without a national party president. Dalton Camp's unsuccessful challenge to John Diefenbaker's leadership the year before had caused a bitter split in the party and resulted in Camp's resignation. The post had been vacant for almost a year while the infighting carried on. Some felt that it was time the party had an MP as president, and Moores had the distinct advantage of being so new to the Tory party that he was in neither camp. Jack Horner, Don Mazinkowski, and a few others decided that Moores was the ideal candidate to both attract new people and charm the veterans. Aside from being disillusioned with life as an opposition backbencher, Moores saw becoming party president as an opportunity to improve the profile of Newfoundland throughout the rest of Canada. Also, the brand new Tory was easily persuaded to go after the party's top job because, after all, the top job was what he was used to.

Once again, losing wasn't part of Moores's vocabulary. Roy McMurtry coordinated the campaign, and Moores called in Charlie White to be his right hand. White took a couple of weeks off from law school, canvassed across Canada, and worked in Ottawa for the summer. Only one secretary was provided for each MP, and that secretary shared the MP's office. White was sort of tacked onto the side of Frank's desk. When Moores was in the House or elsewhere, White sat in his chair. Moores paid White out of his own pocket, and White stayed in Moores's apartment. Once again, Moores proved he could put play on hold to campaign, and when he took a break, White says, he usually stayed in the apartment reading. Moores did a lot of the cooking, too, always setting the table in the correct manner to which he was accustomed, surprising White as much with his attention to etiquette as with his skill in the kitchen.

Jack Horner and Dalton Camp had been bitter opponents in the leadership review in 1966, but now the Horner and Camp factions combined to get Frank Moores elected as president of the party; he won easily on the first ballot over Saskatoon's Dr. Lewis Brand and Quebec's Heward Grafftey. Brand charged that Moores was backed by the power brokers of Ontario, a fact which Moores denied, although it didn't hurt that he was able to campaign extensively at his own expense. Uniting the Progressive Conservative party nationally and strengthening its organization was now the job of a man who, less than two years earlier, didn't know what a nominating meeting was. Back in the Newfoundland House of Assembly, MHA Harold Collins rose to congratulate the MP for Bonavista-Trinity-Conception on his election as president of the national Progressive Conservative Association. "It is completely out of order," said Premier Smallwood. "Who wants to hear about Frank Moores in this House? . . . Frank Moores is not a matter of urgency in this House and never will be."

Not for the first or last time, Frank Moores felt like the proverbial dog that chased a bus and caught it. As president of the national Conservative Party, following in the footsteps of the strongly opinionated Dalton Camp, he had to try to unite the party, yet he really had no personal or political sense of what it was to be a Conservative. He also had no real affinity for politics. He found he hated living in Ottawa and being around political types day and night. He decided to buy a cottage somewhere between Ottawa and Toronto to get away from the city and, in theory, be able to spend more time with Dodie and the children. He heard of a place about sixty miles north of Kingston called Chaffey's Lock and was advised to go see a chap named Jim Alford, who owned the marina there.

Jim Alford was a well-liked larger-than-life personality, and Moores trusted him right away. Alford took him around, pointing out what was for sale. What caught Moores's eye wasn't one of the high-end cottages or homes but a big point of land surrounded on three sides by water, graced with stands of birch and without a For Sale sign. After seeing everything on the market, Moores told Alford he wanted that point of land, picked a cottage design out of a book, wrote out a cheque for $25,000, and asked Alford to look after it. When Alford gave him the green light, he had a few truckloads of sand dumped down by the water, and for a while Dodie and the kids got to see him more frequently.

His learning curve as party president was steep. On his first trip to Vancouver, in a speech to a small group, he noted that the PCs were in the minority because Social Credit was the right-wing party there. He perceived that Social Credit thinking, and therefore trade, was predominantly north-south, and he was intrigued that the Rocky Mountains were almost like a barrier between two worlds. Deciding to make his speech a little more relevant to the BC audience, he waxed eloquent on his observation that while Quebec preached separatism, BC actually practiced it. He got a standing ovation and was quite pleased with himself.

The next day, driving up through Penticton, he stopped at a small store for a pack of cigarettes and saw a big red headline in the local paper: "PC Chief Assails BC Separatism." Thinking, "What in the Christ has Stanfield done now?" he bought the paper and started reading, but he discovered in the first paragraph that Mr. Stanfield wasn't the subject of the story. It was Frank Moores. He made a chagrined call to Bob Stanfield, who said, "Frank where are you?"

"I'm up in the Okanagan Valley."

"How long are you planning to stay?"

"A couple of days."

"Could you make it a couple of years?"

Stanfield was joking, of course, but Moores learned a lesson about being careful of what he said. The dynamics within the Conservative party were difficult and strained to say the least, and the new national president found himself in a unique situation.

"There were two distinct elements within the party—the Bob Stanfield group, who were the progressives if you like, and there were the conservative end, which were mostly westerners but quite a few from Ontario as well—a few from Quebec, oddly enough. When I'd come back from a trip, I'd go to Mr. Stanfield and give him an update on everything that had happened and what I felt should be done. Immediately after leaving him, I'd go across the hall to Mr. Diefenbaker and do the same thing. There was one person leading the party, but there were two people to report to. Diefenbaker still had a handle on everything happening in Ontario, very much so. And conversations would be very different; their interpretation of what I told them was very different. There was a lot of wishful thinking, particularly on Mr. Diefenbaker's part.

I didn't have to go see Diefenbaker, but to keep peace in the caucus it was a wise thing to do. I think Bob Stanfield knew what I was doing. He wouldn't have minded if he had. But Diefenbaker, if he had been in Stanfield's place, would have minded. Diefenbaker was—I was going to say a control freak, but that's the wrong word. But he was very much in control; he didn't tolerate people who disagreed with him very well. It was the damnedest things you ever saw in your life. In caucus meetings, there were seventy-two people, and the difference in philosophies! I look back at Brian Mulroney, and how the hell he ever kept Quebec separatists, the very conservative westerners, and all the rest in one room, I don't know. At the height of the United Nations, they couldn't have pulled it off."

Moores saw the national presidency as a personal opportunity to gain organizational and political experience and also to inform Canada about Newfoundland. He was constantly amazed and appalled at how few of the people he met and spoke to knew anything about Newfoundland at all, but he felt that he himself was well received and respected, and he believed that people were very interested to find out more. In later years, however, he had experiences in which Newfoundland was so maligned that he wondered if his earlier audiences were just being polite to him.

In the first year as national president, Moores made a half a dozen trips across Canada, giving over fifty major speeches. Before the year was out he had also undertaken a complete organizational study of the party administration, produced guidelines for reorganization and programs for building the party at the federal constituency level, organized a policy conference, and drawn up a mechanism for continuing policy development.

He was criticized in the Newfoundland press for the scarcity of his appearances in the House, actually setting a record low with an attendance rate of 8 per cent. Moores didn't worry about it, saying that there were a number of ways to be a good MP, and shooting off your mouth in the House at frequent intervals had little value unless it was backed up with a realistic approach to solving problems. He set up a mobile office that travelled constantly throughout the 189 small towns scattered throughout his huge district, and even in his absence, he felt, his constituents were getting more attention than they had ever had.

John Crosbie describes winning the national presidency as an example of Moores's tremendous political luck. The fact that he hadn't been an active PC before he went to Ottawa should have been a handicap; instead the personable new fellow was the key to avoiding the bloodbath that would have resulted if the Camp and Diefenbaker forces had slugged it out. But achieving the national presidency was only part of that particular piece of luck.

That year as national president was a tremendous preparation for what came later. He met people from coast to coast and made a lot of Conservative contacts. His national office was full of pamphlets about organizing poll captains and area captains, policy conventions, agendas—all the strategies, new and tested, geared to winning an election. While his campaign for the federal seat had been well organized by Newfoundland standards, it was while he was national president that he increased and fine-tuned the knowledge of political organization and timing that made the difference in the subsequent historic Newfoundland provincial election.

Working in the national office as executive assistant to the new president and joining him in a cross-country organizational tour was an attractive young political science major from Manitoba. Janis Johnson, just eight years older than Frank's oldest daughter, was the personification of her Icelandic heritage, tall, cool, and tenacious. As the daughter of a Manitoba cabinet minister, she'd grown up in politics. According to staffers and colleagues who were around at the time, Janis Johnson set her sights on Frank from the very beginning. For a while he seemed totally unaware of her, but not for long, and their affair developed, in his view, as the inevitable result of travelling together. Not only was she attractive and interested, she encouraged him and talked to him with enthusiasm and knowledge about politics. Soon he was finding reasons not to make it even to the cottage, and Dodie started thinking she should probably have gone to Ottawa instead of Toronto. It was too late. The next Mrs. Moores was on the horizon.

When Moores was in Toronto with Dodie and the children, Janis would call him. When he was in Chaffey's Lock she'd show up at Dorothy's Fishing Lodge with some reason to see him, sometimes inviting herself over. Janis's demands on her husband's time annoyed Dodie, but Moores was still as attentive and loving as ever when they were together, and she suspected nothing. One late August weekend at Chaffey's, when Frank announced that Janis was coming by to do some work, Dodie just didn't want to see her, so she decided to go back to Toronto and get some last minute back-to-school things done, leaving the children with Frank. Thinking of her naivety, she ruefully laughs at the thought that she'd probably put more of a damper on Janis's weekend than if she'd been there to keep the children occupied.

A portrait taken that summer in Toronto shows a happy family and a smiling Frank, but the story behind it is that he came home long enough to make the photographer's appointment and left immediately. Incredibly, despite his own behaviour, or maybe because of it, he was jealous when Dodie made an effort to enjoy herself without him. At Christmas that year, he was home just for the afternoon of Christmas Day. He made an excuse for not making it back for New Year's Eve, but he assured Dodie that he'd call at midnight. When Dodie told him she'd be next door at a neighbour's party, he wasn't pleased, calling to check up on her and make sure she was there.

CHAPTER 11

The Revolution Needs a Leader

BACK IN NEWFOUNDLAND, Joey Smallwood was entering the fourth year of a five-year term. With Harold Collins's breakthrough in Gander followed by the massive federal upset, provincial Tories were salivating at the possibility of making greater inroads into Joey's empire.

Smallwood's strength lay in the outports, where a large population of mainly uneducated people credited him personally, and not entirely incorrectly, with the old age pension and family allowance cheques that had come with Confederation. In a cash-poor society, the first Canadian cheque was the most money some people had ever seen, and there would be another cheque every month. It's not surprising that Joey Smallwood's picture hung in a place of prominence on many a front room wall.

In St. John's the more sophisticated voters were predominantly Tory, prompting Joey to label the PCs the rich merchants' party. Ironically his commitment to expanding primary and secondary education and Memorial University was part of Smallwood's downfall, as young educated Newfoundlanders from all over the province were not as easily impressed and controlled as their parents.

Smallwood's devastating weaknesses in the areas of financial management and economic development were becoming impossible to disguise or explain. Under his leadership, the terms of confederation that Newfoundland signed with Canada had been so heavily weighted in Canada's favour that prominent businessman Ches Crosbie, one of the delegates to the National Convention, couldn't bring himself to sign the historic agreement. (Ches Crosbie later advised his son John to have nothing to do with Smallwood, but John had to learn his own lessons.) The inequitable terms of union and Smallwood's subsequent handling of the Newfoundland treasury were dragging the newest Canadian province and its people into a hole they might never get out of. In May of 1968, a week after Frank Moores beat Joey Smallwood's man in Bonavista-Trinity-Conception, Smallwood heavyweights John Crosbie and Clyde Wells resigned from cabinet over Smallwood's use of public funds in his dealings with industrialists John C. Doyle and John Shaheen.

John C. Doyle was an American mining promoter. The story goes that in 1952, on a trip to Newfoundland to seek markets for a coal company he had acquired in Montreal, Doyle had had the good fortune to sit next to Joey's Deputy Minister of Mines, who revealed that the Iron Ore Company of Canada had just released a 24,000 square mile holding in Labrador, south of Wabush Lake, a holding the DM believed had significant ore prospects. It didn't take the smooth-talking, urbane American long to get an audience with Smallwood and convince to hand him over the rights to Wabush Lake and all its ore deposits, along with offshore oil rights and timber rights. More than fifteen years later, when Crosbie and Wells resigned, Doyle's share of the Newfoundland treasury included, among other millions, a $16.5 million bond issue (half the total provincial debt at the time of issue in 1955) to finance a rail line in Labrador. He had also received $120 million in backing for a mill in Stephenville, on the province's west coast, which would produce linerboard, a kind of paperboard used in cardboard boxes. In addition he was collecting $25,000 every three months from the government as consultant fees to his own businesses; eventually he collected $7 million a year in royalties, while the province's share amounted to $3.2 million.

John Shaheen was an American industrialist proposing to build an oil refinery in Come By Chance, Placentia Bay. Evidence of his own investment in the project was hard to find, moving Clyde Wells to observe, "There is no indication that Shaheen put one solitary nickel into the Newfoundland refinery." It was eventually built with over $30 million in provincial funds and a $125 million loan guarantee.

Smallwood reacted to the defection of Crosbie and Wells with typical arrogance. In July of 1968 he unceremoniously dumped another three of his veteran cabinet ministers and appointed seven new ministers, some of whom had never run politically, let alone been elected. Such highhandedness was child's play for the man who, at a dinner the same month, referred to Lenin as "one of the greatest human beings ... certainly in this century," adding, "Hitler was another."

The resignations showed the first internal crack in Smallwood's power. Externally, federal Liberal dollars had dried up, and John Crosbie was in Ottawa meeting privately with the Liberal brass to discuss his replacing Smallwood as leader. Smallwood obliged Crosbie and challenged the dissenters by calling a leadership convention for November 1969.

It was a bitter fight that split the Liberal party badly. The venom between Crosbie and Smallwood had grown so caustic in the year before the convention that Alex Hickman decided to run as an alternative to either of them. Cabinet minister Val Earle publicly supported Hickman, but no one in the caucus was willing to side publicly with Crosbie. Smallwood was more vicious toward the leadership contenders than he had ever been to Frank Moores. He emerged bloodied but victorious and expelled Crosbie from the party. John Crosbie had a lot of support, particularly among the youth, and announced the organization of the new Liberal Reform Party.

By the time the next session of the House began, the opposition had grown to ten, and seven of them had originally been elected as Liberals. Labrador MHA Tom Burgess had left Smallwood to sit as an Independent. Alex Hickman and Val Earle had made their break with Smallwood and joined the Conservatives, and John Crosbie had Clyde Wells, Beaton Abbott, and Gerry Myrden under his Liberal Reform banner. These men, some of Smallwood's strongest and smartest, couldn't stomach any more of his despotism and bizarre approach to economic development. Val Earle, the former finance minister, reported that he had personally contributed only sixteen of the 15,000 words in the last budget.

The provincial Tory leader, Gerry Ottenheimer, was a good looking, somewhat soft-spoken educator with a measured, intellectual manner. Ottenheimer's organizing ability and initiatives in improving the party strength outside of St. John's had been recognized as playing a significant part in both the provincial and the federal victories. Given the close outcome of the future election, it is valid to conclude that the Tory party might not have won it without Ottenheimer's groundwork, and it came as a shock to Conservatives and Liberals alike when he suddenly resigned in November of 1969. Ottenheimer cited the usual family reasons and a long-time ambition to study law as the explanation for his unexpected and oddly timed departure. In his book *No Holds Barred* John Crosbie wrote that Ottenheimer had been set up in a brothel in Montreal. Some people lay the alleged set-up at the door of the provincial Tories, who wanted to force Ottenheimer out and make room for a new leader. Others say it had all the trademarks of a John C. Doyle move to discredit and demoralize the party, either by forcing its leader out at a critical time or, to hedge his bets, by making room for a candidate he could control.

Ottenheimer had a good public image, if not the charismatic personality needed to defeat Smallwood, and the Doyle theory, while seeming more far-fetched, is in many ways the more plausible. Doyle was the kind of man who would put the fox among the chickens and then sit back and watch how the battle played out, believing he'd pick up an advantage one way or another. If indeed Ottenheimer's resignation was orchestrated by Doyle, the scheme backfired when Frank Moores entered the race.

St. John's lawyer Bill Marshall, who had advised Moores when Smallwood attacked his father and also handled the Birds Eye sale, was provincial party president while Moores was in Ottawa, and he became interim leader after Gerry Ottenheimer resigned. Marshall and Gerry Ottenheimer were very close, and Marshall maintains that a year before his resignation Ottenheimer discussed with him his interest in pursuing the study of law. Neither confirming nor denying the story in Crosbie's book, he goes on to say, "Cannibalistic traits seem generic in Tories. Appetites are especially whetted towards their leaders when the aroma of government can be scented on the horizon. This was operative in that era, as the noses of several pretenders, who will remain nameless—except to state Frank was not among them—set them on the scent of their own leadership fantasies."

The chance to unseat Smallwood was not to be squandered, and the choice of a leader was a make-or-break situation. Frank Moores had proven he was an able match for Smallwood on the campaign trail. His wealth, old family connections, and private school education made him acceptable to some of the St. John's Tories, his small-town fish plant roots gave him a chance with the wary baymen who revered Smallwood, and once again, he hadn't been around long enough to be involved in the internal party politics.

Not everyone in the Tory party thought that Frank Moores was the leader they needed or wanted. Among some of the old-guard St. John's Tories, the thought that the only way they could win an election was with a fellow from around the bay with no history in the provincial PC party was too much to swallow. Some looked to the Smallwood dissidents. Tom Williams (the father of Danny Williams, who eventually became premier), was among those who tried to recruit Reform Liberal John Crosbie. Alex Hickman was also considered a good possibility.

Hickman says that Frank Moores was one of those who attempted to persuade him to seek the Tory leadership. Hickman was tempted, but despite the "anything goes" nature of Newfoundland politics, he felt it was a bit much to run for the Liberal party leadership in the fall of 1969 and in the spring of 1970 expect to be the leader of the Conservative party. At that time the only announced candidates were Walter Carter and John Carter. The Conservatives were getting worried; the candidates were not bad, but they were not star quality.

Becoming premier of Newfoundland was never part of Frank Moores's political ambitions. He wanted to get rid of Smallwood, but he didn't see himself as leading the assault. He hadn't been in Ottawa long, and with the prestigious and active presidency of the national party, he faced a significant challenge and was no longer bored.

But the belief that he was the one to do it began to catch on. Moores made a public statement that he wasn't interested. A "draft Moores" campaign began, led by Dr. Kevin Linegar, Ed Neary, Terri and Tom Williams, and Frankie Cole. A subcommittee of thirty, including Terri Williams, went door to door around the province and collected forty thousand names on a petition. Linegar and Eric Martin flew to Ottawa and refused to leave Moores's office until he agreed to come home. Moores joked that he finally capitulated to get rid of the smell of the take-out chicken they kept eating.

CHAPTER 12

The Stage

MOST NEWFOUNDLANDERS HAD NO IDEA about the state of the province's economy, that a mere twenty years after Confederation, Joey's promises of prosperity had been sabotaged by his own egotism and incompetence. Nor did they realize that the rise in popularity of Pierre Trudeau was being matched by the fall from Trudeau's favour of Joey Smallwood. Trudeau had no intention of associating himself too closely with someone who had Smallwood's potential for embarrassment. In March of 1970 a well-known Toronto *Telegram* reporter named Bob MacDonald ran a three-part series examining Newfoundland's economic and political condition. The articles were repeated on consecutive days by the St. John's *Evening Telegram* "to give Newfoundlanders the opportunity to read what other Canadians are being told about Newfoundland." The series had a huge impact because it was the first time such an analysis had been laid out before the Newfoundland public.

Headlined "Ottawa Quiet . . . but Concerned," the first article began by pointing out that Newfoundland had entered Confederation in 1949 with a treasury surplus of $40 million, and it stated, "The province of Newfoundland is sinking into a dangerous financial and economic situation that some top critics feel may lead to a type of federal trusteeship."

The mere hint of federal trusteeship was like a red flag to Newfoundlanders, who remembered their humiliation and loss of self-determination under the Commission government. The article reported that the federal government was planning to bring in a one-year interim program to aid development in Newfoundland. This would normally have been something for Joey to take credit for, except for one very significant detail: the federal government intended to supervise the expenditures. Hackles were raised all over the province.

Listed as warning signals were skyrocketing debt, which had increased to close to $1 billion; unemployment, which stood at more than twice the national average; depopulation—Newfoundlanders were leaving in droves, and an estimated 135,000 now lived in Toronto; maturation in three years of $100 million in short-term debentures, with no sinking funds having been provided; the resignation of Denis Groom, financial advisor to the premier, after only four years of a ten-year contract; the departure of key ministers from government ranks, charging that Smallwood's chaotic one-man show had led to the brink of economic disaster; and the huge concessions given to US industrialists John Shaheen and John C. Doyle.

The Newfoundland people learned that even though the government was guaranteeing loans and giving millions to John Shaheen, he could buy the oil refinery outright any time within fifteen years for $2,000. Another report put the purchase figure at $10 million, still a bargain for a property built with $155 million of other people's money. The land to build on had been sold to him for one dollar, and he was to be repaid for all promotional fees, plus 100 per cent. Shaheen was also given all the timber rights on the island not owned by two paper companies, Price and Bowater, and a big chunk of the Labrador timber rights so he could build a third paper mill on his Come By Chance land.

Newfoundland was richer in natural resources than any other province in its new country, but the ink was barely dry on the

Confederation agreement when Joey started his disastrous and seldom resource-based "develop or perish" policy. He hired Alfred Valdmanis, a Latvian Joey described as a genius, to be the province of Newfoundland's first Director of Economic Development. Joey raved about Valdmanis to the point of declaring on a radio show that he wouldn't want to be premier for ten minutes without him. Valdmanis took Joey on a merry circuit of German and Latvian industrialists and some twenty impractical schemes until Joey found out that Valdmanis's real genius lay in collecting kickbacks, and he had to suffer the embarrassment of sending his genius to prison.

MacDonald pointed out that Joey didn't have to go to Europe or the United States to empty Newfoundland's treasury. His old friend and former MHA, O.L. (Al) Vardy, now Deputy Minister of Economic Development, decided St. John's needed a top quality apartment building, so the province financed the $5 million luxury Elizabeth Towers. Vardy ensconced himself in the penthouse, but the Towers were too expensive for most people, and a year later only forty of 102 suites were rented; the cost to taxpayers was another $500,000 a year. Among Vardy's other enterprises was a supply company that everyone in the hospitality or restaurant business was expected to buy from.

Another of Smallwood's close friends, Arthur Lundrigan, "after me the hardest working man in Newfoundland," was given a contract to build four Holiday Inns in the province. Under Hotel Buildings Ltd., a crown corporation, the hotels were built, tax free, on a cost-plus basis and fee system. Building costs to the province in 1970 were close to $17 million, and operating losses were close to $2 million. Joey explained, "in a backward, isolated province such as Newfoundland, taxpayers' money must be used to help private business or else nothing would get done." Newfoundlanders were to accept that Holiday Inns and Lundrigan's Hotel Buildings Ltd. needed a lot of financial help.

Building was an important business among Joey's friends, such as electrical contractors Arthur Noseworthy and Joe Ashley, who were often awarded big contracts without tender. Unabashed, Joey reasoned, "Art Noseworthy is one of the finest electricians in the province" and "a very ardent campaigner," and "in every election since Confederation Joe Ashley takes six weeks off to campaign for me." These men may well have been good electricians, but being good Smallwood supporters was their key to success.

The major shareholder in the government-sponsored Newfoundland Farm Products was Russwood Poultry, owned by Joey's son. The company operated in a government-owned plant with government-owned equipment for the sum of a dollar a year. The Newfoundland treasury spent $700,000 on renovations, paid the annual heating cost, and in addition contributed a "grant" of $210,000 to help cover operating expenses and $23,000 for "direct expenses." Joey was indignant about criticism. "Just because my son is in eggs and I used to be his partner, should everybody in Newfoundland believe I am a dirty rotten grafter?"

The series of articles included a look at Smallwood's policy of offering cheap power to attract industry, using the Electric Reduction Company of Canada, Erco, as an example. The establishment of the company's phosphorous plant in Placentia Bay was one of the most opposed of Smallwood's development schemes. *Evening Telegram* columnist Ray Guy, a native of Placentia Bay, led the protest against this potential polluter with the kind of biting political satire that Newfoundlanders relished. Guy was right; Erco polluted the bay in short order, and the details of the deal became even harder to swallow.

Smallwood had given Erco a $15 million subsidy plus a guarantee of power at 2.5 mills. Cost to produce the power was estimated at 5 to 6 mills. Clyde Wells estimated that Erco was costing the Newfoundland taxpayer over $3 million a year and was good for twenty-five years. Smallwood responded, "Hogwash. The criticism is ignorant. Industry will not come here without cheap power. So I ask a company, how much do they want to pay for the power – how much can it pay to have an economic operation?" According to Smallwood, allowing businesses to set the amount they wanted to pay for power was standard practice all over North America.

The focus on Joey Smallwood ended with an interview in "the huge living room of his $500,000 home" on Roaches Line, outside St. John's, with the premier predicting he would eliminate eight of the ten opposition members in the next election. The reporter then turned his attention to the upcoming Tory leadership convention and to one candidate in particular. Frank Moores, the writer said, was stressing that "we need to develop skills and industries Newfoundlanders do best. . . . We don't have polluted air and water here so far, except for that caused by the phosphorous plant. We have basically happy people who should not be shoved into huge plants to push buttons."

The message was simple: Moores's ideas about economic development couldn't have been more different from Smallwood's. He was aware that change wouldn't come easily and took pains to repeat that message at every opportunity. He publicly welcomed senior Liberal defectors, he told the reporter, envisioning a total change of government style.

> "Political parties are what people make them. We've got to get people involved who don't even recognize the need that they be involved in their own welfare, their own future, who perhaps after twenty-one years don't even realize they have that right, and we have to get our best people involved, our best academics, artists, businessmen, educators. I want these people to become totally involved in the work that faces us, and to know that they won't be manipulated like puppets but will have major roles to play in reviving the province.
>
> Our best possible role may be in developing our cottage industries, developing excellence in what we know and what we can get better at—logging, mining, fish processing, sheep raising—instead of putting up heavily industrialized

plants. We need to stress vocational training more. Most important, we have to take the stigma out of work. For many there seems to be no better opportunity than welfare when it gives them more than working hard would. To me welfare is just the reverse; it imprisons people because they just can't afford to break loose."

ABOVE: Frank and big sister 'Memo'.

LEFT: The Commanding Officer with his proud mother and sister.

Newfie Boys Travel 11 Days To See Cup Game—'Worth It'

Telegram

HITCH-HIKE FROM NEWFOUNDLAND TO SEE GREY CUP GAME

Left to right, Frank Moores, Dick Sutton, Terry Malone

It took 11 days for two young men to get to Toronto, but the effort was worth it. This afternoon they'll be at the Grey Cup game, after paying $21.30 for the two tickets.

They are Frank Moore and Terry Malone, of Carbonear, Newfoundland. They arrived last night in Toronto, where they were met by Dick Sutton, of Agincourt. The three boys were chums at St. Andrew's College

six years ago and this is the first time they've met since leaving school.

The lads first hitchhiked a ride on a fish freighter to Boston. From there they managed to get to Montreal and took a train to Toronto.

While here they will stay with Sutton in Agincourt. Neither was anxious to predict the outcome of today's game.

LEFT: Early press relations.

BELOW: St. Andrew's football team, Moores second from right front row.

FIRST FOOTBALL TEAM—ST. ANDREW'S COLLEGE, 1950.

LEFT: Still a bachelor with a classy red Buick.

BELOW: *Left to right*: Percy and Elizabeth Pain, Dorothy 'Dodie' and Frank, Dorothy and Silas Moores.

Nineteen-year-old Frank and Dodie with their first child Susan.

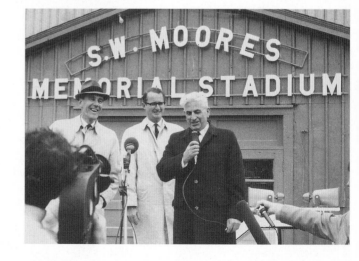

Campaigning with Bob Stanfield and Hedley Kitchen, the mayor of Harbour Grace in 1968.

ABOVE: Six new Tory MPs 1968, (*Left to right*): Walter Carter, Ambrose Peddle, Bob Stanfield, Jim McGrath, John Lundrigan, Jack Marshall and Moores.

BELOW: Moores paid personally for the mobile office and the salary of assistant Bert Ryan.

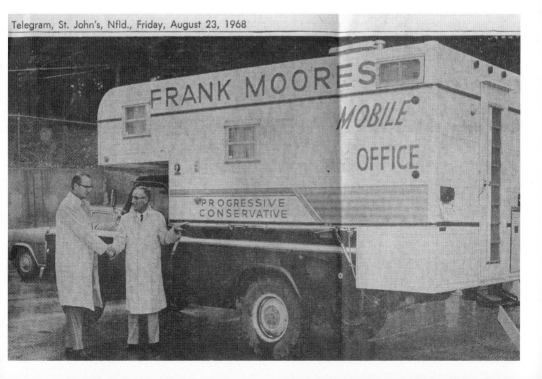

Telegram, St. John's, Nfld., Friday, August 23, 1968

The new leader of the National Tory party and his wife.

Frank was home just long enough to pose for this family photo in 1970. *Left to right*: Andrea, Dodie, Jill, Stuart, Michele, Nicole, Debbie, Frank, Susan seated.

Meeting of the first Progressive Conservative Cabinet (1972) since Confederation. *Left to right*: Gordon Dawe, Tom Hickey, Harold Collins, Gus Rowe, Tom Farrell, Gerry Ottenheimer, Alex Hickman, Moores, John Crosbie, Bill Marshall, Ank Murphy, Bill Doody, Aubrey Senior, John Carter, Ed Maynard.

Official photo of Frank Moores.

In 1973 John Shaheen named a new oil tanker after Moores. It was later renamed the *Kurdistan* and sank the same month Moores left office, in March of 1979.

Daughters Michele and Debbie did the christening honours.

CHAPTER 13

New and Strange Bedfellows

THE NEWFOUNDLAND PROGRESSIVE Conservative Party held its leadership convention on May 16, 1970. There were six other candidates for the role of leader: Dr. Hubert Kitchen, Walter Carter, John Carter, Hughie Shea, Frank Howard-Rose, and Joseph Noel. Moores took 425 of the 612 votes cast on the first ballot. Waving placards proclaiming "Frank's the Man," the exuberant crowd lifted him to their shoulders, and Premier Moores buttons suddenly blossomed everywhere.

The leadership convention garnered enormous attention from the press. The fourteen-page convention special in the *Daily News* bore the huge headline "FRANK'S THE MAN." The reason for this unprecedented coverage may have been articulated in the prophetic and carefully measured opening words of Frank Moores's victory address: *"The times have dictated that we, as a party, will change the course of history in this province."*

Now the man who, two years earlier, had never been to a political meeting had been elected as a member of parliament and become leader of both the national PC organization and the provincial PC party. Dodie Moores packed up her family and moved back to Newfoundland with her husband, telling the press, "Frank calls himself an instant politician. He went into it as a public service, he doesn't have to do this, but he feels he should, and I agree. I am happy to move, and the children are happy to be wherever Frank is content, and Newfoundland is where he wants to be."

The provincial PC leadership election was not without controversy. With ninety-one votes, Dr. Hubert Kitchen, whom he had previously defeated for the federal nomination was Moores's closest opponent. The St. John's power group liked Kitchen even less than they liked Moores, but he had support among the youth and in rural areas. Kitchen was reported to have openly speculated that Moores's return was calculated to stop him and that he would "get" Moores. When a private meeting he held with Smallwood was revealed, Kitchen was expelled from the party, prompting resignations from executive posts in district associations around the province. Moores kept his distance from the controversy, letting the party executive handle it.

The Liberals were in disarray, and Joey was in the fourth year of his mandate. John Crosbie's Liberal Reform Party had a membership of four, one of whom was Clyde Wells. Wells didn't see himself as part of a splinter party, and Joey was showing no signs of leaving, so Wells announced that he was going back to his law practice. Crosbie was said to be considering forming a Progressive Liberal or Liberal Progressive party or a Reform coalition with the PCs to each run candidates in certain districts.

Shortly after Moores's election, Smallwood offered him Gerry Ottenheimer's seat, uncontested. Getting Moores into the House without an election would have prevented him from shining once more as a vote-winner and kept him occupied in a place where Smallwood reigned supreme. It wasn't considered strange at the time for the premier to offer a seat without consulting the constituents. St. John's East was a strong Tory seat, and Moores believed they'd win it anyway whenever a by-election was called. He had no intention of giving Smallwood the chance to label him a St. John's Tory or of spending any time in the House of Assembly being baited by Smallwood. He intended to enter the House as premier, and to do that, he knew, grassroots organization was key.

Once again he involved young people. He recruited six Memorial students, gave them each a car and an expense allowance and sent them out around the province to set up three-person teams for every poll. Tom Marshall, the current Newfoundland Finance Minister, was one of them. Marshall's father Jack had been elected in the federal district of Humber-St. Georges-St. Barbe in the 1968 Tory sweep and Tom was sent to the Great Northern Peninsula where his father was very popular. Even so, when the younger Marshall said to one store owner, "I understand you support the Tories," the horrified man hauled him into the back room telling him he couldn't say things like that in public. Marshall also learned that even though religious lines were blurring, when he found the Catholics in a community, he'd find Tories.

Moores challenged Smallwood to call a provincial election or meet him in a personal debate. Joey refused "for humanitarian reasons because Moores might drop dead if he accepted either challenge, and Moores was too much of an asset to the Liberal party to risk losing him." He called a by-election, and Bill Marshall decided to run for the seat his best friend had vacated. Marshall was active in the Anglican Church, and St. John's East was a staunch Irish Catholic district. Party strategists suggested that Marshall do his door-to-door campaigning accompanied by a prominent Tory Catholic, but Marshall did his rounds accompanied by Frank Moores. The Knights of Columbus and the Benevolent Irish Society were as charmed by the Protestant Moores as the nuns who invited them into the convent for tea, and the Tory seat remained safe. Marshall was surprised but shouldn't have been; during the 1968 federal election two years earlier, the nuns in the convent in Harbour Grace were said to be wearing Vote for Moores buttons.

Moores spent little time in St. John's. He and Bill Doody set off to organize the province and left the House of Assembly to the splintered Opposition. Old-time Tories like Ank Murphy prevailed upon new Tory Alex Hickman to keep pressure on John Crosbie to join their ranks. Hickman told Murphy not to worry about it because Crosbie was going to end up running for the Tories anyway. To Hickman it was logical: "Wells had quit totally and left John high and dry, the other Reformers, Gerry Myrden and Beaton Abbott, had announced they weren't running again, so Crosbie had a party of one. Where was he going to go?"

Active negotiations were going on between Crosbie and Moores, who had more than privilege and St. Andrew's College in common; they were also each more committed to getting rid of Smallwood than they were to party allegiance, and unbeknownst to dedicated Tories like Bill Marshall, many of their conversations were focused on strategies to achieve that goal.

John Crosbie was so obsessed with Smallwood that he had tunnel vision concerning his own political career. The Tories had never been a force to be reckoned with, and joining them was a last resort that he didn't expect to have to take, but he had failed in his bid to depose Smallwood and had let the Tory leadership opportunity pass by. As he admitted in *No Holds Barred*, he thought that opportunity would always be there if he wanted it. The public wit that he developed in later years was nowhere to be seen, and now he had two charismatic leaders between him and the premier's office.

Crosbie knew that Frank Moores and the changing times were steadily undermining Smallwood, but he was still counting on a chance to establish his Liberal Reform Party in the upcoming election. The only way to do this was to run candidates, and the best way to defeat a Smallwood candidate was to avoid splitting the vote with the Conservatives. Moores knew Crosbie would be an invaluable ally against Smallwood in the House of Assembly, the election wasn't on the horizon, and promises were easy to make.

Although questions were not permitted in the House of Assembly, as leader of the Liberal Reform Party, Crosbie was entitled to speak without a time limit on certain pieces of business, while other members were permitted to speak for only ninety minutes. An insightful article by St. John's political columnist Dave Butler, headlined "Frank Moores, the Silent Leader," commented on "the seeming presence of Frank Moores in the House of Assembly without his being physically present." It told of exchanges in which Smallwood called "Frankie Baby" Crosbie's true leader. Butler wrote, "Mr. Crosbie just smiled, and once again the spirit of Frank Moores floated across the chamber while the body was hard at work outside the House, preparing for the election campaign." In another tirade, Smallwood accused Tory House leader Ank Murphy of being jealous and afraid of Crosbie. "Crosbie smiled." Smallwood said that Crosbie made him sick and accused him of loving Frank Moores, adding, "a little more love from you and he's dead." "Again Crosbie smiled," reported Butler, "and again Frank Moores was in the House."

Party leader Bill Marshall was not aware of any agreements between Moores and Crosbie. He was sitting in his law office in the Royal Trust building one day in early May, reading the paper, when to his shock he saw an article quoting Moores as saying he was not hung up on running candidates in every seat. Marshall immediately drove to Moores's house on Riverview Avenue, walked into his den, slapped the paper down on Moores's desk, and asked for an explanation. Moores denied knowing anything about it, but Marshall didn't believe him.

Marshall, as party policy chairman, was a pure Tory, and he informed Moores that while Moores might be leader, he was the president of the party, and there was no way in hell that the Tories were not going to run a candidate in every seat. He advised Moores to inform Crosbie that he would be welcome as a Tory candidate for the St. John's West seat he had won as a Liberal, but if he intended to contest it as a Reform Liberal, he could forget any deal with Moores. Moores didn't admit to any deal and, in typical fashion, pulled out a bottle of Scotch to calm the troubled waters. Moores then reported the collapse of the deal to Crosbie, blaming it solely on Marshall.

Meanwhile the House of Assembly devolved into chaos. On Thursday May 27, 1971, Bill Marshall rose in the House to read a list of 'slum' landlords, and one of the names was Clara Smallwood, Joey's wife. Joey's son Bill, MHA for Green Bay, rose from his seat, walked across the floor, and hit Marshall in the head. Marshall's colleagues intervened and there was no more physical violence, but by Monday the shouting in the House had become almost hysterical, and it culminated with Bill Marshall, John Crosbie, and the normally mild-mannered Val Earle being suspended for three days. With Tory Ank Murphy storming out in protest and Tory Tom Hickey already serving a three-day suspension for unparliamentary language, there was no opposition left in the house, and Joey calmly proceeded without them.

In a press conference a few days later, flanked by Frank Moores and Bill Marshall, John Crosbie announced he was joining the Conservatives. In response to a reporter's question, Crosbie said that he had been in active negotiations since February. In my general conversations with Frank Moores for this book, he promised, "I'll tell you more in spades later about what I had to do to get Crosbie to come across, because that was pivotal," but later never came. John Crosbie offered no illumination, telling me at first that he couldn't recall having had any discussions with Moores prior to joining the Tories, and then, perhaps realizing how ridiculous that sounded, he remembered that there may have been "some talks."

When Crosbie joined the Tories, many of the Liberals who had supported him in the leadership race against Smallwood followed him, some of them also becoming Conservative candidates. Still, when the election was called, the Tories barely squeaked through. If the agreement not to run Tory candidates against Liberal Reformers had been carried out, the anti-Smallwood vote would have been split, and Smallwood would certainly have been elected once again. Most likely he would have headed a minority government, as Crosbie would have taken some votes from Liberals who didn't want Smallwood but couldn't bring themselves to vote Conservative.

Bill Marshall's intervention can be said to have saved the day and altered the course of Newfoundland history. John Crosbie observed at the time that Bill had gotten his own bloody way, but the fact is that Frank Moores was neither surprised nor dismayed at Bill Marshall's refusal to go along with the promise he had made to Crosbie.

CHAPTER 14

Raising the Army

SMALLWOOD DELAYED CALLING the election as long as he could. It was a huge error because the delay gave Moores time to put into place the first organized political machine the whole province of Newfoundland had ever seen. While Smallwood was posturing in the House of Assembly, Moores immersed himself in the Herculean task of getting candidates, assembling experienced organizers from his days in federal politics, criss-crossing the province, holding general meetings, setting up district associations, and meeting with potential candidates, and doing it all in a few months. With John Crosbie on board, finding people to run suddenly became a whole lot easier. Nominating conventions were held for the first time in districts where the Tories had previously had trouble scraping up one sacrificial candidate.

Smallwood's venom against Crosbie during the leadership convention had split the Liberal party more than either Smallwood or even Crosbie realized. Young, idealistic lawyer Fred Stagg was one of thousands of anti-Smallwood Liberals looking for a home. Stagg was the quintessential Newfoundland Liberal; his father had been Liberal, his grandfather had been Liberal, and he had never considered being anything else. He had been a Crosbie supporter at the Liberal leadership convention, and his conversion to the Tories was typical of what was happening all over the province.

Stagg was from Boswarlos and had started a law practice in Stephenville, both in the Port au Port district. The member for Port au Port was Bill Callahan, Minister of Mines, Energy and Resources. Under Callahan's representation the district had recovered from the shock of losing its biggest employer, the huge Ernest Harmon United States Air Force Base; John C. Doyle was building the liner-board mill, and thanks to Smallwood's largesse, he had taken over the O'Dea family brewery. There wasn't a Tory around who wanted to run against Callahan, so Crosbie asked Fred Stagg to take him on. Stagg discussed it with his wife and his father. Even Stagg's father, who ran the lone polling booth in Boswarlos and "taught the crows to say, 'Vote Liberal,'" gave his blessing, and Fred Stagg took the enormous step of announcing he was seeking the PC nomination, much to the surprise of the local PC association, some of whose names he didn't even know at the time.

Frank Moores called the candidates who ran in that first election "the heroes who laid it all on the line," observing that while he had more good candidates in the second election, it was only because the fear of running had gone. Some of the real Tory candidates, like Al Evans in Burgeo-LaPoile, looked askance at Crosbie and other former Liberals, and loyal Tories who were excited and optimistic about actually getting elected weren't happy about being ousted from the nomination by people who had been Liberals a month earlier. To Moores it was simple. "The obligation I had was to win. You could take the best guy in the world, but if we thought he couldn't win the district, we'd say, 'We'll see what we can do to help you after we're elected, but in the meantime, so and so should run.'" Some of the former Liberals embraced Moores as the leader, but other members elected under his banner were really under Crosbie's. This distinction dogged Moores's premiership, but it was the only strategy that could beat Smallwood.

This toleration of divided loyalty was another indication that wielding the power of the premier's office was never what the crusade was all about to Frank Moores. The prize was to rid the province of Joey Smallwood. This goal had brought him and John Crosbie together, but Moores was decidedly more careless than Crosbie about his own political fate. He announced months before the election was called that he would run against Joey in Humber West. Smallwood was the most invincible Liberal Moores could have taken on, and he could quite conceivably have lost the seat. "I thought I had an outside chance of taking Joey out," Moores said, "and if I didn't, I would tie him down for the campaign so he couldn't go anywhere else."

It also helped that Humber West was in Tory Jack Marshall's federal district. Marshall was very well liked because, as Moores told me "There was no party without Jack, they were all his people. He worked for all the people of the west coast and for veterans and did more in his time than any individual member of parliament I've known." Knocking on doors in the district with Jack Marshall practically guaranteed Moores a welcome, even by die-hard liberals. (Marshall was so well thought of that Pierre Trudeau appointed him to the Senate in 1978 in what was seen as the only chance of winning back the traditional Liberal district, which Brian Tobin accomplished by a slight margin over Tory Michael Monaghan.)

It was a bold, dramatic, and possibly foolish move that, thanks to Smallwood's reaction, turned out to appear politically brilliant: Joey switched districts. He may have thought moving to another district would deprive Moores of the press attention he'd get as Smallwood's direct opponent, or he may have wanted to show that he was in control and could foil Moores's strategy. For whatever reason, he announced that there were a number of districts wanting him to run for their seat and that it wasn't fair that the people in Humber West should have him all to themselves. He then took a long time to settle on Placentia, unfortunately giving the impression, correct or not, that he was afraid to face Moores but couldn't find a district that really wanted him.

The Humber East and Humber West districts met in the middle of Corner Brook, Newfoundland's 'second city.' Practising medicine on the Humber East side of town was a fellow Moores thought would be a big help, Tom Farrell, the good-looking, affable Irish doctor who had travelled to Gander to help Harold Collins make his breakthrough. A municipal councillor, Farrell was also well known all over the west coast by patients who came into Corner Brook for medical treatment, and he had driven up the coast with Moores searching out candidates. Farrell liked a drink and a laugh, and he clicked with Moores, who decided he wanted Tom Farrell to run for Humber East. Farrell was vocal against Smallwood, but with a medical practice and a young family, he had always refused to run for office, and party president Bill Marshall told Moores not to waste his time.

They both underestimated Moores's persuasiveness. He kept at Farrell until Farrell came up with the excuse that he had a responsibility to the partner who had just invested in a new medical clinic with him. Moores then went to work on Farrell's partner, convinced him that Tom should work for the common good, and Tom Farrell was out of excuses. He left a lucrative medical practice and followed the Pied Piper.

It wasn't hard; Farrell saw Moores as "a very bright, a very attractive candidate, physically, mentally." He was impressed with Moores's quick grasp of facts and figures and his political instincts for the broader picture. Farrell also had the revolutionary fervour. "All of that first crowd were freedom fighters. Some of them had money, but a lot of them didn't; people gave up their businesses. There were people who went in there and left a lot of money behind them, lawyers, doctors, these fellows put it all on the line. I had six kids to raise, and I was making a fair bit of money in the medical business, four times what I made in government." Tom Farrell was to become Moores's best friend, but the financial sacrifices would come back to haunt him.

Moores brought in George McLean, of Mclean Public Relations, a Toronto agency, to help with the organizing. Mclean was a large man, well over three hundred pounds, and attracted a lot of attention. Political organization in Newfoundland was in such a rudimentary state that Mclean held schools for campaign managers and candidates. Educating the troops was an uphill grind. Alex Hickman was one of the more experienced candidates, but having previously been one of Joey's anointed, he had never had to actually campaign and had no district organization. It wasn't easy to get people like him onside. Hickman says he thought most of Mclean's ideas were a waste of time and he wouldn't be able to get people to go along with them, and he remembers Moores arguing with him and the other candidates that it was at the poll level that they were going to win this election. One day Moores came up with some figures showing that if the Tories had picked up an extra thirty votes in every poll in the 1966 election, which Smallwood won by all but three seats, the Tories would have won the government. Hickman allows that Moores may have made that up, but the statistic got the point across.

Smallwood finally called the election for October, 1971. The Liberals still had no idea about political organization, while the Tories had reached the stage where they had accurately estimated numbers on every poll in every district in the province. Moores, a natural organizer, had fine-tuned his skills on the federal scene, he lived and preached them, and he insisted on a high level of detail. He said, "The numbers had to be right on. We didn't want wishful thinking in this, we wanted exact numbers. Out of the forty-plus polls, I had three that were absolutely exact, which is incredible. It hadn't been done before. Every voter in the province was covered one way or another, and it worked big time."

Moores's surprise opponent was ex-PC leader Noel Murphy. At one point Moores had actually named Murphy to his shadow cabinet with the expectation that Murphy would be running in Humber West for the PCs, but it had become obvious that Murphy was no longer in the PC fold long before Moores decided on Humber West for himself. Instead Murphy, generally considered to have his sights on the lieutenant-governor's office, was sworn into Joey's cabinet without having been elected. After the feelers he sent out for the nomination in another district were rejected, he was presented to the Liberals of Humber West as their candidate, armed with blue-prints for a massive development plan for Corner Brook and the Marble Mountain ski facility.

The Liberals' development plan had everything people in the district could have wanted, but early in the campaign, Moores learned he had nothing to worry about. One night when he was out campaigning, he crossed paths with Murphy and stopped to have a chat with Murphy's driver, Jack McCarthy, one of Joey's west coast henchmen. McCarthy told Moores he might as well go home and go to bed. At first Moores thought McCarthy meant Murphy had it sewed up, until McCarthy went on to say, "You don't have a thing to worry about. He's fucking up every door he's knocking on."

With an estimated 93,000 Newfoundlanders on social assistance, Smallwood based his campaign around a documentary film called *The End of the Beginning*, which reminded Newfoundlanders of his twenty-two years of accomplishments, especially the pension and family allowance that came with Confederation. He addressed the employment crisis in his usual fashion, announcing mega-projects such as a fifth paper mill, even though the trumpeted third and fourth mills hadn't been built. When questioned about wood supply, he blithely claimed it was cheaper to import wood from Labrador than cut it on the island. Right up to election day in late October, Joey's paving machines were preceding or following Moores into each town, once even paving a wooden bridge.

Moores began a series of press releases meticulously coordinated with the Tory advertising. Consistently, throughout the province, candidates would get a call advising them to start emphasizing a certain message or distributing a certain poster on a certain day. While claiming to be above personal attacks, Moores did pick up on some of Smallwood's style, labelling Smallwood's cabinet the Hush Puppies—"You buy them, lace up the tongue, and find them comfortable to walk on." He reserved his greatest disdain for Social Services Minister Steve Neary, "the flunky extraordinaire … master of gutter politics and hatchet man," and Justice Minister Les Curtis, "a sanctimonious hypocrite … the original minister of injustice."

Name calling was nothing. Reports of bribery and intimidation were coming out of every community. The Liberals were accused of promising everything from a television relay station to job appointments and liquor licences, and if a voter didn't need a liquor licence, he could at least take a bottle for his trouble. Depositions of proof were being quietly taken by the Moores people, who often had difficulty in booking hall space or even getting signs erected because the fear of Smallwood confronted them at every turn.

Gerry Ottenheimer had decided to re-enter politics and run in St. Mary's Bay. The Liberals resurrected and embellished the rumours about him, passing them along to the priests in the predominately Catholic district. Charlie White was doing his articling with Bill Marshall, who willingly dispatched him to help Ottenheimer. White didn't leave St. Mary's Bay for three weeks, going door to door with Ottenheimer and a service station worker named Ray MacDonald, who, with artist Christopher Pratt, was one of the few prepared to be openly Conservative. Ottenheimer personally visited every home in the district in three weeks and drank hundreds of cups of tea with people who had never had a politician come to their door before.

The Liberal candidate wasn't concered about visiting the district; he was Liberal, that was it, they would vote for him. It didn't hurt, for a bit of insurance, to tell people that Joey could find out how they voted and to offer a small favour or token of our appreciation, a flask of rum or ten bucks. Reports of this got back to White from people who were afraid to support Ottenheimer publicly. White managed to collect some sworn affidavits, just in case, but Ottenheimer won the district, although by fewer than a hundred votes.

As the campaign progressed, it became apparent from the turnouts at rallies all over the province that something new and huge was happening in Newfoundland politics. The rising fervour climaxed in a joint rally for Moores and Farrell at the stadium in Corner Brook.

Smallwood had held a big rally of about a thousand at a local high school, and Noel Murphy's radio station reported that the Tories would be hard pressed to beat that number. By the evening of the Tory rally all roads into and around the small city were blocked with cars. The crowd was estimated at four thousand and overflowed to fill the stadium parking lot. It was so enthusiastic that the organizers decided they couldn't safely proceed with the formal speeches.

"There was the organized motorcade and then a spontaneous one that joined it that was unbelievable," Moores told me. "I drove over the ridge in Humber West where you see Corner Brook in the valley for the first time. I could look behind me and see these cars and car lights, and here coming down the other side of the hill in Humber East was another solid chain. I felt like Wellington arriving with the Prussian army.

It was a momentous night, and the rink was absolutely blocked. I pitied the poor guys in charge of the ice. I couldn't make a speech because everyone was bawling and roaring so much—forget speeches. There was one little old lady down in front of me, she muddled through the ice, up above her ankles. I knelt down and I said, 'Ma'am, you're going to freeze to death. You should get off the ice surface.' She looked at me and said, 'As long as you'se here, I'se here. Suppose this comes right up to me, you know what, I'm not moving an inch.'

It was very emotional—incredibly emotional. The vision of the cars, that motorcade, I don't know if there was a car left in Corner Brook, honest to God. Oh, I was incredibly proud—ecstatic. If there was a single moment of ecstasy in that whole thing, it was that moment."

CHAPTER 15

Giant-Killer

SMALLWOOD DEPENDED HEAVILY on his old style and past glory, particularly in the outports, where he was still revered. He and Moores ended up one night both holding rallies in the tiny community of Flower's Cove on the Northern Peninsula. Press reports estimated that each attracted some 450 people from up and down the coast. While Moores was preaching reform, Smallwood was asking the little children to sit on the stage by him to "get close to Joey," calling them the true riches of Newfoundland, and describing himself again as the instrument through which God had worked to bring them into the great country of Canada. Smallwood's candidates campaigned in the usual way, under Joey's umbrella, dealing with local issues, promising pavement, culverts, or whatever the particular community wanted. The Moores message was consistent: reform in just about every area of government and resource development.

Campaigning with the slogan 'The Time Has Come,' Moores held rallies in every district. His nervousness about public speaking rarely showed, and he was a natural campaigner on a one-to-one basis. He continued to hammer home the message of focusing on development to suit the historic culture of Newfoundlanders, repeating his message: "We need to develop excellence in what we know, rather than continually trying to change the personality of the Newfoundland people. Someone who works in a smelter in Pittsburg doesn't know much about setting a cod trap, and a fisherman doesn't know much about working in a smelter."

It was a message rural Newfoundlanders could relate to, and they also related to Moores's approachable style. Moores felt he dressed "with respect for the office and the people" by wearing a jacket and tie, but usually the tie would be loosened or off altogether before long. He was often seen in a powder blue Grenfell parka with a fur-trimmed hood, contrasting with Smallwood's predominantly black outfit of homburg, long overcoat, and bowtie.

Smallwood was a renowned orator, but he talked at people and down to them with his trademark exaggeration and repetition. Moores talked with them and to them in a well modulated voice, using the colourful colloquialisms of the Newfoundland language that came naturally to him. One on one, Joey was Mr. Smallwood; Moores was Frank. When Joey entered a hall with his entourage, the effect was intimidating and people didn't readily approach him. When Moores arrived with his entourage, the effect was the opposite. He seemed to have total recall of people's names, their families, and his previous conversations with them, whatever their station in life. "Ah! Jack," he would say, "how are you doing? How's the young fella's arm?"

Some Crosbie supporters were won over to Frank Moores by this rapport with people. "I remember introducing him to a guy named Fred Retieffe," Fred Stagg said. "That's all it was, an introduction—this is Fred Retieffe, this is Frank Moores. Not another word because there was quite a crowd. The next time he came back to Stephenville months later, there was another whole lot of people around, and this man walked by. Frank reached out for him and said, 'Hello, Fred, how are you doing?' It was uncanny. Fred Retieffe was a fisherman from Three Rock Cove who died tragically a few years ago, but I'm sure, all his entire life, he remembered that Frank Moores, after meeting thousands of people, said, 'How are you doing, Fred?'"

By this time Susan and Debbie, the oldest Moores children, had left home for university, but Dodie Moores still had five children at home. Having no real interest in politics, she was seldom seen during the provincial election campaign. Janis Johnson had gone from being Moores's assistant in the national office to being his assistant in Newfoundland, set up with an office in Corner Brook, and she travelled everywhere with him. On Thursday October 28, 1971, on the most important night of his political life, Frank Moores watched the election returns from a hotel suite in Corner Brook. Janis Johnson was there, and his wife was at home in St. John's.

The whole province was glued to their television sets and radios when the polls closed at eight o'clock. Joey Smallwood watched the early returns in his Roaches Line residence. It was immediately apparent that the usual Liberal sweep wasn't going to happen, but it was early, and defeat still seemed impossible. Joey left as planned, with his driver and two reporters, for the forty-five-minute drive to St. John's to join Liberal supporters for the celebration. By the time they reached St. John's, even Joey could tell that something momentous was happening. Instead of going to Liberal headquarters, the car carrying the premier and the turkeys and hams for the party started driving around St. John's, its passengers listening to the radio; eventually it turned around and drove back to Roaches Line.

An unprecedented 87 per cent of the 265,000 eligible voters turned out to the polls. The voting age was now nineteen, and 50 per cent of the voters were under twenty-five. Young Newfoundlanders who had never been politically involved before weren't impressed with Joey's rhetoric and imperiousness, and many of their parents wanted change. When the count was over, Smallwood's Liberals were reduced from thirty-nine seats to twenty, Frank Moores's Conservatives held twenty-one seats, and there was one New Labrador Party member. The popular vote was a little more telling: 52 per cent for the Tories, 44 per cent for the Liberals, 3 per cent for the New Labrador Party and 1 per cent for the NDP.

Moores defeated Noel Murphy by a count of two to one, while in Placentia East, Smallwood won his seat by only 790 votes. The winning margin for the Tories in five of their seats combined was only 350 votes.

It wasn't strictly a Frank Moores win or even a Tory win. In Fred Stagg's opinion the vast majority of the people who voted for him were former Liberals, Crosbie people who became Tories when he did. "They were voting against Smallwood. All they needed was a warm body that hadn't disgraced himself or herself, and I was that person, and they didn't feel they'd be throwing away their vote. With Crosbie and his supporters on board, the old Tory party was gone forever. To say there were two definite factions is perhaps just a little strong, but there were two groups with two streams of thought that coalesced with a common ideal and managed to get twenty-one of them elected."

Tory campaign worker Terri Williams danced on the new premier's desk on election night, as she would do decades later, at the age of eighty, when her son Danny Williams became Premier. The time had come.

CHAPTER 16

Not Quite

WHEN SMALLWOOD FINALLY MADE a statement the next day, it was to say that while the people had made a terrible mistake, he was still the premier because Moores did not have a clear majority. He later voiced the opinion that he had lost because, since he was Newfoundland's first premier after Confederation, the voters had nothing to compare him with except perfection.

It was hard for people to take in. When Moores, accompanied by his daughters Susan and Debbie, arrived at Confederation Building in an open convertible cavalcade the next day, he found the premier's parking spot occupied by an avid Smallwood supporter who refused to move her car, nearly causing a riot. His first press conference was to announce that "any deals, borrowings, or any other kind of understanding entered into by the Smallwood government after the election will be subject to review when the lieutenant-governor asks the PC Party to form the government."

The stand-off had begun. While Smallwood had only twenty seats, Moores, with twenty-one seats out of forty-two, did not have a majority. Tom Burgess of the New Labrador Party became a very important man. Joey was fighting for his life, and John Doyle was quick to cut short a trip to Europe to help out. The election was on a Thursday; by Saturday Doyle's leased DH-25 jet was in Labrador, where he graciously offered to transport a giddy Tom Burgess to Stephenville to connect with the Lundrigan jet to take him to St. John's, where Burgess could consider his options as Doyle's guest in a three-room suite in the Holiday Inn.

Ensconced in the suite, just a few doors from Doyle's, Burgess entertained the press, announcing his demands for a cabinet post and many concessions for Labrador, but John Doyle was still busy elsewhere. The reason his jet had been unable to take Burgess all the way to St. John's was that Doyle had another hook to bait. With the linerboard mill under construction in Stephenville and Bison Brewery going strong, Fred Stagg, a recent defector from the Liberal party, was considered to be a good prospect.

On Saturday night Stagg was home watching *Hockey Night in Canada*. When the phone rang, he thought for a moment the voice on the other end said, This is Tom Doyle, who had been elected for the Tories in Ferryland. Instead it was John Doyle, inviting the new member down to the brewery to get acquainted with his district's most important businessman. When Stagg arrived a couple of the local fellows who worked for the brewery showed him to Doyle's office, where Doyle was sitting behind the desk with a person he later found out was a lawyer from Montreal. It was Fred Stagg's first glimpse into the world of power and money and he didn't even realize it at the time. "We spoke for about three hours, and I didn't know that everything was being recorded. Years later people down at the brewery used to play the tape, because it was fascinating, I suppose. We weren't long into it before he dealt with the real issue, which was the election and how easily a person could walk across the floor, but I think he picked up early in the conversation that what he was dealing with here was an idealistic damn fool. I was so pleased with what I had done that I actually thought he was there to congratulate me. It was days later that I put it all together and found out he was making the rounds of all the MHAS and feeling them out about crossing the floor. He offered me legal work from Javelin, but I'd only been in practice less than two years and I thought that stuff would be a little complicated for me, so I wasn't interested in that. There was no mention of money, but of course the legal work was a front for that. He could have paid me anything."

For some reason Doyle also decided that Port aux Basques MHA Al Evans was a good prospect. Evans was a life-long Tory, but his antipathy towards John Crosbie may have attracted Doyle to him. Also, Evans was rough around the edges and didn't care what he said. Doyle may have thought this meant he wasn't very smart, but those who got to know Al Evans knew he was a lot smarter than he appeared.

Evans showed up one day in Alex Hickman's office, visibly nervous and upset. He told Hickman that as he was having dinner alone the previous night in the Newfoundland Hotel, a man asked if he could join him, congratulated him, told him what a splendid future he had, and generally buttered him up. The man was John Doyle. After chatting for a while, Doyle invited Evans up to his suite for a drink. Evans went along out of curiosity and to see how far it would go. After a few drinks, Doyle suggested that Evans would be smart to talk to Smallwood, and Evans said he wasn't interested. Then, he said, Doyle had tried to get him drunk, continuing to persuade him, but by the time Evans left, it was Doyle who was the worse for wear.

Evans told Hickman that there were other people going after him, too, and he thought he was being followed. Hickman called the RCMP, and they assigned someone to keep an eye on Evans. Hickman said, "I didn't think someone would actually get rid of him, but Evans was totally new to the political arena and he was scared; he didn't want people coming up and half-threatening him."

The affairs of the province were at a standstill. Moores publicly and privately appealed to Lieutenant-Governor John Harnum to ask for Smallwood's resignation or instruct him to call the House together to prove the strength of his administration. Harnum, who had been appointed by Smallwood, refused.

A constitutional debate raged at the federal and provincial levels. In the parliamentary library of the day, there were only two documents dealing with the role and power of the lieutenant-governor: a memorandum from the Justice Department, produced in 1955, and a report by John Saywell, produced in 1957. According to the Justice Department document, "It is the duty of the lieutenant-governor to seek impartially to obtain a government in accordance with the wishes of the electorate," and Saywell wrote, "Common sense and good practice alike suggest that when the result is in doubt the government should meet the legislature as soon as possible to test its strength." With the Liberals having received only 44 per cent of the popular vote, many argued that Harnum could have acted if he wanted to.

However, Senator Eugene Forsey, a Newfoundlander and Canada's recognized constitutional expert at the time, announced that the lieutenant-governor was acting properly and that he would not be constitutionally right to intervene unless Smallwood called the House together and was defeated amongst the caucus. Forsey was a cousin of Alex Hickman's, and Hickman wrote him a strong letter pointing out that people were holding him responsible for keeping Smallwood in power. Forsey wrote back that he had devotedly prayed for the last decade for the political demise of Smallwood, but regrettably the lieutenant-governor's position was correct, and that if Smallwood had any sense of decency at all he would have resigned well after the election; however he reiterated that the lieutenant-governor could not intervene until Smallwood called the House together.

Moores spent two days in Ottawa attempting to meet with Liberal Justice Minister John Turner to discuss the situation, but Turner wouldn't meet with him, and Moores was told that the minister was too busy even to talk to him on the telephone. He then wrote to the governor general asking for intervention, but there was no appetite anywhere at the federal level to become involved in a provincial mess of such proportions.

Appeals were made to prominent Liberal cabinet ministers, such as future lieutenant-governor Ed Roberts, but although some privately cringed at what was going on, no one in Joey's cabinet was willing to break ranks with him. Smallwood continued to act like the undisputed premier, attending various meetings with federal and industrial officials and making decisions and commitments on behalf of the province.

Newfoundlanders were embarrassed about being made a laughingstock by Smallwood, and the Newfoundland press took to reporting how the mainland press was assessing the situation. Political observers across the country went as far as to describe it as an illegal seizure of power by a deposed government, and they openly accused Smallwood of playing for time in order to cover the tracks of twenty-three years of despotism and financial mismanagement. As one paper observed, in any other democratic country it would be incredible and, in any other province, inconceivable.

November 1971 was probably the most bizarre month in Newfoundland's political history. The month began with Tom Burgess, calling himself Kingmaker, holding fort from his Holiday Inn suite, issuing demands daily, making remarks about activities "that would make James Bond look like a Boy Scout," and boasting of what he was being offered, including "a cool million." Moores quickly stated that he was not prepared to offer Burgess special concessions, and Liberal MHA Steve Neary accused Burgess of blackmail. Recounts were in process, and on November 11, Smallwood announced in a province-wide television address that, regardless of the outcome, he would be stepping down as leader and calling a leadership convention in January. On November 12, Burgess announced that he would support the Tories when the House of Assembly opened, and on November 15, John Doyle accused Burgess of trying to obtain $35,000 from Javelin for his election campaign. On November 16 the *Daily News* broke a copyright story linking Moores with the August bankruptcy of the Toronto brokerage firm Malone Lynch.

The *News* reported that on the previous August 11, Moores had transferred securities valued at $200,000 from Malone Lynch to Grand Johnson Securities. On August 12 Malone Lynch was suspended from trading, and on August 13 the company's telephones were cut off and its staff of 125 put out of work, leaving behind a deficit of over $2,500,000. It quoted executives of the firm who alleged that the Moores account was the only one that had been moved and speculated that Moores was in fact a partner. It was a more serious allegation than the one that would land Martha Stewart in jail forty years later. Moores in turn accused the Liberals of planting the story, denying any affiliation with the firm other than being a friend of Terry Malone's and a client, and pointed out that as one of the firm's more than 3,000 clients, he would have been reimbursed for any losses by the financial industry's National Contingency Fund anyway. No charges were ever laid.

On November 17 Frank Sinatra Jr. performed at the Atlantic Police Association Benefit and Ball at St. John's swanky Old Colony Club and thanked "Premier" Moores for his hospitality. On November 19 subscriptions addressed to 'The Honourable Tom Burgess, Minister of Agriculture and Resources,' began arriving at Confederation Building, and on November 22, the recount of the ballots from St. Barbe South hit the news like a bombshell.

Over the first two weeks in November, recounts had been done in ten seats. The counts were uneventful, and nothing changed until the count for St. Barbe South, which showed that former Crosbie Liberal Ed Maynard had defeated Liberal Trevor Bennett by eight votes.

When the clerk put his hand in the envelope for the ballots from Sally's Cove, the thirteenth poll of the thirty-four in the district, the envelope was empty. The returning officer from Sally's Cove had done what she had always done with the ballots after an election: she put them in the wood stove in the kitchen and burned them.

Missing ballots were certainly unusual, although not unprecedented, but then nobody had ever challenged the results of an election in Newfoundland before, let alone demanded a recount.

Moores observed that Smallwood had been far too confident as he awaited the results of the recounts, and speculation was rampant that the Liberals had had a hand in the Sally's Cove fiasco. But Charlie White, who was in court when the distressed woman made her statement, doesn't believe that there had been any undue influence in what he now calls a great piece of Newfoundland history. White describes her as the salt of the earth and added, "Not for a moment did she think she was doing something she wasn't supposed to do."

The original count in envelope thirteen was fifty-five votes for Maynard and fifty for Bennett. Maynard's lead from the recount of the first twelve polls had been reduced to five, but Judge Arthur Puddister stopped the recount and declared Maynard's election valid. Section 91 of the Elections Act stated that the Supreme Court judge counting the ballots shall, within two days of the final count, certify the results to the District Returning Officer, who shall then immediately declare to be elected the candidate with the most votes. Puddister could have reported the situation to the DRO, as some argue he should have, the election would then have been declared null and void, and a by-election would have been called. Instead Puddister certified that Maynard was leading when the count was stopped.

Before the end of the month both parties had appealed to the Supreme Court on the issue of St. Barbe South. Melvin Gilley, the District Returning Officer, passed the certificate on to Howard Strong the Chief Electoral Officer, without the proper documents declaring Maynard elected. The Liberals immediately made application to the Supreme Court under the Contraverted Elections Act to have the election of Ed Maynard set aside; then the Tories applied to the Supreme Court for a Writ of Mandamus directing Gilley to declare Maynard elected.

Meanwhile, Tom Burgess wasn't getting the attention he felt he deserved and started having second thoughts about supporting the Tories in the legislature. Moores and Farrell went to see him.

Moores recalled Burgess as a bright, devious Irishman, a delight-ful character, but said

> "You couldn't trust him as far as you could kick him. Tom Farrell and I spent six hours with Tom Burgess persuading him why he should join us. We told him, you can join us and get elected again as a member of the government, or you can sit as an Independent, but if you join the Liberals, you'll never get re-elected again, which is exactly as it turned out. We had this long, long session, with me doing my best and Tom, being Irish too, laying it on him. There was never any talk of money. He wanted to get into cabinet; I said I could go along with that, because we didn't have any representation in Labrador. We left at three o'clock in the morning. He shook hands when we went out the door, totally agreed, going to announce the next morning he was joining us. Next morning about eight-thirty, I turn on the radio: Tom Burgess is saying he would join the Liberal party.
>
> Obviously, Doyle got to him after we left at three—the only reason he could have possibly changed his mind. I mean, fifty grand to Tom was much better than a promise to be in the cabinet, where you'd earn $15,000 a year. Doyle was the man going around handing out the money, with Joey's concurrence I'm sure, but I can't prove any of that."

Smallwood later claimed to have been approached by two Conservatives who wanted to join the Liberals. Moores never did believe it. "If they approached him he would have grabbed them. The people who ran for the Tory party and got elected were not about to go over to Joey unless they were paid off. They worked too hard for what they got, and the ones who had left the Liberal party weren't going to go back to it, after what they had gone through and the abuse they took. No, it was more about being bought off. Anyone who was approached by Smallwood was via

John C. Doyle. He was his secretary, he had the money. There was always that worry."

The other worry many of the Tories had was whether Moores's personal behaviour would bring the shaky house of cards down upon them. In the months immediately following the October election, Moores was spending his nights at Elizabeth Towers, supposedly in his mother's apartment with Tom Farrell, in reality with Janis Johnson. Even though during the campaign Janis was usually by his side, it was then that the legend of Moores's exploits with women all over the province began. Tom Farrell probably knew more than anyone about Frank's behaviour with women, and while he points out that Frank wasn't always the instigator and quips that "he didn't want to be rude," he says, "A lot of it was the gospel truth. He was a terrible case altogether, he was never faithful to anybody. But he was pursued, too, and it wasn't just being premier, it was more than that. He would be up and down the coast, and it was like being with a rock star. We would go to dances after meetings, and there would be guys offering him their wives, guys saying, 'Frank, take her off for a drink, and I'll be back later.' I'm not making that up."

At home with their mother, in a house less than five minutes away on Riverview Avenue, were fifteen-year-old Michele, thirteen-year-old Jill, ten-year-old Nicole, eight-year-old Stuart, and six-year-old Andrea. Nineteen-year-old Susan, the oldest of Dodie and Frank's seven children, and her eighteen-year-old sister Debbie had returned to university in Nova Scotia. Dodie Moores became clinically depressed, but she says she didn't understand for some time that she was ill and needed help. Remembering that period, she realizes now that she was too ill to fight back. Knowing her husband's basic reluctance to hurt anybody, in the hindsight of the years that followed, she regretted it.

CHAPTER 17

Let the Games Begin

THAT FRANK WAS HAVING AN AFFAIR with Janis Johnson was taken for granted, but the fact that he and Dodie were actually living apart was not public knowledge. It was a tense time for Moores's caucus. With the unprecedented constitutional wrangling and the drama of Joey's refusal to leave, the eyes of the Canadian press and political watchers from all over the country were trained on Newfoundland. Nevertheless just after Christmas, while Dodie tried to hang on and explain to the children why Daddy wasn't home, Frank decided he needed a break and took off for the Caribbean with Janis, Tom, and Marg Farrell.

While Frank was unwinding in casinos down south, higher stakes were being played for back in Newfoundland. Alec Dunphy had been elected for the PCs in St. George's, on the province's west coast. Dunphy ran a successful fish business in the area but lived in Steady Brook, a few minutes north of Corner Brook. He was a reformed alcoholic who had been dry for over a decade. Perhaps the heady stuff of victory was too much for Dunphy, or perhaps, as rumour had it, John C. Doyle had a finger in the pie; whatever the cause, at a Federal Tory convention in Toronto in November, Dunphy had started drinking again. He was a very unpredictable drunk.

Ed Poole and businessman Ed Kearsey, who had been Tom Farrell's campaign manager, were at the convention, and they took on the task of keeping an eye on Dunphy. It wasn't an easy job; he got away from them briefly when they were changing planes in Halifax, but they rounded him up again. Once back in Newfoundland, under the watchful eye of his wife Mary, Poole, and Kearsey, who was a fellow AA member, Dunphy appeared to settle down.

Over thirty-five years, many versions of the Alec Dunphy story have been told, with no major variations. This version comes from two key players, Alex Hickman and Ed Poole. Hickman and John Crosbie were making a point of stopping by Moores's office regularly to keep tabs on things while he was away. A few days after Christmas, Barbara Nugent, Moores's secretary, told Crosbie that Mary Dunphy had been trying to get a hold him all day and that she sounded very serious. Crosbie, who knew Mary Dunphy personally, called her, with Hickman listening on the other line.

The parish priest in Dunphy's district was Father Ron Kelly, the son of Hubert Kelly, who was a great Liberal organizer. Hickman says that Father Kelly had been asked to do something about Dunphy. Worried and frantic, Mary Dunphy told them that Alec was drinking again and had been since Father Kelly had invited him to the Holiday Inn on Christmas Eve. In a curious turn of circumstances, the same Father Kelly, later charged with sexually abusing boys in his parish, left the church and became a millionaire property developer, raising speculation about where a parish priest might have gotten the backing for such ventures.

Mary said that Alec was coming in to St. John's to meet with Smallwood that very night, even though she had told him that if he did, he was not to come back. She put Alec on the phone, and he admitted that he was indeed being taken in Lundrigan's plane that night to meet Smallwood. When Crosbie asked him why, the belligerent Dunphy replied that Smallwood was the premier, and if the premier invites you to come to see him, you can't say no. Dunphy insisted that he had made the commitment to go and he was going, but Crosbie was relentless and finally extracted a promise that he wouldn't go. Before the call ended, Mary Dunphy came back on the line and warned Crosbie not to believe her husband.

Any members of Dunphy's St. George's riding association who might have been able to help were over an hour away, so Crosbie and Hickman called Ed Poole in Corner Brook and asked him to get up to Dunphy's right away. Poole told them flat out that he didn't want to hear anything about Alec Dunphy. Trying to keep Dunphy sober had ruined Christmas for both him and Ed Kearsey, and even after hearing that the Lundrigan jet was on its way to take Dunphy to St. John's and understanding the significance of Dunphy's ending up in the hands of the Liberals, Poole wanted to wash his hands of Alec Dunphy. He finally agreed to help, but before he left he called Smallwood's office. Leading Smallwood's secretary to believe he was a Liberal who was in on the plan, he got conformation that the jet was indeed on the way.

Ed Kearsey had also heard from Mary Dunphy, and he and Poole set off on the fifteen-minute drive to Steady Brook, stopping before they got to Dunphy's house to pick up Dwayne Ross, a younger, heftier Tory supporter. They found Dunphy outside his house with his travel bag, leaning over his fence. In the dark and in his condition, Dunphy thought it was the car Smallwood was sending to take him to the jet and started to get in, but he backed away quickly when he discovered his mistake. The three men got out, manhandled him into the car, and drove off, turning back onto the highway just as Lundrigan's car was turning in.

In the meantime, in case Poole didn't get there in time, Crosbie and Hickman had broken the news to the media in St. John's, telling them they should have someone at the airport to meet Lundrigan's jet, and Crosbie got in touch with Bill Rowe, another of Smallwood's young Turks, and threatened to bring charges, although for what it wasn't clear.

Then in early January, 1972, while Moores was still away, the Liberal member for Fortune Bay, former magistrate Gus Oldford, resigned. Oldford, like all other magistrates, owed his job to Small-wood, and Smallwood had decided Gus Oldford would run in the October election. Oldford had been a magistrate in Harbour Breton for a long time, and Alex Hickman had appeared before him. The Sunday following the election, Hickman was in his usual place at St. James United Church, and he noticed Gus Oldford on the other side of the church. Hickman had never seen him there before and was pretty certain Oldford was Anglican. When the service was over, Hickman was surrounded by people in the parking lot, congratulat-ing him, but he could see Gus Oldford waiting. Oldford approached Hickman, who congratulated him on getting elected; Oldford replied, "I wish I hadn't been." Hickman sensed Oldford wanted to talk, but someone else came up and there was no opportunity that morning.

Moores swore he never talked to Oldford and didn't know of any of his people who did, adding, "Gus was a very honourable guy. He didn't cross the floor, he just resigned, he'd had enough. The stuff that had gone on was not a magisterial type of behaviour, and he quit in disgust. It would have been a lot more key to us if he'd crossed the floor, but he just wanted out."

In the meantime, the Liberals' application to have the St. Barbe election thrown out was making its way through the system. There were four Supreme Court judges in Newfoundland at the time, and the application had to be heard by two of them. Puddister was automatically disqualified, which left Arthur Mifflin, James Higgens, and Robert Furlong.

Hickman recalls that a *Telegram* reporter named John Carter had covered Smallwood during the election campaign and through all the speculation in November about what was going to happen with Tom Burgess. Carter had written an opinion piece advising people not to underestimate Smallwood. He gave as an example a previous general election in which one of Smallwood's cabinet ministers, Max Lane, was defeated. That same night, he observed, Arthur Mifflin, who had been re-elected in Trinity North, "conveniently" announced that he would resign so that Lane could run in a by-election to regain his seat; Smallwood had then rewarded Mifflin by appointing him to the bench. Mifflin was furious and determined to prove he was not under Smallwood's influence. In a conversation with Bill Marshall just before Christmas, Mifflin had talked about Carter's article and told Marshall that even though he was suffering ill health and hoping to go south for a while, he was determined not to miss his chance to hear the Liberals' application.

A few days before the hearing was to open, John Crosbie paid a visit to Alex Hickman's office, voicing the opinion that the Tories were going to lose. Hickman answered that the courts were going to sustain Maynard's election; in fact, he was so certain they were going to win that somebody should call Moores and tell him to get back to the province. Hickman's confidence had nothing to do with the law and everything to do with the article by John Carter and Mifflin's desire to demonstrate that he wasn't Smallwood's man.

Regardless of who would prove to be right, other events were unfolding. On January 8 frantic phone calls to Moores in St. Lucia informed him that the front pages of Canadian newspapers were trumpeting both his own whereabouts with Janis and news of Dodie's petition for divorce on the grounds of adultery and mental cruelty. Moores had no choice but to head home, although he did not do so as discretely as he might have. In order to get him a flight immediately, someone had the brainwave to tell the airline that Moores was the prime minister of Newfoundland and had to get back for an urgent matter of state. The incident grew over the years into a story in which Moores and Farrell got off the plane at a stopover in Barbados accompanied by two floozies, complete with spike heels, short skirts, and big hair. The actual women, Marg Farrell and Janis Johnson, would not have been amused at the downgrading of their appearance, let alone their status.

Tom Farrell remembers what actually happened. "We got off the commuter plane, and it seemed like the whole government was down on the tarmac, waiting to receive the prime minister of

Newfoundland. We had to go down and walk through the receiving line and meet people. Of course we'd had a few drinks and I was half cut, and they asked me what minister I was. I said, highways or something, and then I went on to the next one and forgot what I had told the last one. I was telling everybody I was a different minister. I said to Frank, 'If this gets out we will all be ruined.' Frank thought it was the funniest thing and never said a word. When we went out to get on the next plane, all the crew was lined up to salute us on board. They had expected the prime minister of Newfoundland, and that's who they got."

No one in the PC Party was very happy about Frank's being away from the scene, but that he would jeopardize their precarious position by openly turning his back on his wife and seven children was almost unbelievable. John Crosbie quietly started meeting with the members of the Tory caucus. Today Crosbie explains that he was concerned about John Doyle, but in the same breath, he somewhat contradicts himself. "Everyone was concerned because Doyle was trying to get in with Frank, and Frank disappeared south and saw Doyle down there.... There was nothing John Doyle wouldn't stoop to. He was the type who'd set you up with a call girl and take pictures, anything, so there were tensions caused by the fact that he had even seen Doyle, even though he couldn't do anything with Doyle even if he wanted to. Doyle was so obviously a crook Frank would have lost control of the party. The PC Party would have been split." In other words, if John Crosbie had any evidence that Moores was meeting John Doyle, it would have been just what he needed to get rid of him. Tom Farrell says unequivocally that there was no meeting with Doyle, that it would have been impossible for Frank to meet with Doyle without his knowledge, and it just didn't happen.

Crosbie may have used the Doyle rumour to strengthen his argument that Moores might not be able to form a government, he was unlikely to win another election, and he was unfit to run the province because of his personal behaviour. In his excellent book, *Smallwood: The Unlikely Revolutionary*, Richard Gwynne reported that after a long, heated cabinet meeting, ten of the fourteen ministers present voted to ask for Moores's resignation. Today Crosbie gives an ambiguous denial, Gwynne doesn't recall his source, and Tom Farrell, adding up the ministers he believed to be firmly on Moores's side at the time, doubts those figures. There's no doubt, however, that there was a movement to get rid of Moores and that John Crosbie was stoking the fires and leading the revolution. However, some Tories who had finally reached the Promised Land largely because of the charisma and leadership of Frank Moores were having none of it, and Moores was well informed about what Crosbie was up to. Members not in St. John's at the time were contacted by phone about Frank's lack of attention to the job and urged to support a move to get rid of him. Thirty-five years later, no one I spoke to wanted to admit having been part of it, and a Tory who claims that he didn't go along with it won't identify the person who called him, except to say that it was not John Crosbie.

It was the night of January 10. Timing was with Moores again. Because of the crisis with Dodie, he had been on his way home while those calls to mutiny were burning up the wires. Moores and Farrell arrived "hung over and working on another one." They expected to have the night to recover, but Crosbie demanded that Moores meet with him immediately at his house. Moores wasn't in a position to refuse. In all probability Crosbie knew the Maynard decision was coming in the next couple of days, but Moores didn't. Crosbie may not have known what it would be, but if Alex Hickman's prediction was right, he was running out of time to force Moores to resign.

Tom Farrell accompanied Moores, both for moral support and as a witness. They thought it odd that Crosbie was alone. There was no mention of Moores's supposed meeting with John Doyle. Crosbie focused on "a lot of vitriolic stuff about adultery and marital problems—how it was a disgrace, the leader of the party getting a divorce, cavorting with his girlfriend while his wife was here with seven kids." Crosbie demanded that Moores announce his resignation. Moores refused. It was a very volatile, heated session, with a lot of "jumping up and shouting and all." Moores knew he was in a very weakened position and hadn't been back long enough to assess the division of caucus, but he held his ground and his luck held out.

On January 12 the judge found for the Tories in the Maynard case.

The next day Moores dismissed rumours that his leadership was being challenged, Tom Burgess announced he was loyal to the PCS, and Dodie Moores announced that she was not divorcing her husband. Frank had charmed her one more time. A bemused John Crosbie admits that not only was the reaction to Frank's blatant adultery not what he had expected, but if anything, being a playboy seemed to be one of his assets. Moores made no apologies to anyone for his behaviour.

"Don't forget, governments lose elections; oppositions don't win them, as a rule. I think we did more to win that election than most oppositions, but the fact was, Joey's time was up. We were in the right place at the right time. I knew it was only a matter of time before it had to happen; we had the popular vote. I think Joey couldn't give up because he just couldn't admit in his own mind that he'd lost. I got to know him pretty well [later], but he never talked to me about that. I think he probably just got tired of it. He didn't have one person in the world that was agreeing with him, including the people he had around him, people like Ed Roberts, who he was close to. Even the hangers-on couldn't agree with him. So finally, I suppose, he got isolated.

Our caucus just wasn't focused. They were poisoned because they were not the government, not getting their just desserts for being elected, and of course they were frustrated. A few of them, I suppose, like Crosbie, who thought making loud noises was important, blamed me for not getting in there and kicking up all hell. They were very impatient with me, but there was nothing we could do about it, not a damn thing, and they couldn't see that or maybe they didn't want to see it. Unfortunately some of them were more emotional than logical. Doody and I had spent a year and a half, non-stop, organizing across the province, we had just been through a hectic campaign, and I knew what we had ahead of us: there had to be another campaign. I just figured I would go and have a little rest before the real battle started."

Moores was planning what some have called the greatest political ploy in Canadian history.

CHAPTER 18

The Time Finally Came

IN THE SECOND WEEK of January 1972, newspaper reports spoke of "nocturnal visits of Brinks vans to Confederation Building and Elizabeth Towers ferrying god knows what to Roaches Line" as a sure sign Joey was planning to leave, but Moores learned about the plan through the media. On January 14, almost three months after the election, Joey Smallwood announced he would be handing the government over to Frank Moores on January 18, and Frank Moores stated that Tom Burgess was highly unlikely to be invited into cabinet.

Joey Smallwood refused to communicate with Frank Moores. His apparent intention was to leave the government of Newfoundland in limbo, with no transition whatsoever to the next premier. Alex Hickman contacted Jim Channing, Clerk of the Privy Council, who said Smallwood refused to discuss the matter. Hickman then contacted Ed Roberts, who wasn't prepared to make a firm commitment on behalf of Smallwood. Hickman requested a meeting with Jim Channing, and Roberts said he'd ask the premier about it. Hickman was flabbergasted. He told Roberts, "Don't ask the premier, tell the premier." A few minutes later Jim Channing called and said that the premier had given him permission to come down to see Frank Moores on the day he left.

Moores was shocked when he first entered Smallwood's office. "There was a console beside his desk with about forty or fifty keys on it; each key was directed into a minister's office. He could turn a key and listen into the conversation without them knowing. If he wanted to, he could push another key and interrupt the conversation. . . . He didn't trust anybody, even his own crowd. He had to have control over everything. I didn't find anything of a personal nature except a staff that was terrified."

The Newfoundland public service had been in a state of suspension and shock for three months. No one knew any other way but Joey's, and Joey's way was to get rid of people who didn't support him. Jim Channing had served with Frank Moores on the Fisheries College board, but when he walked into the premier-elect's office he was trembling so much that he could barely hold on to his cigarette. Moores greeted him like an old friend, started a little small talk about the days when they worked together, and asked Channing for advice and direction on what they had to do for an orderly changeover.

Jim Channing visibly relaxed, and he confessed the trouble he had been having since the election. He said that Smallwood was attempting to destroy a lot of the records, and Channing felt that as the senior civil servant he had some responsibility. He'd protest the destruction or removal of certain documents, and Smallwood would threaten to fire him. Channing took to returning to Confederation Building late at night and photocopying documents that Smallwood was preparing to take. Hickman recalls that there were many deals with little or no paper trail, but some of the deals the Tories did manage to uncover were exposed thanks to Jim Channing's integrity and diligence. Through Channing, Moores sent out a message to the entire public service to say that he needed them and wanted to work with them and that no one should be scared because of the change in administration. Reviews would naturally be taking place, but other positions would be found for anyone not suited for the job he or she was in.

On the morning of January 19, a very ebullient fifteen-member cabinet assembled at Government House to be sworn in, and the first Progressive Conservative cabinet meeting in Newfoundland's history was held that afternoon. But on January 26 the political situation heated up again. An eccentric shopkeeper named Hughie Shea, one of Moores's opponents for the party leadership, had been elected in St. John's South. Piqued because he wasn't in cabinet, he announced he would be leaving the Tories to sit as an Independent. Moores was unmoved. "The man was a lunatic as far as I was concerned. Put him in the cabinet to salvage the government? No. I knew there was another election coming and I knew we were going to clobber them. It was a matter of how to get the election—that was the whole modus operandi where I was concerned."

On February 1 Tom Burgess and Hugh Shea joined the Liberal Party. The odds were mounting against the longevity of the Moores government, and Moores knew he was up against more than just the Liberal party. "Of course we knew Doyle was really involved. I can't prove it, but the rumour was Shea was paid $50,000 by Doyle to cross the floor. Whatever, Shea had gone from our shop, and other stuff was going on but nothing had reached fruition." The backroom Tories were working on their own deals.

Under pressure to call the house together, Moores had reasons to delay: there was a lot of work to do to get ready for the House, the Liberals had a leadership convention to go through, and most importantly Moores needed time for the "other stuff" to ripen. On February 7 Ed Roberts was elected leader of the Liberal Party, beating out three other candidates, including week-old Liberal Tom Burgess.

The Tories were spending the first weeks trying to making sense of files and find paper trails to deals that Smallwood had brokered and no one else knew much about. One of these trails led to the realization that John Doyle was in Europe and about to borrow $20 million on a Newfoundland government guarantee, a deal which was stopped in the nick of time with the help of Ed Roberts.

One of the most sensational, complicated, and difficult deals that began to unravel involved the ownership of seven provincial liquor stores. These buildings were leased to the government by Banker's Trust, a subsidiary of the Royal Trust Company, on behalf of a company called Investment Developers Ltd. The construction cost of the stores was determined to be under $200,000, and the twenty-year leases committed the government to paying more than twice the going rate per square foot plus all the operating costs, taxes, and maintenance. The deal was extremely lucrative for the owners; the problem was that nobody seemed to know who the owners were. In February Moores established a Royal Commission into the Leasing of Premises for the Use of the Newfoundland Liquor Commission, under the chairmanship of Fabian O'Dea, QC, a former lieutenant-governor.

On February 28 Moores called a press conference to announce a by-election to replace Gus Oldford in Fortune Bay. He also said that the House would not open until after the by-election and that the government would resign if the PCs lost. The next morning he surprised everyone by calling another press conference to announce that the House was opening March 1.

The first Speech from the Throne from the Moores government was the longest one ever read. As Alex Hickman describes it, "There was nothing left out. If there was room for motherhood, it would have been in there." The speech was televised live. Only Frank Moores knew it was an election speech.

The tradition was for a reception to be held following the throne speech for all members, senior government officials, and invited guests of the government. Hickman was sitting next to Moores in the House and was astounded when Moores told him out of the side of his mouth that as soon as the House rose for the day he was going straight to the lieutenant-governor to ask him to adjourn it. Hickman thought the idea was crazy and pointless, and he protested that Moores had to go to the reception before he asked for dissolution because Tories had waited a long time to meet a Tory premier, and Moores couldn't disappoint them. Moores, who could never be bothered with the details of how parliament was run, asked Hickman, "What is that thing again I have to ask for?"

Moores went to the party for a while, partly to keep both the Tories and the Liberals from suspecting something was up, and then he quietly slipped out and headed for Government House. The 'stuff that had come to fruition' was in Moores's pocket, a letter of resignation from Carbonear Liberal MHA William Saunders. Saunders's resignation was the point on which the future of the Newfoundland government turned.

Liberal leader Ed Roberts later claimed to have been informed on March 28 that a Liberal was about to break ranks and that he suspected Saunders, who had financial problems. Roberts called Smallwood, in Florida, who called Saunders, and then both called Roberts back to assure him of Saunders's loyalty. Not convinced, Roberts drove to Carbonear on March 29 to see Saunders, who, Roberts said, appeared "very shaky, weary, weepy," but once again he assured Roberts he had no intention of resigning. At this time Moores had had Saunders's letter for twenty-four hours.

Maynard's confirmation had given Moores the majority he needed to form the government, but even with Oldford's seat vacant, Burgess and Shea's joining the Liberals left Moores with twenty seats to the Liberals' twenty-one before the House opened. The election of a Speaker would further reduce the government numbers to nineteen. As early as the day after the House opened, the Liberals could defeat the government and constitutionally had the right to ask to form the government themselves, even though their election of a Speaker would result in a tied house which could accomplish little or nothing. However, if both sides had twenty seats *before* the Speaker took his seat the day after the throne speech, the House could be dissolved at once.

Had Bill Saunders sat in the House for just one day, he would have received $10,000 in session pay and been eligible for his pension. For some reason it took Ed Roberts two years to request a royal commission to look into the resignation, on the basis that "any man who had knowledge of that letter . . . and did not tell the lieutenant-governor or Speaker is guilty of a vile constitutional fraud . . . on the Crown, the House and the people." His request was denied and the question of "vile constitutional fraud" never went anywhere. Moores explained it this way:

> "I grew up in Carbonear, and a lot of the people who sup-ported Bill, including his close relatives, were also friends of mine, and when the thing turned out as it did, with the way Smallwood acted, there were a lot of very upset peo-ple. People who voted for Bill didn't vote for Bill to help screw up the province. There were about eight or ten of them that put incredible pressure on Bill Saunders, and I knew who they were.
>
> I got a call from a dear friend of mine who was related to Bill. He said, 'Frank, I have something here for you. What do you want me to do with it?' I said, 'That depends on what it is.' He said, 'Bill Saunders's resignation.' So in he came and we had a few drinks and I kept it. No one knew except the committee who put the pressure on him, Bill Saunders, and myself, and that was it. There were people saying, If Doyle is paying $50,000 a head maybe we should be paying more; when it got down to it, it was the survival of the fittest. They said money changed hands, and I would not be surprised one bit if that were the case, but I have ab-solutely no proof if it was done or not, and I wouldn't touch that with a barge pole. There are lots of people I would want to be compared to in this world, but John C. Doyle is not one of them."

After all these years Moores still didn't identify the 'dear friend' who delivered Saunders's resignation to him, but on the plane with the west-coast MHAS who had flown to St. John's a few nights earlier for the House opening was a man most of them knew well. William MacDonald Brown, a prominent Corner Brook Tory and a good friend of Moores, let drop that he was on his way to visit his brother-in-law, Bill Saunders.

Moores had asked Jim Channing to draw up the necessary papers to take to the lieutenant-governor. Channing advised Moores that it was a waste of time. Moores told him to just draw up the papers as if he had a majority and ask for an appointment to see the lieutenant-governor after the throne speech. He says, "I didn't discuss it with a soul. I was premier. If you discussed it, then you had too many opinions on the same subject, and it was the only logical thing to do."

Lieutenant-Governor John Harnum had been appointed by Smallwood, and he was loyal. Moores believed that even though Joey was no longer premier, Harnum would check with him, if he had the chance, to see which way he should handle Moores's request for a dissolution. Moores's strategy was not to give him the opportunity. "I hammered him and hammered him, saying, 'You know we got 54 per cent of the vote and they had 45 per cent, you should give us the dissolution, it's unfair,' etc. etc. It was a charade, and what I was hoping was going to happen, happened. After about an hour and a half I said, 'Your Honour, under what conditions *would* you give us a dissolution?' He said, 'If it was tied I would definitely do it,' and I put my hand in my inside pocket and said, 'Here, sir, is Mr. Saunders's resignation. The House is now tied. Jim, will you give Mr. Harnum the papers?' He could do nothing but sign them, but he would never have done it otherwise. He thought he had a foolproof answer; not knowing about the letter, he wasn't expecting it to be tied ten seconds after he finished speaking. I finished with him about eleven o'clock, and I sent out the sos. I wanted all the cabinet as fast as possible."

Alex Hickman was watching a hockey game when the phone rang. Moores's opening words banished all thought of hockey: "I got the fucking thing, what do you call it, dissolution.

The lieutenant-governor just signed it and Channing witnessed it. I want to meet with the cabinet."

Hickman said, "When?"

"Now," said Moores. "There's one group at the Colonial Inn and one group at the Starboard Quarter, and the third is down at Crosbie's."

Hickman phoned around, and sure enough, all were where Moores had said they'd be. One by one they straggled into the cabinet room. It was cold and starting to snow, some of the ministers were still in their morning suits, a lot of them were liquored up, and all of them were asking Hickman what they were there for.

They all stood up and applauded when Moores came into the room, but they were speechless when he said, "Gentlemen, the situation is, we are no longer a government. I have just dissolved the House, and polling day is March 21. We have a lot of work to do, so go home and go to bed and get your campaigns ready. It's not just your own riding, it's everyone's riding you're going to have to watch as well, and help out."

Alec Dunphy was the only incumbent who had to face a nominating convention. He won the seat but later resigned, claiming that Moores had reneged on a promised fisheries portfolio. He then went public about the goings-on the previous Christmas. At that time a person who had been treated for a mental illness could not serve as an MHA. Dunphy claimed that he had found out that the Liberals had planned, with booze and drugs, to reduce him to a state where he could be committed to the Waterford Mental Hospital, and that there was a bed there all ready for him. The Liberals dismissed the charges as the ravings of a drunk. Ex-Tory Hughie Shea then charged that it was the Tories who were plotting to have Dunphy committed, and he added that he himself had been offered $200,000 by the Tories for his loyalty. It was a ludicrous charge, but the bottom line was that Alec Dunphy's life was never the same after the machinations.

A Tory campaign letter outlined how busy the Conservatives

had been in the six weeks they had actually been in power. Moores's government had recovered $24 million for the province by taking control of the linerboard mill, eliminated the 7 per cent sales tax on children's clothing, regulated minimum wage equity for women, increased the minimum wage by fifteen cents an hour, halted the controversial resettlement program, and begun drafting legislation for public tendering, a landlord-tenants act, a labour relations act, a labour standards act, a consumer affairs division, and an all-party public accounts committee. Some of the future plans as outlined in the Speech from the Throne included conflict of interest legislation, the introduction of a question period in the House of Assembly, collective bargaining, and a substantial increase in teachers' salaries.

On March 21, 1972, five months after the cliff-hanger election, after a campaign described by *Time* magazine as low key to the point of boredom, Frank Moores, unopposed in his own district, led his PC Party to a substantial victory, winning thirty-three out of forty-one seats. On election night, another of Moores's legendary talents showed itself. When he arrived at the CBC television studio in Corner Brook after the returns were in, it was obvious that he'd been calming his nerves with Scotch for a number of hours. His speech was slurred and he was staggering just a little. As the anchor, I was horrified that he'd be seen in that state on such a historic and momentous occasion, and so was guest host Michael Monaghan, but there was nothing we could do. We managed to get him seated, albeit a little slouched, and his microphone attached. The camera light went on, and an apprehensive Monaghan asked Premier Moores how he felt about the election results.

The instant the red light came on, Moores drew himself up to full stature, looked straight into the camera and said, with his trademark salutation and not a trace of a slur, "Ladies and gentleman, it is obvious tonight that the government of Joseph R. Smallwood has gone down to ignominious defeat." We couldn't believe he could even say "ignominious," but the interview went on from there in the same manner; nobody watching would ever have guessed the newly re-elected premier had had a drink.

The next day front pages all over the country carried the picture of a smiling Frank Moores being kissed by his wife Dodie, while a letter to the editor of a St. John's newspaper warned that no one should expect the new premier to let the job interfere with his personal life, such as travelling around with a private companion. While Moores's honeymoon with the Newfoundland people was about to begin, his marriage was almost over. Nothing had changed since Frank had persuaded Dodie to retract the divorce action; he wasn't exactly living openly with Janis, but he wasn't home either. Nor was he being faithful to Janis.

CHAPTER 19

"He Haf to Haf It."

EVEN WHEN JANIS WAS WITH HIM at public or private functions Moores would often slip away for an hour, or be an hour late following their travel from one place to another, and there was never any doubt in anyone's mind what was delaying him. As one old timer put it when Moores disappeared from a function in Bonavista Bay, "He can't help it, b'y. He haf to haf it."

Any of Moores's executive assistants could be put on the spot when Moores would point out a woman in the audience and ask the hapless fellow to arrange for them to meet. Even the more strait-laced members of his caucus were somewhat in awe of the effect Moores had on women. Bill Marshall often found himself "defending the indefensible" and finally decided to let the premier handle his critics himself. "There were three dear friends of mine, ladies, who had heard the stories about Frank and didn't approve, and they asked to meet with him. They went into his office ready to let him know what they thought. After an hour or so they came out of Confederation Building, and I can see them now, laughing and giggling like school girls. He had 100 per cent charmed them."

By the fall of Moores's first year in office Dodie Moores had had enough and filed for divorce again. This time no one was shocked or paid much attention, not even John Crosbie. She accepted a lump sum payment from Frank, which she later regretted as she realized the increasing expense of raising the five children left at home. The following year she entered nurse's training in St. John's.

Tom Farrell and his wife Marg got on well with Janis, the two couples travelled together, and for a few months after the election he and Moores shared Dorothy Moores's suite in Elizabeth Towers. Moores and Farrell were on the fifth floor, and he had moved Janis into a suite on the sixth floor. Moores would spend the night with Janis and go downstairs in the morning to get dressed for the day. His clothes started gradually to move up to her apartment, but they fought too much for him to get too comfortable. It was the old story: Moores had cheated on Dodie and lied to her about Janis; now he was cheating on Janis and lying to her. The difference was that Janis knew what he was capable of.

Farrell had an up-close and personal view of the rocky affair with Janis. "They'd have a racket, and she'd be in a terrible state." Moores would ask Farrell to go up and talk to her. Even when Moores didn't ask, Janis would often end up crying on Farrell's shoulder. Even though he depended on Farrell to smooth the waters and placate Janis, Moores's natural suspicion that others would do whatever he would do soon showed itself; after a few of Janis's tearful episodes with Farrell, he asked Tom if he had put the moves on her. Farrell maintains he was no more interested in Janis than she was in him, but that was how Frank Moores thought.

His suspicions didn't stop him from continuing to count on Farrell to help him stay out of hot water. In those days there was no chief of staff or person in any other position designated to accompany the premier on business trips, and more often than not, the role was filled by Tom Farrell. Farrell, who had a wife and six children he was close to, was damned by association, but Farrell joked that he wouldn't even be able to keep up with Frank's rejects.

Accompanying Frank Moores was not for the prudish or fainthearted. On one trip to Europe, he had three women in one hotel at one time. Janis had stayed back at the hotel in London while Moores and Farrell took a side trip to Hamburg on fisheries business. The mayor of Hamburg had a ravishing blonde assistant, and Moores couldn't resist. He took her back to London for the weekend, where another big, good-looking German blonde, a stewardess, was waiting for him. Tom Farrell had his work cut out for him. "They were all on the same floor, never mind the same hotel. *Desperate Housewives* has nothing on it. These blondes, me trying to talk to Jan, and he was going from one to the other, and it didn't knock a sweat out of him. This was in the fall, and the following spring, when the fishing season opened, we went in for a couple of days in the woods. Who arrived in the camp but the one from Hamburg. I flew out, not that I was passing judgment, but they were delighted to see me go, anyway."

I had interviewed Moores on a few occasions between the two elections. Some time after the March election he invited me to his hotel room at the Holiday Inn in Corner Brook to discuss something of interest. I had no idea what the meeting was about, and, young and naive, I assumed other people would be there. I was wrong.

Frank had uncorked the wine and pre-ordered dinner. I wasn't there long when there was a knock on the room door. Frank opened the door narrowly and stepped outside, and I recognized the voice of Ed Poole, who happened to be my cousin. Then their voices lowered, and although I could hear the intensity, I didn't know what they were saying. Finally Ed went away, and Frank came back in and picked up the conversation as if there had been no interruption.

The party had been watching Moores carefully, trying to keep his womanizing under wraps, and they knew he was up to something because of his evasiveness about plans they had made for him for that evening. When I was seen going up to his floor, Ed had been chosen to intervene, perhaps under the correct assumption that I would be pleased to see him and think it quite natural that he show up while I was there, but Moores blocked him. I was single and had a vague understanding that he was separated, but I didn't succumb to the famous Moores charm that night, when he didn't actually make a pass at me, or later, when he did.

He told me he was setting up a new department called Newfoundland Information Services, and he offered me a job in it that would involve a lot of travelling with him. This was an exciting if somewhat unusual offer to make to a twenty-two-year-old with eight months' media experience. I said I'd think about it, and he suggested I fly to St. John's to meet a few people and look at an apartment that was available if I took the position.

The apartment he had in mind for me was directly below his in Elizabeth Towers and currently occupied, so he showed me the identical one that he was sharing with Tom Farrell. I had no idea that Janis Johnson occupied the apartment above. When I admired some beautiful built-in book shelves, he told me that I could have the same ones installed in the apartment below. Those same book shelves later became part of a public accounts inquiry into accepting gifts from contractors.

That night the premier invited me to dinner at the Woodstock Inn. We were accompanied by his driver, Stafford Crummy. After dinner, when I asked to be dropped off at my hotel, Frank suggested we all go back to his place for a nightcap. Crummy went to put away the car and didn't come back. When I questioned that, Frank became very boyish, sat by me on the couch, put his arm around me, and said, "You know I'm strung out on you, don't you?" I didn't know. While I found him charming, I wasn't attracted to him romantically or sexually, and I had never gotten the feeling that he was attracted to me. He did kiss me, then, once, but when I told him I needed time to think about everything, he made no attempt to persuade me to stay. Ever the gentleman he picked up the phone, and Staff Crummy re-appeared to drive me to the Holiday Inn alone.

Back in Corner Brook I went to see Ed Poole and asked his opinion. Ed was uncomfortable and hedged until I finally asked, "If I were your sister instead of your cousin, what would you say?" He answered, "I'd tell you not to touch it with a ten foot pole." Added to my mother's caustic remark about going down in history as Frank Moores's paramour, my answer to the generous job offer was no.

At the time I was surprised that Moores would risk the controversy such an appointment would have caused, but it wasn't until I interviewed Tom Farrell for this book that I learned that Janis Johnson was in the apartment above, and I remembered that this occurred just a few months before their wedding. At first I thought about the story of the three women on the same hotel floor and marvelled at his nerve, but then I realized that Janis would have had to have known about his arranging for me to move in below him and would never have stood for it. Knowing now how close he came to leaving her at the altar, it seems quite possible that he was trying to extricate himself from his relationship with Janis. I don't think he ever seriously wanted me for that job, and I don't believe he was the slightest bit "strung out on me."

He took no for an answer very gracefully and never made another pass at me, and we remained on good terms. I knew my conversation with Ed Poole had probably gotten back to him, but he never referred to the incident until twenty-five years later, after I became communications director for Ed Byrne, the leader of the PC opposition. Frank called one day when I was in Ed's office. I hadn't spoken to him for almost two decades, and Ed passed me the phone to say hello. "So he finally got you where I couldn't get you" was his opening remark. "Oh, but Frank," I said, "the terms of reference are different." He laughed and replied, "Just make sure I don't hear any talk of him trying to set you up in an apartment in Elizabeth Towers."

Second- and third-hand accounts of Frank Moores's womanizing wats would fill a book by themselves. On one occasion he suggested to a well-known member of the Newfoundland theatrical community that they spend the night together in a nearby motel. She decided that if she was going to spend the night with the premier, she wanted to stay in the Newfoundland Hotel, and so the courtly Moores drove the two hours back to the city. While he could be very discreet and usually tried to shelter his activities from the disapproval of the party and caucus, he was often totally indiscreet. Roy McMurtry recalled a time when he was in Newfoundland for a meeting of the provincial attorneys general. "Frank was standing in a group talking to three or four of the attorneys general, along with a young CBC woman who was there. Frank took her aside and clearly, within the hearing of the AGs, told her he had an apartment in New York and there was a weekend coming up and why don't we go down and take in a couple of shows? He didn't even really try to hide it, but she was very flustered." McMurtry stopped in the telling of this story and asked, "It wasn't you, was it?" to which I was able to answer, "No."

Tom Farrell was always amazed at the way Moores managed to love 'em and leave 'em without leaving a trail of bad feelings behind him. "He seemed to keep friendly with them all, and that was the secret to staying out of trouble, I think. No one seemed to dislike him enough to cause him any trouble. Most men, if they break up with someone, do it badly, it's so final and they hurt somebody; Frank never did it that way."

Obviously he hurt the women who were unlucky enough to fall in love with him, and his behaviour sometimes shocked and hurt men who looked up to him. It was said that Frank Moores could charm the pants off the Mother Superior, but he had no compunctions about choosing his women from the other end of the moral scale. On a trip to Bay d'Espoir for a public meeting, he and a couple of other members were put up in workers' cabins outside the town. After the meeting he invited a couple of local "loose women" back to the cabin. One of the group that night was a hefty, decent man who had followed Moores into politics like a disciple. When he found out in the morning that Moores had had one of the girls stay overnight, he sat down hard, stunned. Then he said, "She had dirty fingernails," and this big, burly man began to cry. Tom Farrell tried to convince him that the woman hadn't been with the premier, but a hero had fallen that night.

Moores never stopped thinking about women, it seemed. Following a meeting one Tuesday night in the small town of Bay Roberts, when everyone was preparing to go home, Moores rubbed his hands together and said to Eric Dawe, "Now let's go find some women." It took a bit of persuasion to convince him that there was virtually no place open to find women in Bay Roberts, Newfoundland, at eleven o'clock on a week night.

Frank Moores may have been a sex addict or, as one close friend said, "just a real horny guy"; another theory suggests that his role model in this, as in other matters, may have been his father, whom he adored and who could do no wrong in his eyes. Si Moores had quite a reputation as a womanizer. According to the conventions of the times, when everything was known but nothing was said, he attended to much more than business on his many trips away from home; he was said to have had another woman and a child in Boston. If his own mother was able to accept this behaviour in a man, surely other women could be expected to do the same. Whatever the reason for it, Moores accepted his womanizing as part of his personality.

With his amazing charisma, Moores just attracted people period. St. John's businessman Mark Dobbin tells of going into pubs on George Street with former Ontario premier David Peterson, a number of other businessmen, and Moores. Over twenty years after Moores had left office, people swarmed around Moores, delighted to see him. Peterson, out of office for a much shorter time, couldn't believe Frank's celebrity status, remarking that he would never have gotten that kind of reception in his province, even when he was in power. Dobbin, too said it was like being out with a rock star.

CHAPTER 20

The Team

FRANK MOORES WAS A KEEN OBSERVER of men as well as women and a master at getting them to work for him. He was fortunate to have a formidable pool of talent to choose from. To this day political observers and historians credit the cabinet Frank Moores had put together by the of 1972 with being the most talented cabinet Newfoundland had ever had. He commented on some of the members and his style of leadership during our last session together. Off the cuff and not a complete analysis by any means, his remarks are nonetheless illuminating.

"I probably did have the strongest cabinet in our history," he said, "and one reason for that was the members wanted to do the right thing. After the Smallwood decades, they had to correct all that had been done wrong; they made changes slowly, but they made them well." The group was very diverse. There were the old Tories—Bill Marshall, a rock-solid, almost fanatical Conservative, a pain in the arse sometimes and Ank Murphy, who both knew the traditional St. John's view well, and Tom Hickey from St. John's East Extern, who was important for knowing what a certain not always desirable crowd were thinking."

Whether the way they influenced each other was academic or not, he felt Farrell did a good job. Moores described Gerry Ottenheimer as an extremely bright and exceptional minister, but by far the best minister, he thought, was Bill Doody. Doody understood not only his own portfolio but the workings of both the government and the unions; however tough the union men, Doody held their respect and was welcome to have a drink with them. When trouble seemed to be brewing in a union dealing with the government, Doody would call the boys, outline the bigger government picture, and ask them for their opinions. "All of a sudden we would have a call," Moores said, and "the representative of the department in danger of union trouble would say, 'The guys from the union just called, and they are rethinking their position.' Then I would say to myself, Why am I surprised?" Tom Farrell was Moores's best friend in politics, and Moores recognized that they may have had a little difficulty separating their personal relationship from the differing responsibilities of their jobs.

There were the Crosbie Liberals. Brian Peckford, for example, Moores said, "was very bright, and he ran a good department, but he was not a Conservative; he wasn't even a Liberal—he was more of a socialist. The natural party for Peckford was the NDP, not the Conservative Party," at least with respect to how Peckford thought. Another one was Ed Maynard who Moores said was underestimated and "the most logical, common-sense guy in the whole cabinet room, when he wasn't drinking, which, "to give him his due, was most of the time. If the cabinet was deadlocked and I wasn't sure how I felt, I'd ask Ed what he thought. Many times he helped make decisions for the government that I'm not sure would have been made the same way if he hadn't had an input."

And then there were Joey's former ministers. "Alex Hickman really believed in the system, and as Minister of Justice, he was terrific," Moores said, adding that he was one of the brightest members of Smallwood's cabinet as well. Val Earle was "a rock of common sense"; Moores felt confident that Earle's opinions would be balanced and solid. And of course there was John Crosbie, "brilliant but uncontrollable."

"All of them played an important part," Moores said. "I was never a person who needed the limelight, I just didn't. I needed to get a job done, and that was the most important thing. I had good people in cabinet, and they knew if they didn't take the responsibility they would be moved. They didn't need me looking over their shoulders."

Many of the new MHAS had mixed feelings about Moores; worried about some aspects of his personality but impressed with his leadership and organizational style, which allowed others to contribute. They were a mixed bag; one described the early caucus meetings as "a mixture of erudite speakers, bumbling speakers, blasphemous, profane, obscene, incoherent, very coherent, and academic speakers." Once they all found their feet, Moores started bringing in people from different departments and industries to explain their areas of expertise. Fred Stagg, who became Deputy Speaker and later served under Brian Peckford, felt that Moores was unique in how strongly he involved his caucus in running the province. "Ministers still looked after their departments," he said, "but when we went to a caucus meeting, everyone was equal, nobody spoke as a cabinet minister, and everybody felt absolutely free to disagree with each other. We were very much involved in where we were going and how we were getting there."

Moores asked each member to do a four-year priority plan in consultation with his district and submit it to the premier's office. He made it clear that it was up to them to get the information in, and to the extent that it was possible, the plans would be implemented over the next four years. This was revolutionary in post-Smallwood Newfoundland, even for some of the newly elected revolutionists. Some didn't do it and others had trouble selling the concept to an electorate unaccustomed to being consulted, but those who submitted a plan found that the government attempted to follow through and that some projects were more successful than they ever anticipated.

Nevertheless, from the beginning of his tenure Moores had cabinet problems. While campaigning he had pledged to reduce the cabinet size to twelve. Chronically unable to say no, he ended up with nineteen cabinet ministers at one point, shuffling his cabinet four times in the first two years in his efforts to maintain peace and efficiency.

Bill Marshall refused a portfolio, pleading a young family and a growing law practice. He wanted to retain his independence, but he agreed to become House Leader. Moores thought that that compromise might be letting him off too easily, and during the press conference to introduce the new cabinet, he announced that Mr. Marshall would be a Minister without Portfolio in charge of reviewing the contracts of the previous administration. It was the first time Bill Marshall had heard of it, but he took it on with such diligence that he became known by the Liberals as Witch Hunt Willy.

Newfoundland's civil service was full of people who were either not up to the job they had been given or had not been allowed the opportunity to develop in their jobs and do them well. Moores began a full-scale professionalization of the civil service. Some deputy ministers who were within two or three years of retirement were offered a layoff with full salary until they reached pensionable age. Managers and others were moved to positions more suited to their abilities. The opportunity to bring in badly needed new blood while dealing humanely with people who had spent their lives in the public service was considered well worth the cost.

Smallwood's executive assistant in the Humber West office which Moores now occupied, a man named Frank Colbourne, was given the job of managing the newly opened Interfaith Seniors' Home. It was a plum job and many Tories were very unhappy. Moores responded that you can't get rid of a man with a family just because he is a Liberal. There was also pressure on Moores to dismiss all Liberals from paid positions on government boards and to crack down on Joey's friend Art Lundrigan and his Corner Brook-based construction empire. Lundrigan's headquarters was in Tom Farrell's district, adjacent to Moores's, and at that time employed over a thousand people in its various enterprises. Some of the old-guard Tories continued to raise the matter at caucus meetings until Moores finally reminded them that they wouldn't be sitting there if half the Liberals in the province hadn't voted for them. In spite of Bill Marshall's nickname, there was no witch hunt. For many Tory partisans who had been left out in the cold for over twenty years, the new government's treatment of Liberals marked the beginning of a disgruntlement with Moores that never went away.

Moores had to develop a government organization almost from scratch, beginning with the budget process. Joey, with little or no understanding of financial policy, had set government priorities based on whatever he wanted them to be. Within a few weeks of taking office, Moores set up a government reorganization committee, through which was developed the system of separate cabinet committees—treasury board, social policy, and others—that still operates today. By the end of 1972 Moores had created one completely new portfolio, tourism, completely revamped nine others, created over twenty new department divisions, and dismantled eleven superfluous agencies and boards.

Political loyalty was no longer the main qualification for the civil service. Moores retained Vic Young, Smallwood's Deputy Minister of Treasury Board, and made him his unofficial assistant. Young says that Frank Moores profoundly affected the civil service in Newfoundland and Labrador for generations to come. "Joey hired a lot of his cronies, and from outside. Frank wanted to give smart young Newfoundlanders a chance. He had a lot of faith in his fellow Newfoundlanders and put them to the test, and that was a huge strength. Part of his legacy is his professionalizing of the civil service. There are people there today, lifelong public servants, who Frank brought in and developed, who went on to make a big contribution because he gave them the chance. Everyone liked him, he was a very easy guy to work with, and a great motivator, especially of young people, and he never got credit for that. Not many public servants smile about their jobs anymore, but between Frank,

John Crosbie, Bill Doody, and Alex Hickman, even the tougher times were always very enjoyable."

CHAPTER 21

The Inheritance

IN JULY OF 1972, the findings of the O'Dea Royal Commission were made public: the shareholders of Investment Developers Ltd., owner of the seven liquor stores leased to the government under exorbitant conditions, were J.R. Smallwood, O.L. Vardy, and Arthur Lundrigan. Other inappropriate leases were uncovered as well, and the paper trail led to an even more shocking revelation: shares of IDL had been used as collateral for over $1.5 million in loans from the Bank of Montreal (of which Lundrigan was a board member) to the three shareholders for the purchase of shares in Brinco. After this purchase, Smallwood had granted substantial mineral concessions to the company, and he had also negotiated the terms of the Churchill Falls hydroelectric power development and the sales agreement with Hydro-Québec with Brinco. Smallwood bought his first shares in 1963, the year negotiations began for the sale of power to Hydro-Québec, and the bulk in 1965. The following year he capitulated to Hydro-Québec's demands and agreed to disastrous terms in order to get the project going. Hundreds of thousands of dollars in interest on this joint loan and on other loans made to Smallwood and Lundrigan were forgiven by the Bank of Montreal, which was also the province's banker. On a slightly different note, the commission also revealed that in the summer of 1971, about to take on Frank Moores again, this time more directly in a provincial election, Smallwood tripled the province's order of bulk rum.

The findings of the O'Dea commission made for scandalous reading and prompted an outcry for charges to be laid against the three. Smallwood denied any knowledge of owning shares in IDL; defending his purchase of Brinco shares, he said that he had suggested that all Newfoundlanders invest in the company but that he had in fact lost over $100,000. Moores engaged Toronto lawyer John J. Robinette to determine whether civil or criminal action or both should be taken. There was conflicting evidence about Smallwood's knowledge of the company, with both Vardy and Lundrigan changing their statements, and Moores felt reluctant to see the man who had led Newfoundland for twenty-three years brought down to such a level. Robinette found grounds for both civil and criminal charges, but, against intense pressure, particularly from John Crosbie, Moores decided there was little to be gained in dividing the province by pressing criminal charges against Joey Smallwood. It was just one of the many times when he would lose support for being too soft, but he never regretted it, and the years tempered his view of Smallwood somewhat.

"I don't think he was crooked as much as I think he was a maniac. Money wasn't important to him, power was. He had a farm built, with a house that was worth a lot of money. I think Art Lundrigan built the house because he felt the premier deserved a house. Is that a kickback? Yes or no, but as for taking cash and stashing it, I don't think he did it. His lifestyle didn't change, his kids' lifestyle didn't change. He was all about power. I had figured he was being paid off by John Doyle, huge sums, which in hindsight turned out to be incorrect, I think, but I just couldn't figure out why he would possibly be doing the things he did otherwise. Why would he give away the timber and mineral rights for all of Labrador? He was so insane, the things he gave John Doyle, total madness."

Today John Crosbie admits Moores probably made the right decision. "I thought Joey should have been prosecuted. It didn't make sense politically, but that didn't matter to me. Frank had a different temperament, and he knew you would have had a hell of a time finding a jury in Newfoundland that wouldn't have at least one person dissenting."

The government brought criminal charges against O.L. Vardy for fraud, accepting bribes, and breach of public trust involving some $760,000. Vardy skipped to Panama, where he was arrested and imprisoned, prompting him to have Moores served with a writ claiming damages for kidnapping. Released on bail pending an extradition hearing, Vardy escaped once again.

Moores implemented the recommendations of the O'Dea inquiry, including revamping the entire Board of Liquor Control, making it a crown corporation. At the same time, he was always very conscious that the civil service around Joey had had little choice in what they did and that many felt they owed their jobs to him, as indeed most of them did.

The other two immediate big issues in Moores's first year as premier were a complicated deal with John Shaheen, worth some $188 million in guarantees and loans for the partly finished oil refinery at Come By Chance in Placentia Bay, and the $75 million in guarantees to John Doyle for the linerboard mill in Stephenville. The inherited obligations oppressed the administration from the outset, and the public never quite understood why the same people who lambasted Smallwood's dealings with Doyle and Shaheen would continue to have anything to do with them

John Shaheen was bookended with John C. Doyle in the Newfoundland consciousness. The American industrialist, described by Richard Nixon as the greatest salesman in the world, was just the type to appeal to Joey Smallwood's grandiose visions, but his polished pitch also found a receptive ear in Frank Moores. What few people have ever realized about Moores was that, for all his privileged upbringing and external sophistication, he was still a boy from the bay, and high rollers like John Shaheen impressed and attracted him. Only too well aware of John Crosbie's feelings toward him after Crosbie's split with Smallwood, Shaheen saw right away that Frank Moores was an easier sell and set about wooing him. Just a few months after taking office, Moores and Alex Hickman accepted a trip to Cape Kennedy as guests of Shaheen for a first-hand look at a moon shot. To the Newfoundland people, almost overnight Moores had gone from calling Come By Chance a classic example of Smallwood's megalomania to hobnobbing with the devil behind the deal. Then while his finance minister, John Crosbie, was out of town, Moores pushed through a deal with Shaheen for a second refinery.

Moores differentiated between Doyle and Shaheen by saying that John Doyle was a crook, whereas John Shaheen was a businessman who played close to the edge, and he saw no evidence of his being a crook. Crosbie agrees with this, but he didn't trust Shaheen and clashed heatedly with Moores over the second refinery deal. It wasn't as bad as Crosbie feared; the second deal forgave $135 million in loan guarantees tied to the first refinery deal, and, while the second refinery was never built, the $135 million was still saved. Over the course of the next two years the original project would see-saw from near bankruptcy to plans for expansion, finally going into receivership in 1976.

In the years leading up to the receivership, Shaheen met with Moores frequently, pitching more ideas such as a petrochemical complex, all of which required more and more money from the province. John Crosbie was not invited to any of these meetings, and so he made sure that Vic Young, who sat in on meetings in the premier's office, was well versed in Shaheen history and all of Crosbie's concerns. Crosbie painted Shaheen as a shady character at the very least, and nothing Young saw or heard in their meetings contradicted that. He didn't believe anything Shaheen said and tried to buffer Moores's inclination to accept Shaheen and continue to do business with him. Shaheen eventually told Moores that the young fellow from across the hall was an aggravation and that he didn't want him attending any more of their meetings. Young didn't attend any more meetings, but Moores ultimately did not involve the province in any more business with John Shaheen, either.

Smallwood's dealings with industrialist John C. Doyle, Javelin, and the linerboard mill in Stephenville were many and intricate. Javelin's 1970 annual report listed Newfoundland holdings as "vast forest tracts in Labrador, Labrador iron holdings, on shore and off shore oil and mineral rights, and thousands of square miles of mineral concessions." When Moores took office, $132 million from the Newfoundland treasury had been spent on the linerboard mill. With so much public money already invested and Stephenville suffering from the closure of the American air force base, the government was under great pressure to finish the mill. The cost to the Newfoundland government to get rid of Doyle and regain the assets was reported at $5 million, a seemingly reasonable investment but hugely controversial at the time. Internally, public service officials were advising against finishing the mill. The concept of importing a wood supply from Doyle's holdings in Labrador was ridiculous to begin with, and there were no markets in place. But for every brief written against it, there was a consultant's report saying it could work, and in the end walking away from $132 million was just too hard for the government to do; the mill was finished. In some people's opinion, and in hindsight, it was the worst decision that Moores and his cabinet made while in office.

The operation provided 650 mill jobs and over twice that number in full- and part-time logging, but the mill lost money from day one. The salespeople kept asking for more and more time to build markets, and the tens of millions of dollars in debt kept building up. The final amount that the government invested in various ways to save the mill was almost $500 million. By the time the linerboard mill was finally closed down, it was the largest make-work project and the biggest industrial disaster in Newfoundland history. Linked to everything from shady deals to prop up federal Liberal governments to the Gerda Munsinger sex scandal, Doyle, like Vardy, also fled to Panama to avoid criminal prosecution.

CHAPTER 22

The Greatest Development— the Greatest Giveaway

EVEN WHEN SMALLWOOD focused his determination to develop on a tremendous natural resource like Churchill Falls, the initiative was ruined by his belief that he needed no advice in making the best decisions about anything and everything that affected the province. To no small degree, the aftermath of this conviction defined the Moores's administration's work. Blaming shortcomings on previous governments has become cliché in democratic societies, but few have been forced to spend the bulk of their time, effort, and talent to actually create a working democratic system while trying to undo disastrous economic contracts.

Of these, the Churchill Falls disaster was the worst. So secretive and so exclusive to Smallwood were the negotiations that no one in his government, including John Crosbie, was aware of the details of the agreement until they were uncovered by the Moores administration in June of 1972. From his initial visit to 10 Downing Street in 1952 to present the potential of Labrador's riches to Winston Churchill, through the formation of the British-Newfoundland Corporation (Brinco) with Anthony de Rothschild, the Rio Tinto Company, and the Anglo-American Company of South Africa, to the discussions with Canada and the signing of the power contract with Hydro-Québec in 1969, Joey Smallwood, a man with no financial background and no track record of business success, was the sole negotiator for Newfoundland.

There's no doubt Smallwood was cravenly and despicably betrayed by the Canadian government he had embraced with such fervour. Canada's National Energy Policy mandated a free flow of oil and gas across provincial boundaries, but it was less definitive about hydroelectric power. Quebec, under Premier Maurice Duplessis, decided it would not allow Newfoundland power to be transmitted across its boundaries to reach the markets in the US and Canada.

The federal government had the power to overrule provincial jurisdiction if the issue was deemed to be "for the general advantage of Canada or for the advantage of two or more of the provinces," which clearly this was. Allowing Quebec to hold Newfoundland ransom was unprecedented discrimination and is still unheard of today against any other Canadian province, but Liberal Prime Minister Lester Pearson wasn't about to take on Quebec. The story goes that when Smallwood protested, Pearson told him there would be no point in erecting power lines through Quebec because they'd be torn down as fast as they went up. Newfoundland had to sell its power to Quebec or nowhere.

There was one more opportunity for a fair deal. In 1964, resisting the 3 mills per kilowatt hour Brinco was proposing for the power, Quebec Premier Jean Lesage suggested that the project be developed jointly with Newfoundland under a crown corporation, excluding Brinco altogether. Smallwood wouldn't hear of it. Brinco was Newfoundland's friend. It was one year after Smallwood had purchased his first Brinco stock. The following year he would purchase more.

Hydro-Québec became a major participant in the financing of the project under a partnership called the Churchill Falls Labrador Corporation (CFLCO), of which Brinco owned 56.6 per cent, Hydro-Québec 34.2 per cent, and Newfoundland 9.2 per cent. On June 17, 1972, five months after he took office, Frank Moores, Quebec Premier

Robert Bourassa, and Pierre Trudeau officiated at the opening of the largest underground powerhouse in the world, with an output of more than seven million horsepower, at Churchill Falls, Labrador, Newfoundland. It should have been the beginning of a new prosperity for Newfoundland and Labrador, but as Moores and his government began to unravel the details of the contract, it became clear that it was Brinco and the province of Quebec that would reap the economic and energy benefits of Newfoundland's tremendous resource.

A letter of intent had been signed between Hydro-Québec and the parent company CFLCO in 1966, allowing only four years for the first delivery of power with a price of 3 mills or three-tenths of a cent per kilowatt hour. CFLCO began construction immediately while the details of the final contract were being worked out. Three years into the construction, CFLCO still had no contract with Hydro-Québec and was running out of money. Hydro-Québec then drastically changed the terms agreed to in the letter of intent from forty years with an option to renew in 2016 to an automatic twenty-five-year renewal. A sixty-five-year contract was bad enough, but instead of including an escalation clause for the price of energy, the price Quebec would pay de-escalated to 2.5 mills after twenty-five years and 2 mills for the twenty-five-year renewal period. In 2007 Hydro-Québec paid just over one-fifth of a cent for power it resold for around eight cents. For every million dollars' worth of power produced by Churchill Falls, less than a day's output, Quebec got $980,000 while Newfoundland and Labrador got $20,000.

In today's perspective, over the sixty-five-year term of the agreement, the export of energy from Churchill Falls will equal 3.3 billion barrels of oil, more than three times the output of the Hibernia and Terra Nova fields combined. Newfoundland will have received from a high of 4 per cent to a low of 2 per cent of the income from this power. Successive federal governments, accepting no responsibility for the agreements of their predecessors, have done their best to insure that Newfoundland never recovers from its dependence on Ottawa by deducting this amount from equalization payments.

Smallwood had signed away Newfoundland's first and best chance to become financially secure, but Moores rightfully laid most of the blame at the door of the government of Canada for allowing Quebec to deny Newfoundland a corridor to transport its hydroelectric power. Moores understood the position Smallwood was in and said he would probably have signed the same deal, with one critical difference: a formula to follow the price of energy. "Quebec would have gone along with a fifty-fifty split of profit over and above the basic return they expected," he said. "No sane person would have disagreed with it, and today Newfoundland wouldn't have any debt."

In spite of threatening to "pull the plug" or leave the federation, Moores and his ministers came to the conclusion that the best chance of renegotiating the Upper Churchill contract was to get Brinco out of the picture so that the province could deal directly with Hydro-Québec. Burns Bros. and Denton, the province's fiscal agents were asked to assess the financial ramifications of nationalization. Expropriation of energy resources was not new in Canada, but Finance Minister John Crosbie was very conscious of Newfoundland's need to borrow money and anxious to avoid looking like a "banana republic," so the province was prepared to negotiate.

On Monday March 11, 1974, in a carefully coordinated plan with Industrial Development Minister Bill Doody acting as time keeper in Newfoundland, the province released a statement in Newfoundland that it had suspended trading on the market; Finance Minister John Crosbie and Energy Minister Leo Barry walked into the office of Brinco President Bill Mulholland at Brinco headquarters in Montreal; and Frank Moores, accompanied by representatives of Burns Bros. and Denton, walked into the London head office of Rio Tinto Zinc Corporation Ltd. RTZ, Brinco's largest shareholder. Moores told a startled secretary who he was and that he was there to see the chairman, Sir Val Duncan, whose morning schedule showed no appointment with a Mr. Moores.

When Moores was finally shown into the chairman's office, an unruffled Sir Val asked to what he owed the honour of such an unexpected visit. When Moores finally got through to him what the government of Newfoundland intended to do, Sir Val impressed Moores. "He walked to the adjacent office of the vice-chair, Sir Mark Turner, and said, as cool as could be, 'Mark, could you drop in for a moment. Something of interest has come up.'"

Cool or not, Brinco was fighting for its corporate life. The next day Sir Val accompanied Moores to Montreal to begin negotiations with the province in the Ritz Carlton Hotel. Leo Barry and MHA John Collins went to the United States to present a pamphlet explaining the province's position to investors in the US, where it was well accepted that the province had very little choice considering the inequities of the Upper Churchill deal. At the end of almost two weeks of intense negotiations, the province was offering $6.90 a share and Brinco had come down to $7.50 from $8.70. Things were stalled and at one point Joey Smallwood even showed up in Montreal, reportedly at the request of the erstwhile unflappable Sir Val Duncan.

Moores and his team went back to Newfoundland and began the process of introducing takeover legislation, at which point the Brinco negotiators arrived in St. John's to start the gruelling process again. Their experience with the easily manipulated Smallwood may have accounted, in part, for the arrogance with which the Brinco people, notably Sir Val Duncan and Bill Mulholland, approached the negotiations. Frank Moores was no Joey Smallwood, but he had the fatal flaw of wanting to get along with everyone. In *No Holds Barred*, John Crosbie writes of Moores's waffling and the negotiating team's constant efforts to strengthen his resolve between sessions, but estimates $10 million as the difference that stronger negotiating might have made, not insignificant by any means, but not extreme in a deal of this magnitude.

They must all have been nearing the end of their ropes because according to Moores, the base share figure was reached anticlimactically. In a late night session, one of Brinco's negotiators, anxious to get back to business in New Guinea, said that deal or no deal, he was going to be on his 707 the next day, at which point Moores said that 707 made as much sense as anything. Thus the share price of $7.07 was arrived at and, after a few more rounds of fine-tuning, a deal was reached in which the province acquired control of the Churchill Falls Labrador Corporation for $130 million and the company's Labrador water rights for $30 million. The initial offer from Brinco had been $200 million.

The province's original proposal was to expropriate Brinco in its entirety, including both the energy and mineral resources but as a compromise, Brinco retained its mineral rights which included 20,000 square miles in Labrador, 4,500 on the island, and oil and gas exploration rights of some 6,000 square miles in western Newfoundland. Energy Minister Leo Barry and his department officials were not happy with the deal or the process. Today Barry says, "We accepted it. We all had our chance to make comments and have some input, but to a large extent it came out as 'here is what we have, now cabinet should accept this to bring down a budget.' That's where I felt it broke down somewhere. Any number of times as a cabinet minister you have to ask yourself 'is this the breaking point? Is this where I have to resign?' I didn't. When it comes to that type of bargaining, you can't negotiate by committee all the time. You have to have an individual who is able to go in and do the deal. Even though I would have liked a tougher deal with Brinco, and even though some of us might have been prepared to push further, I'm not prepared to say that it was the wrong thing to do, to settle and reach compromise the way Moores did. Some people feel he didn't go far enough. What else could he have done? I'm not sure if these people would be able to give you an explanation on how the province could have survived in terms of having to borrow money every year after, that if investors felt that if they loaned money, the province might not be responsible. The more I see things develop the more satisfied I am that it was the proper thing to do."

The wisdom of the deal is still under debate. Bill Marshall maintained at the time and still does, that all the province needed to do was spend the $30 million for the water rights and that Moores was listening to bad advice from others when he made "the mistake" of buying CFLCO. Marshall's argument is that the province's ultimate position, that expropriation was not possible because Brinco's subsidiary CFLCO was incorporated under federal legislation as a crown corporation, was fundamentally incorrect. "Reasoning like that," he said, "anyone could shield themselves from provincial expropriation purely by having the property put in a federally incorporated company—just pay your money and get your certificate." John Crosbie reiterates that the advice the province received was contrary to Marshall's opinion. He does not recall Bill Marshall or anyone else arguing that the legal opinion was wrong at the time, and he does not acknowledge any change in his own opinion. However, whether the legal opinion was correct or not, Frank Moores eventually came to regard the purchase as a mistake and regretted in later years that he hadn't put the time and money elsewhere.

In early 1975, less than a year later, CFLCO started negotiations with Hydro-Québec to develop the Lower Churchill as part of an extension of the Upper Churchill project. Moores intervened with legislation insuring that the Lower Churchill could only be developed with the agreement of the government of Newfoundland. With the ground rules in place, he set about trying to get the Lower Churchill underway and bring a power transmission line to the island of Newfoundland. Trying to keep the momentum going and to put pressure on the government of Canada to get involved, he commissioned studies on the feasibility of a tunnel under the Strait of Belle Isle to bring power to Newfoundland. It was a serious study done by highly reputable consultants, but Moores had decided to call an election by that time and jumped the gun before all the Ts were crossed. There was great fanfare over turning the sod, with photo ops of Moores and Leo Barry digging holes on both sides of the strait. Barry was defeated in that election, the federal government refused any assistance, and hope for the tunnel disappeared.

An untold story has profound financial implications for the province. In 1978 Moores had a deal with René Lévesque to develop the Lower Churchill that would have seen the profits from 800 megawatts of the Upper Churchill power going through Quebec being returned to Newfoundland, beginning the following year. At the time Newfoundland Hydro was a much more autonomous entity, developing and following its own policy rather than being directed by the Minister and Department of Energy. When Brian Peckford became the minister, he felt this seriously impeded the government's ability to make good energy decisions and prevailed continuously upon Moores to take away some of Hydro's control. In the head offices at Newfoundland Hydro, Brian Peckford was not a popular man.

Peckford's views against any compromise in the fight for redress of the wrongs inflicted by the Upper Churchill deal were also well known. Moores was desperate to do something, anything, for the economy, and so, with Newfoundland Hydro head Wally Reid, he met secretly with Lévesque and his minister of energy for months while Peckford, as Newfoundland's energy minister, was busy working on the emerging offshore oil industry.

Only at the last minute, with Lévesque and his ministers in St. John's and a press conference scheduled for eleven a.m. on March 11, 1978, was Moores ready to present his big breakthrough to cabinet. "This was an additional 800 megawatts, which, until we needed it, would be sent over the Quebec grid," he said, "and the market price would come back to Newfoundland, as opposed to going to Quebec. That was a lot of dollars for Newfoundland, almost a million dollars a day on the low end at the time. It was a big concession that Lévesque didn't have to make, and I thought everyone would be excited because we had gotten something out of nothing." He couldn't have been more mistaken.

Brian Peckford was stunned and horrified, and the cabinet meeting disintegrated into pandemonium. Moores retreated to his office, accompanied by the ministers closest to him, Tom Farrell, Bill Doody, and John Lundrigan, shortly followed by Brian Peckford, who physically pushed his way into the office. After a heated exchange, Peckford was eased into Vic Young's office while Moores and the others conferred. A short time later Young watched as Moores and Doody did everything they could to convince Brian Peckford of the wisdom of the deal. Peckford's response was that if Moores went ahead with the press conference, he would follow with another one immediately to announce his resignation, and he informed Moores that most of the cabinet would resign with him.

The most objectionable part of the agreement for Brian Peckford was a clause that said Newfoundland would never again attempt to reopen the Upper Churchill deal. Peckford believed that all legal challenges had not been exhausted and that Newfoundland was going to be sold down the river again. As far as Moores was concerned, the chance that any court would overturn the deal was slim, and "it was that or stick to what we had, which was zero."

While René Lévesque waited down the hall and local reporters plus some twenty from Quebec, waited downstairs, the press conference was delayed by an hour and then another hour. Brian Peckford was so passionately against the deal that in the end he broke down and cried in frustration in Young's office. To Young, Peckford's emotional reaction wasn't a sign of weakness but evidence of the intensity of his opposition to making what he believed fervently was another huge mistake with one of Newfoundland's biggest resources.

Moores says he felt he didn't have time to poll the cabinet and caucus, and he knew that Peckford was "brazen enough to go ahead on his own, assuming he'd get people to join him." Moores actually had had over two hours, plenty of time to check the pulse of cabinet, if not the entire caucus, on a matter of such urgency, and he could have taken as long as he needed; he was the premier and the press conference could have been postponed, but he choked. He walked down the hall and told Lévesque the deal was off and why. Lévesque responded, "We're all politicians, Frank, and politicians do what they have to do." The two went out to meet the restless press with grim faces and a non-story about future cooperation that fooled nobody, even though nobody knew what the real story was to have been.

Thirty years later Moores regretted backing out of that deal far more than the purchase of Brinco. "I should have called Peckford's bluff. Cabinet said I should not have gone as far as I did without them in on it, but I doubt if I would have lost the government on it."

In Newfoundland and Labrador today, oil has much greater resonance than hydroelectricity. Annually, 800 megawatts of power is roughly the energy equivalent of four million barrels of oil. Allowing for the different degrees of variation in market prices for both commodities and recognizing that different formulas could be used, Memorial University economist Wade Locke estimates the loss to the Newfoundland treasury from 1978 to 2008 to be in the neighbourhood of $4 billion. With another thirty-five years left to go on the contract and with the price of energy continuing to rise, the total loss can only be imagined, and all because Brian Peckford thought he could do better and Frank Moores backed down.

Brian Peckford still believes he took the right stand. The negotiations with Quebec had been what Peckford accurately describes as a very unusual departure from successful procedures Moores himself had established. Peckford also believes that if Moores had really felt comfortable with the deal, he wouldn't have backed down, and he points to the fact that Moores went on to trust him in the offshore negotiations as proof of Moores's continued respect for his opinion and ability.

Perhaps the ideal course of action lay somewhere between the paths Moores and Peckford chose. Leo Barry, who admits he had moments when he considered resigning over the Brinco purchase negotiations, later became a minister in Peckford's government and did resign over disagreements on negotiating style and authority. Barry compares the two by saying Peckford could fight but couldn't bring himself to close a deal, while with Moores they had to make sure he didn't close the deal too quickly, before the province got as much as it could.

When he became premier, Brian Peckford's attempts to find other avenues to get around the Upper Churchill contract were unsuccessful, and thirty years later there is still no deal.

CHAPTER 23

The Honeymoon Ends

IN LATE 1972 Moores dropped three cabinet ministers in what was generally considered a strategy to break up a 'dump Moores' movement, and in March of 1973, when John Crosbie presented his second budget, Moores lost his first cabinet minister by resignation. In a portent of things to come for decades later in the fisheries, Moores's first fisheries minister, Roy Cheeseman, resigned, stating that federal and provincial policies did not coincide, the provincial government did not have the necessary funds to cope with the needs of the fisheries, and he was not prepared "to go on deluding the fishermen into believing that I, as their minister, can bring about any significant changes to the situation."

Having started so high, there was nowhere for Moores to go but down, and his descent had already begun. A by-election to re-place Cheeseman in the Hermitage district was called, and Moores recognized that in by-elections people often cast protest votes against the government. He was so anxious to win the election that he lost it by mounting a campaign with uncomfortable similarities to the Smallwood campaigns he had so recently condemned.

It was said that a plough would come down the street clearing away the snow for the paving machine coming along behind. The joke was, 'keep your doors closed or you'll get your floors paved.'

In spite of that, some people thought Moores wasn't quite enough like Smallwood in other ways. Moores would spend an hour or so at the kitchen table explaining party policies, while the Liberals would put a bottle of rum on the table and say, 'get out and vote for us.' Moores sent George Hutchings to the district for six weeks, flying in his wife and children one weekend rather than let Hutchings leave the district even for a few days.

Then Moores decided to fly every cabinet minister he had into the district. Hutchings knew it was a mistake and tried to talk him out of it. "The boys felt pretty important, but in the halls of small communities, nobody was impressed with a couple of so-called big shots in the back of the room, sometimes a bit loud, with too much to drink, maybe telling an off-colour joke or two." Hutchings saw all his hard work and time spent away from his family going down the drain, and the Tories lost the by-election for Roy Cheeseman's seat to Liberal Roger Simmons.

In the early 1970s, governments in every province were facing double-digit inflation and interest rates, an energy crisis, and wage and price controls. World conditions and a recession meant nothing to people who had hailed a saviour, and the Newfoundland press was unforgiving. Before the end of 1973 Moores had started legal action for defamation against NTV and was publicly lambasting the *Telegram*'s "screwball" and "yellow" journalism, while the paper was accusing Moores of maintaining a band of PR and glad tidings men to keep polishing the image. Ironically, polishing the image was one aspect of politics that Moores never did get right. The lavish Come By Chance opening in October of 1973 was a public relations disaster for him.

The budget that had caused Roy Cheeseman's despair over lack of funding for the fisheries included $37.4 million for Labrador Linerboard and $25 million for Come By Chance. The refinery opening was celebrated with the biggest party in Newfoundland history. Shaheen charted the *Queen Elizabeth 2* to take 1,200 guests from New York to Come By Chance. Hundreds of Newfoundlanders were flown to New York to make the voyage, including Smallwood and John and Jane Crosbie, Crosbie maintaining that he wouldn't have gone "but Jane insisted." Moores was unable to make the trip from New York but boarded the vessel as Smallwood was leaving after it docked in Come By Chance. A few MHAs boycotted the opening of the refinery. Moores soothed both sides by pointing out that he had gotten the government out of the guarantee for the indebtedness of the refinery and encouraging them to keep speaking their minds. One MHA did just that, saying, "If Shaheen was a cunt in '69, then he's still a cunt."

The two-day cruise included unlimited food and drink in the ship's numerous bars and restaurants. There was an orchestra, a band, a quartet, a duo, and other entertainers. Gambling, gymnastics, golf, bridge, movies, trap shooting, table tennis, and wig and beauty treatments were just some of the amenities. Guests were given sealskin souvenir bags and a flask of Screech. The event was extreme to the point of decadence, and even though the cost of the two-day spectacle was borne by Shaheen (reportedly the QE 2 bill was never paid), the very idea of Moores and 'his crowd' living the high life with the man they had been vilifying just a year before was too much to swallow, especially for a public being prepared for restraints. To make matters worse, the night the ship docked in Come By Chance, Moores hosted a reception for a thousand, paid for by the province, at which the new Mrs. Moores made her first official appearance.

A few months earlier, in response to a reporter's question, Moores had stated emphatically that he had no intention of getting married again anytime in the near future, but on August 25, he was in Manitoba on his way to the ceremony. This time Tom Farrell was his best man. Farrell, Terry Malone, Dick Sutton, and Dorothy Moores were in the car with the bridegroom. Terry Malone knew things were different this time. "I don't think he was sure about that marriage from the start. We were driving him to the wedding, and he was saying he wasn't sure if he should be doing this, so Dick

Sutton said, 'We'll get you out right now if you want.' We got to the church and Frank said, 'Keep driving.'" They drove right on by. Moores's mother was horrified. As they drove around Winnipeg she told him over and over that he could not leave Janis at the altar, that it was simply unacceptable behaviour. Her properly brought up son did not let his mother down.

CHAPTER 24

Government Reform

MANY OF THE CIVIL LIBERTIES taken for granted in Newfoundland and Labrador today either did not exist before the Moores administration or were significantly advanced by it. It is easy to say, and not without validity, that many of his government's reforms were ideas for which the time had long since come, but it is also easy to forget what things were like before he came to power and to underestimate the will needed to change a political culture. This was especially true with respect to awarding government contracts.

Bill Marshall was the father of the public tendering act. To Marshall, providing Newfoundland with a public tendering act was the Holy Grail and the primary goal in his political life, followed closely by introducing an apolitical public service act. A committed student of Newfoundland history, Marshall saw that as far back as the Amulree Report, which preceded the loss of self-government in 1933, Newfoundland had been used by governments whose main purpose was to line the pockets of a chosen few, and he was dedicated to seeing that disastrous practices of the past weren't repeated.

Marshall had prepared the policy resolutions supporting the two acts and made sure they were in the Tory platform. They were in fact major planks, but the ideals that sounded so earnest and unshakable from the Tory opposition were very restricting to a new

Tory government with legions of its own supporters clamouring to get some government work at long last. When, within a few months of the election, there was no sign of movement toward introducing either a public tendering act or a civil service act, Marshall complained to Moores, who advised him to slow down because the issues needed more time. Marshall was adamant that the legislation go through just as he had proposed it, but the feeling in caucus was that Marshall was simply too uncompromising in his determination to insure that the government would never again be able to use the province's treasury to hand out political favours.

John Crosbie considered himself dedicated to seeing that the corruption of the Smallwood era wasn't repeated, but he supported Moores's reticence, recalling "The Public Tendering Act was too restrictive, in my opinion, and put a chain around the government's throat. I'm sure Frank didn't want it. He delayed it as much as he could, but when he could no longer delay, he did it. He was afraid of losing Marshall over it, and it wouldn't have looked very good."

As more time passed, Marshall, who was a Minister without Portfolio, decided to take matters into his own hands. He initiated interviews with the unions; he obtained copies of the public tendering and public service acts from every Canadian province and some from the UK and the USA; and he drafted the two acts for Newfoundland and bought them to cabinet. Marshall was impinging on other departments, but as far as he was concerned those were cardinal conditions that were not being addressed. He had some support from Gerry Ottenheimer and a few others, but most saw Marshall's version of a public tendering act as a hindrance to party financing and his civil service act as a hindrance to the provision of jobs for Tories, particularly since the civil service was already full of Joey's appointments.

Marshall persevered and got the acts through the way he wanted them, but he couldn't ensure compliance. Given Moores's inability to say no, the introduction of the public tendering act probably saved him from himself many times over, but it was an irritation. In

1973, shortly after Roy Cheeseman resigned, Marshall became aware that a contract had been let for a hospital in Twillingate without public tendering and he confronted Moores in his office. Moores gave him a complicated story about the foundation and electrical work's having been started in Joey's time and added that tendering at this point would cost more money. He was so convincing that Marshall left satisfied. Once away from Moores, however, Marshall began to have second thoughts, got into his car, and made the more than five-hour drive to Twillingate. On the site he found basically just a platform, with no electrical work of any description. Back in Moores's office the next day, Moores put the blame on the minister and assured Marshall that it would never happen again.

A few months later Marshall got wind of another untendered contract, this one for a project in Churchill Falls, and he exploded, walking in on Moores and tossing his resignation on his desk. Moores professed ignorance again and prevailed upon Marshall not to resign, promising that the agreement to let the untendered work would be cancelled. Marshall took back the letter of resignation, and the two had a long talk about policy, public tendering in particular. Marshall left feeling happy that the air was finally cleared and that the unpleasant meetings over tendering practices were in the past. Within twenty-four hours the controversial contract was cancelled, and for a couple of years things settled down again.

Another of Moores's notable reforms that became a thorn in his side was the provision of a daily oral question period in the House of Assembly. As a major reform it is almost overlooked, because a legislative assembly without an oral question period is unthinkable today; opposition members' freedom to question governmental initiatives in the people's legislative body is at the core of democracy in the parliamentary system. That right did not exist in Newfoundland under Joey Smallwood. Every question had to be submitted in writing so it could appear on an order paper, and then the government answered it when and if they felt like it. Attempts to ask questions from the floor would be met with the response from the government benches, "Order paper! Order paper!"

Before the first sitting of the House, Moores had the standing orders amended to provide for a daily oral question period. He believed fervently that it had to be done, but few appreciated the irony of a leader deliberately unleashing a monster determined to bring him down. While behaviour motivated purely by politics in the legislature's question period is now accepted as a part of life, Moores was the first premier in Newfoundland to experience it. The Liberal MHAS had never had the opportunity to grandstand under Smallwood, even privately, and some were almost rabid in their desire to grab the spotlight. One in particular got to Moores. Bell Island MHA Steve Neary quickly learned that attacking the government and hurling scandalous accusations, regardless of substance, was the best way to get press coverage. Neary's mud slinging seemed to know no bounds, he had no qualms of conscience about creating the mud from innuendo, and the press, having never been in such an arena, loved it.

Some of the mud stuck, and Moores quickly came to hate question period and to regard it as "a colossal waste of time." He was by nature a lover, not a fighter, in more than just the sexual sense; he hated confrontation and liked being liked. The flashing smile and the gentleman's stiff upper lip belied a thin skin that bruised every time he was attacked. It was a serious weakness in a politician and compounded as time went on. The more he was attacked, the more he avoided the House. Soon any excuse at all would keep him away, and when he was there, the heckling and goading from the opposition was worse. Moores would go out for a smoke and not come back. The subsequent press about his absences fed the image that the opposition was relentlessly cultivating: Moores was nothing but a playboy wastrel who didn't care about his job or his responsibilities.

In Alex Hickman's opinion, not only did Moores dislike the legislature, he didn't really understand it and didn't want to understand it. He also set a bad example; as soon as Moores left, some of the others would disappear as well. Hickman would plead with him to show up more often and stay longer, worried that absenteeism could get to the point where the government could be defeated on a motion. Moores would promise to be there whenever he was in the building, and then he would say he'd gotten tied up in his office but would rationalize that he had listened to all the proceedings, which were piped in over Joey's sound system, and he could have been there in a minute if he was needed.

When he was in the House, there was another problem: he said what he thought with little care for the political consequences. This habit made his ministers very nervous. Early in his first year as premier, Opposition Leader Ed Roberts asked him a question pertaining to education, and Moores observed that in his opinion it was time to get rid of the denominational education system that had always existed in Newfoundland. At that time the mere thought of taking control of schools away from the churches would have been considered political suicide. It fell to Gerry Ottenheimer, Minister of Education, to explain that the premier didn't really mean what he said. Moores was unfazed, and in fact he was ahead of his time: twenty years later, education was indeed taken out of the hands of the churches.

CHAPTER 25

Rural Development

ONE OF THE EARLY ACTS of the new government was to put an end to the Newfoundland Resettlement Program, a government transfer of people that historians have compared in size if not in cruelty with the expulsion of the Acadians or the internment of the Japanese during the Second World War. The theory behind resettlement was that government couldn't afford to provide services to every community, particularly on the islands that dotted Newfoundland's rugged coast that had been settled because of their proximity to the fishing grounds. Moving people to 'growth centres,' it seemed, would benefit everyone.

In 1965 Smallwood announced that as part of a new development strategy, he had persuaded the federal government to partner with Newfoundland in establishing a community resettlement program, with Ottawa picking up most of the bill. Families who moved to the designated growth centres would receive assistance of $1,000 per household, plus $200 for each person in the household. To traditionally large families with a way of life that saw little cash, it seemed like a lot of money. Many jumped at the chance, but if they didn't, the pressure to move was intense, and if over 80 per cent of a community signed a petition, everyone was forced to move. By the time Moores ended the program, some 20,000 people in 4,000 households had left behind almost 150 deserted communities. Merchants were not compensated for their loss of business property, and fishermen were not compensated for wharfs and fishing stores and sheds they had built themselves. The best fishing grounds in their new communities were reserved for long-time residents, and most fishermen didn't know how to do anything else even if there had been other choices.

To Moores, it was just one example of how the federal "benefits" derived from Confederation destroyed the independence and self-reliance of Newfoundlanders and started them on a dangerous spiral into dependence on the state; even when time saw many people prospering because of the move, he remained passionate about the resettlement program and its long term effect on generations of Newfoundlanders. He felt more strongly about the damage caused by resettlement than about almost any other issue. "A man would have a house that he'd built himself and paid for," he said. "He had a way of earning a living—a convenient way, because that was where the fish were. But he was a nuisance to the government because it cost too much to put a school teacher there or deliver the mail—that's about what it was. So instead of taking a central island where they could go to pick up their mail or send their kids to school, even if they had to board, they took up the whole shebang and towed them up to the head of the bay or somewhere." Even if fishermen could continue to fish, housing cost more; some ended up with a mortgage, which they'd never seen before in their lives, and ended up on welfare to pay for it all. Resettlement, in his view, started the generational cycle of dependence on welfare and "did more to suck the moral fibre out of Newfoundlanders than any other single thing."

Moores's government didn't have the money to send people back to the islands, of course, and in fact he estimated that half of them wouldn't have wanted to go back anyway, some because they were doing well, some because they had had time to forget their independence and become used to the government cheques. Even so, he said, "I couldn't stop it fast enough." On one occasion his daughter Jill, a teacher, asked him to speak to her class, and one of his topics was resettlement. After he finished, "this little girl, about nine or ten years old, came up, laughing, tickled, scared. She said, 'Mr. Moores, that was a wonderful speech, sir, and I want you to know we go home every summer.' I said, 'Where's home?' She said, 'Merasheen Island.' Merasheen was settled in the 1700s, and two generations after anyone has lived there, they still refer to it as home." It reminded Moores poignantly of a line in a song by the Newfoundland duo Simani: "They left without moving and never arrived."

The second phase of the resettlement program was to have covered 1970 to 1975 and historians give 1975 as the year it ended when in fact the last twenty-nine families moved early in that five year time period, having already begun the process. Effectively the program ended when Moores took office. He then changed the regulations so that in the future, 100 per cent of a community had to agree to resettlement, and the compensation structure would be based on individual circumstances.

Moores was convinced that the secret to a successful Newfoundland economy was to enable its people to come up with their own initiatives related to the fishery and other natural resources which were rural in nature. He called on Newfoundlanders to submit their commercial ideas to him for possible financial or resource assistance. Rurual development became a full-fledged department under Minister Jim Reid and a Rural Development Authority was set up to encourage development associations in every region of the province. By late 1973, under what was dubbed the Premier's Faith in the People programs, 128 small rural industries emerged, ranging from trout farming to casket manufacturing. Some employed only one or two people, but they created over six hundred jobs in total, at a cost to the government of less than $1 million. The craft industry blossomed, and entrepreneurs and community activists from rural Newfoundland had the premier as their champion at the cabinet table. To further increase accessibility, Moores began the practice of holding at least one cabinet meeting a year outside St. John's.

An early rural development initiative was the establishment of a royal commission with a broad mandate to examine and make recommendations on the economic and social conditions of Labrador. The report took eighteen months to prepare and was submitted in March of 1974. It contained 288 recommendations in areas such as communications, health services, housing, utilities, legal services, oil exploration, tourism, cost of living subsidization, and pollution and environmental control. Two years later Moores claimed that the government had implemented almost half of them, but he always felt impotent to effect real change. At the heart of the problem, he believed, were the disjunctions between the government and its community agencies, comprised almost entirely of people of European heritage, and the population of Labrador, which was largely native; he came to realize that only the aboriginal people could decide what was their best course

With the OPEC oil embargo in January of 1974, the world-wide recession began. Since there was little money to invest, the enthusiasm for rural development was hard to maintain, and in no time the promising movement became compromised through the emergence of government job creation and make-work projects. Most of these projects were short-term, geared more towards qualifying people for unemployment insurance than towards the long-term diversification of the local economy. In direct opposition to Moores's objective of self-help, development associations often became little more than agencies for soliciting government projects and perpetuating the dependence he wanted to change.

Another unforeseen stumbling block developed. In 1959 Memorial University of Newfoundland established an Extension Service (ES) with a mandate to work in rural areas, facilitating continuing education and participating in community development. Rather than complement each other, the ES and the Rural Development Associations fought over turf. Nevertheless by February 1975, twenty-three Rural Development Associations had been formed in Newfoundland and Labrador, and 733 businesses had been assisted by the Rural Development Authority. It was never enough.

Critics had been saying since the early months of the Moores administration that the province would be much better off if the government spent more time at home actually making things happen than traipsing around the world "observing and learning." In 1976 Moores and his ministers of Industry and Rural Development, Forestry and Agriculture, and Fisheries returned from a trip to Europe with yet more hopes for solid achievements in rural manufacturing, handicrafts, shipbuilding, sheep farming, bakeapple and blueberry industries, and fresh and salt water fish farming. After the trip, Moores said, "I'm the first one to admit that the government has provided very little follow-through in the development of its resource policies in the past. I guess it's a little embarrassing to see how little we as a government have been able to do to capitalize on our natural resources." He couldn't explain why it was so hard to make things happen, and no doubt he would have appreciated the observation made in the *Evening Telegram* after he died by one of his political foes at the time, the Smallwood Minister of Mines, Agriculture, and Resources, Bill Callahan, who had been defeated by Fred Stagg. Callahan wrote, "It must have been a very frustrating period for Mr. Moores because most of the things that he tried to reverse or change were really intractable problems that didn't lend themselves well to reversal."

He did make lasting changes in forestry management. Prior to Moores's government, paper companies could use their vast tracts of wood as they saw fit, cutting or not, with no obligation to replant. Moores introduced the Forest Land Act, forest management units, and mandatory reforestation regulations, and he expanded and revamped the Crown lands offices, with the first legislated system of leasing, granting, and clearing of titles. He was appalled by the lack of resources on the ground to manage the province's wildlife and introduced a wildlife management division with forty-eight new positions—biologists, trained technicians, and wardens—with greater authority, new trucks, and a helicopter. The fact that he enjoyed the use of the division's resources for accessing his favourite rivers did not lessen the appreciation of wild life officers, who credit him with bringing the province's wildlife management into the twentieth century.

The fishery was the resource that Moores understood best. Brian Peckford describes the Department of Fisheries under Smallwood as having only a skeleton crew, and he credits Moores with establishing the first genuine fisheries department in Newfoundland, a place whose very existence depended on fisheries.

Moores's taking office in January of 1972 had coincided with the expansion of the Unemployment Insurance Act to cover fishermen. Suddenly the dangerous and demanding seasonal cod fishery became a lot more attractive. Moores had a vision of what the fishery should be: joint venturing with the Europeans, Germans mainly, and a big-boat super port, probably in Harbour Grace, where all of the fish would be landed, sold at auction, and taken to central plants for processing, along the lines of the English model. Few people understood the concept, and it sounded suspiciously like one of Smallwood's megaprojects. A super port and central plants would take years to accomplish and wouldn't provide work in individual communities, so the idea was very unpopular with both the electorate and those hoping to be re-elected.

Thus, despite his personal belief in a centralized model for the fishing industry, Moores embarked on a community-based expansion program. By providing financing programs for new boats to take more men to the fish and new processing plants to provide work at home for the women, the government transferred thousands of seasonal workers from annual months of welfare at the expense of the province to annual months of unemployment insurance at the expense of the federal government. Fishermen could get financing to strengthen their boats against ice so they could catch northern species that hadn't been caught before; participation in the industry almost doubled, and no one foresaw the stock collapse to come. All the new programs were supported by the federal government, which welcomed the increase in fish exports. Moores spent much of his fisheries efforts in the early years on making sure there would be enough fish to keep everyone going by trying to persuade Ottawa of the need for a 200-mile fishing limit, stricter foreign fishing controls and enforcement, and more provincial authority

At the First Ministers' Conference in Charlottetown in 1973, Moores was credited with writing and playing a major role in winning acceptance for fisheries resolutions. Surprised at his sophistication, reporters referred to the other Atlantic premiers as yahoos in comparison. He was a constant leader in the fight for the 200-mile limit, but it wasn't until 1977, near the end of his premiership, that the United Nations declared it law.

In 1975, under Fisheries Minister Walter Carter, the government undertook a wide-ranging study of the fishing industry in order to be ready with a complete development strategy when the anticipated 200-mile limit was announced. The study took almost three years to complete; it produced a six-volume 1000-page seven-year plan called "Setting a Course" and a glossy sixteen-page booklet called "Fish Is the Future," which highlighted the programs and initiatives from the report.

The booklet, put together systematically by people experienced in all aspects of the fishery, reads like a blueprint for every aspect of a successful fishing industry. When Moores resigned the following year, he was confident that the fishery was on the road to expansion and prosperity. His successor, Brian Peckford, had his own ideas, however, scrapping Carter's plan and commissioning another one. More importantly, even though no one realized it, the fish were in trouble.

When the stocks collapsed completely, part of the blame was laid on the number of boats and plants Moores had licensed. Vic Young, who went on to build the government-sponsored Fisheries

Products International into a steady, successful enterprise and become an expert observer of the industry, defends Moores.

> "I studied everything about the fishery that I could before I joined FPI in 1985, six years after Frank left, and fish stocks were still not recognized as a problem. Michael Kirby's report in the early eighties said the biggest problem would be marketing all of the fish that we were going to have, yet I remember a vicious attack against the company in 1986 by the inshore fishermen who were not catching any fish. People paid very little attention to them because they had all these scientific reasons for why the fish were not coming ashore, water temp, currents, stars, anything other than the fish were in trouble, and of course the fish were in trouble."

Young pointed out that, in all the reports about the greatly increased fish catches the 200-mile limit would produce, no one ever asked the question, where would the fish come from, given that the reason Newfoundland needed the 200-mile limit was that there were no longer enough fish closer to shore? The time when a moratorium was needed was not 1992; a moratorium was needed in 1977, as soon as the 200-mile limit became international law. "Of course," Young says, "this is hindsight. All the advice Moores was getting was about how to catch and market these huge quantities of fish. I can see them now, in the cabinet room, the Germans and countless European fish companies, discussing all this fish."

Moores did know that some federal trade deals made no sense, even in a healthy fishery, and he was constantly frustrated by the federal attitude of complete indifference to informed opinions from the province. When Ottawa announced a contract allowing the Russians to take 400,000 tons of caplin, a prime source of food for cod, Moores called the decision despicable and objected strenuously, to no avail. Right up until his death, Moores remained frustrated. "People who talk against the seal hunt say seals don't eat cod. That used to be basically true, though not any more; what they do every day is eat forty pounds of what cod eat. Cod that would go from one pound to five pounds in a year would go from one pound to a pound and a quarter because the nutrition just wasn't there for the fish, and once you get a weak strain in anything, they're going to have a down cycle."

CHAPTER 26

Legal Reform and Education

ANALYZING AND DESCRIBING Moores's contribution is somewhat different from going through the same exercise with subsequent premiers. Every premier since has had the strong base laid by Moores's government to work with and build on, and some of Moores's ministers, such as Alex Hickman, were very much the architects of their department's reforms. In that sense the contribution was theirs, but Moores attracted and kept valuable people around him, and while nothing proceeded without Moores's support, he allowed and enabled them to do their jobs with minimum interference.

Legal reform was a huge initiative of the Moores government. While Hickman was in Smallwood's cabinet, he had set up a commission under Justice Raymond Gushue to examine the law in Newfoundland. Some of the reforms recommended by the commission were quite controversial, and none had ever been implemented. Moores gave Hickman the green light to do what he thought should be done, and Hickman set about introducing sweeping changes in the province's legal system, implementing everything that was in the Gushue report.

One of the most politically sensitive issues was the matrimonial property act, giving women equal rights to marital assets. There was a lot of opposition to it from within the entirely male caucus, but Moores instructed Hickman to go ahead. Under the new law, Dodie Moores would have been entitled to considerably more than the lump sum he had settled on her. Hickman divided the court system, creating the first Unified Family Court in Canada and a Court of Appeal separate from the Supreme Court. He also introduced legal aid to Newfoundland, expanded the circuit court system, and set about upgrading the network of magistrates that Joey had appointed, few of whom had any formal qualifications for the job.

St. John's lawyers and judges were not anxious to travel outside the city, and the chief justice at the time particularly disliked circuits. People wanting to have a case heard had to travel or send their lawyer to St. John's or else wait until the circuit came around. For Hickman, getting the message through that it was the Supreme Court of Newfoundland, not the Supreme Court of St. John's, was not an easy task. Even so, under his guidance, the circuit court system grew: instead of three circuits of two weeks duration annually to Corner Brook and two circuits to Grand Falls, there would be circuits in three additional locations, Gander, Labrador, and Grand Bank, to occur whenever there was a demand.

The magistracy was under the control of the Department of Justice in the Smallwood government. None of the magistrates, except for those in St. John's and Placentia, were legally trained, and some were little more than figureheads who routinely phoned the department for advice on how to dispose of their cases. Some had served for years with no post-secondary education. Hickman developed an innovative plan to phase out the untrained magistrates without dismissing any of them. He approached the Dean of Law at Dalhousie University in Halifax and asked him to admit two magistrates a year, on Hickman's recommendation only, without any reference to their academic qualifications. Having reached an agreement, Hickman came back to St. John's and implemented a program to send the magistrates to law school and pay their tuition and transportation to and from Halifax, while maintaining their full salary.

In return they had to agree to work as relief magistrates during the summer and sign a contract to serve for nine years after graduation.

The majority agreed. Some felt they were too old to go back to school; some were afraid. Of the group of twenty who went though the program, only one failed to get through, and he was ill. It was an imaginative and humane way to deal with the problem, a tremendous opportunity for the magistrates, and also a good investment for the province. The result of the program was that by the time Moores retired, Newfoundland had a provincial magistrate's court made up of legally trained magistrates with a wealth of experience. Salaries were increased, and a new Magistrates Act enshrined the independence of the magistrates, who had previously been controlled by the Deputy Minister of Justice.

Hickman also decentralized and facilitated the administration of justice by overseeing the design and construction of several new courthouses. The one in Grand Bank is considered to be one of the finest courthouses in Canada. Its design allows for accommodation, without conflict, of the Supreme Court and a jury and the Provincial Court, and it has since been copied by other provincial jurisdictions.

The new courthouses were not typical of Moores's political priorities. Many politicians feel the need to erect monuments to themselves and show their constituents physical evidence of what they have done, placing more emphasis on building structures than on the people who will operate in and from them. Moores didn't have that need himself and never based the construction of anything his government built on the political ramifications.

Practically every member of caucus could make a case for at least one new school in his district, but Moores's priority was teachers. His own experience in a four-room school with what he described as "magnificent teachers" had convinced him that buildings were secondary to good, committed teachers. With salaries 40 percent lower than the salaries of teachers in Nova Scotia and Prince Edward

Island, however, Newfoundland's teachers were discouraged, their ranks were thinning, and there was no lineup of new graduates to take their places. A delegation of the province's teachers met with Moores and put forth their case, hopeful of getting a raise of some sort. After listening to them plead their case, Moores astounded them by telling them they would be getting a 40 percent raise all at once. They had no idea that the decision had been made before they even walked into the office.

In post-secondary education, though, there simply weren't enough facilities to prepare the province's students for career opportunities. Smallwood had developed Memorial University in St. John's, but outside the capital city, and in vocational training, there was almost nothing. Memorial was becoming crowded. In the four-year plan consultations in his and Farrell's Corner Brook districts, as well as in other districts on the west coast, community leaders had pressed the need for a satellite campus of Memorial, a junior college, where area students could complete the first two years of a university degree without having to travel to St. John's.

The democracy of Moores's cabinet was such that he and Farrell had to fight hard to get approval. The Treasury Board and John Crosbie were diametrically opposed to it, arguing that splitting the post-secondary resources was counterproductive and a waste of money and that the benefits to students from other areas of being exposed to the culture of St. John's far outweighed any expense and inconvenience. Moores and Farrell finally got cabinet approval, and in 1975 the Corner Brook campus of Memorial University was opened. In 1979 it was renamed in honour of Sir Wilfred Grenfell; today it serves some 1,300 students and grants degrees in fourteen disciplines.

There was a strong lobby from Stephenville to have the junior college located there. Instead Moores announced the establishment of the province's first community college, housed in buildings left vacant by the closure of the American air force base. The community college system Moores began with that first Stephenville campus has been enormously successful. Eventually renamed the College of the North Atlantic, it offers more than ninety full time courses on seventeen campuses around the province and one in the Middle East state of Qatar.

CHAPTER 27

Offshore Oil and Minerals

MOORES TOOK THE LEAD on offshore oil. He had discovered that the man who had brought about and negotiated the largest hydroelectric project in the world had no one in his government with any real expertise in energy of any form; Moores basically had to build an energy division from scratch. At the time, as Moores pointed out, experts such as geophysicists and economic energy analysts were not found on every corner, but found they were and persuaded to come to Newfoundland. At the end of 1972 the new Department of Mines and Energy was introduced, with Leo Barry as its first minister, and a division known as Energy Resources was created to assess the value of the province's offshore hydrocarbon resources.

Oil and gas exploration had been carried out to some degree off the coast of Newfoundland and Labrador since the mid-1960s, and it escalated in the mid-1970s with the search for new sources of energy. Moores recognized the potential for a new industry that could mitigate the losses of Churchill Falls, but here too, Smallwood's largesse stood in the way. Pieces of paper existed, handed out by Smallwood to John Doyle and Shaheen and some other 'friends' of government, giving them extensive rights to offshore oil and gas. Moores's government approached cleaning up that situation very delicately, ultimately making it clear that these concessions had no legislative backing and succeeding in having them nullified. The fact that there was very little protest confirmed that holders of the so-called rights were probably aware that they had no legitimate claim upon the resources.

Determined to avoid the difficulties experienced by Scotland in its hasty, ill-advised development, Moores set up an Offshore Advisory Council with representatives from the fishery, labour, municipalities, education, and industry to assist government in policy making. He also instigated an aggressive campaign to prepare the province for the new industry, looking closely at the Norwegian experience and what was happening in the North Sea as well as in North America. Leo Barry supported the more radical Norwegian approach to regulation of the offshore, a model which recognized that the industry spinoff could be as significant as royalties. His department developed a set of oil and gas regulations based on the Norwegian experience, which they considered to be among the most progressive in the world. These regulations included the Petroleum and Natural Gas Act, which required oil companies to disclose full information about their exploratory activities in the province's waters to the Energy Resources Division, information that, up to this point, had not been forthcoming. Ultimately the federal government adopted many of the same approaches, and the oil and gas regulations in place today are based largely on the groundwork of the Moores administration.

Between 1973 and 1975 Leo Barry and Newfoundland lawyer and energy specialist Cabot Martin held meetings around the island and in Labrador. With a slide presentation, they explained what was going on in Newfoundland waters in the field of energy, and how to take advantage of the opportunities it presented, at the time and in the future. The meetings were well attended, but to the average person, offshore oil and gas development was another slice of pie in the sky. While gas discoveries were made in the 1972-1975 period off the coast of Labrador (discoveries that are still undeveloped), the low level of activity resulted in a lot of "eyes glazing over," the same eyes, Barry observes, of many of the people who then had to be re-educated when Hibernia was discovered.

The most important aspect of offshore development to be settled was jurisdiction. In 1968 Pierre Trudeau had declared federal sovereignty over the minerals under the continental shelf and ultimately proposed a fifty-fifty sharing formula with all the Atlantic Provinces. The position taken by the Moores government, after extensive research and the retaining of leading international and constitutional lawyers, was that the minerals lying under the continental shelf adjacent to Newfoundland's shores belonged solely to the province.

When other Canadian provinces entered into Confederation, the ownership of their natural resources was transferred to the federal government by the British North America Act. However, Newfoundland had been granted this ownership by the Crown when it became a self-governing Dominion, equal in status to Canada, long before Confederation. Term 37 of the Terms of Union states: *All lands, mines, minerals, and royalties belonging to Newfoundland at the date of union and all sums due or payable for such lands, mines, minerals, or royalties shall belong to the province of Newfoundland.* There was obviously no doubt about the province's ownership in the mind of Joey Smallwood, who negotiated the terms, as he felt he had the right to give a significant portion of those resources away to speculators.

Ottawa's claim was based on a 1967 Supreme Court decision that awarded the mineral resources under the territorial sea off British Columbia to the federal government. Trudeau eventually agreed to a 75-25 split in favour of the provinces, at which time Moores decided to remove Newfoundland from the joint negotiations on the grounds of Newfoundland's distinct constitutional status. The stand taken and the case prepared under the Moores government established the foundation for a fight that would last almost four decades before it was finally won under Premier Danny Williams.

Conservation and the race for new energy sources were responsibilities not even contemplated when the Mines and Energy department was formed. Barry had to make a conscious effort to
ensure that the mines division was not ignored when, within a year,
events in the Middle East resulted in the cost of oil quadrupling
and energy becoming the critical issue. In 1973 Moores set up a
royal commission to investigate the "inconsistencies, inequities,
and shortcomings in the methods by which the province derives
revenue from the mineral industry." The commission reported that
concessions previously granted were too large, they lasted too long,
and development commitments were too low. Over twenty-five
million acres granted to four companies—Reid in 1905, Labrador
Mining and Exploration in 1938, Javelin/NAL in 1951, and Brinco
in 1953—were still being held.

Companies incorporated outside the province were able to
apply losses and exploration and development costs anywhere in
the world against income from Newfoundland. There was no lim-
itation on head office expenses or allowances for processing assets.
The tax regime was insignificant, and it was not unusual for a company to declare no profit in a given year and to pay no taxes. Between 1964 and 1979, 346,745 short tons of copper, plus zinc and
gold, were shipped from Rambler Mine in Baie Verte, and Brinex,
to whom Smallwood gave the concession, and never declared
enough profit to pay dividends to the ore discovers and original
holders of the expropriated mining rights, the Wells and England
families.

Following the commission's report, the government brought in
a new royalty regime, significant amendments to the Mining Tax
Act, a Regulation of Mines Act that required regular inspection of
environmental and safety practices, and new regulations on how
operations should proceed. The zinc mine in Daniel's Harbour was
an example of a successful partnership between government and
industry. Leo Barry thought that, from start to finish, this mine may
have come into operation more quickly than any other mine in

North America. "There was no nonsense," he told me. "We said, this is what the province wants"—infrastructure that could be used by the general population, such as hydro lines and improved roads—"and this is what we can give you in terms of support. We reduced the cost to the company starting the mine, and we had an infrastructure that could be used by everyone. It was great to drive up there a year or so later and see newly renovated homes, new boats, etcetera." The mine operated for twelve years, which, although not as long as the company had hoped, it was still longer than the government had anticipated. In the end both the company and the government were satisfied with their deal.

Sometimes Moores didn't make negotiations easy. "There were times we had to undo deals that Frank had done, because he was too eager to please," Barry told me, "but where we felt he had gone further than the regulations would permit, we'd say, 'We know the premier said this, but you have to face up to the fact that, here is the reality.' To give Frank his due, he would permit that to happen"; he allowed his ministers to save him from himself.

The Moores government also negotiated a federal-provincial agreement to develop up-to-date geological maps of both the island and Labrador and to publish them so private prospectors could get involved in doing further work. Such mapping was particularly significant in Labrador, where the scale had been one inch to fifty miles compared to one inch to one mile on the island. The mapping done in the Moores era provided the basis for the information leading to the discovery of the huge nickel deposits at Voisey's Bay.

CHAPTER 28

The Premier's Style

FOR A POLITICAL LEADER in tough financial times with tough decisions to make, being Mr. Nice Guy was a disaster; when Moores was making someone happy he was making someone else unhappy, usually one of his cabinet minsters. Handling calls in Moores's district, George Hutchings saw it all the time. "Regulations, departmental policy, or budget didn't mean a thing," he said. "The requests were usually for things that would have been done eventually anyway, covered in the next year's budget perhaps, and often they didn't require huge amounts of money. If it was for something like a woman needing a stove so she could cook food for her youngsters or something, he'd get emotional over it. He'd say, 'She's got to have a stove, George.' I'd say, 'Well, the minister said she doesn't qualify.' He'd say, 'Bullshit,' and she'd get her stove. The ministers used to go berserk, but I think sometimes he did it on purpose to irritate ministers who he thought were losing touch with the people and to remind them who was premier."

Sometimes there *were* huge amounts of money involved. When Finance Minister Alex Hickman told Moores there was no money in the budget for an expansion to the trade school that he had promised on a trip to Stephenville, Moores replied, "Damn you and the budget. If I had to run a business like you run the budget, I'd never get anything done."

To add insult to injury, Moores really was apolitical, and he was interested in listening to people's ideas no matter what their stripe. It endeared him to the populace, but it didn't endear him to his own party. When someone like Liberal MHA Eric Dawe was able to get the premier to overturn a fishery department decision to deny a processing licence to a constituent, it didn't win Moores any points with his caucus, even though the enterprise was very successful.

The legislative changes and reforms that Moores and his ministers introduced did little to change the economic status of most Newfoundlanders. Because of the recession, many people were worse off, but the public saw no evidence that Frank Moores's lifestyle had suffered. His attacks on Smallwood's patronage and corruption had insured that his own government would be closely watched by the deposed Liberals and the press. His travel, expenditures, and staff were under constant scrutiny; he and his ministers were assailed regularly for frequent trips to Europe with their wives and for generally playing fast and loose with public funds. The bon vivant style that was attractive in a revolutionary was far less attractive in a premier, but Moores was as unaccustomed to curbing his tastes as he was to being attacked, and he never really tried to live in a style that did not provoke controversy.

He didn't relish the day-to-day routine of running of the government, and with competent ministers in place, he saw no reason to be chained to his office. The press, accustomed to government's virtually coming to a halt when Smallwood was away, made much of Moores's absences from the House and the province. At one point he took to having an aide frequently park his Cadillac Eldorado in his spot at Confederation Building, and he had the lights of his office left burning late into the night to give the impression that he was there.

Times were different then, and a certain amount of privilege for elected officials was taken for granted and accepted. Politicians and voters routinely did things that would be unacceptable today. To Frank Moores the good life was as natural as breathing, and he was generous to a fault. I was involved in an event that was perhaps typical. At the ski club in Corner Brook one afternoon late in his term, he invited another couple and my husband and me to have dinner in Montreal that night. He was flying there in the CFLCO jet for a meeting and returning the next day. On the jet, the friendly and handsome pilot apologized for not having sufficient hors d'oeuvres on board because he wasn't expecting us, but we managed by sharing the premier's ample allotment of shrimp and other delicacies, and there was no shortage of wine and Scotch. We had a great night in Montreal and didn't see Frank until we were ready to go back to the plane the next day. This time the jet was well stocked. It touched down in Deer Lake, we got off, and Frank continued on to St. John's.

The jet was going to Montreal anyway. To us, the extras were the food and drink on board. We didn't even think about the cost in jet fuel for the diversion to Deer Lake, possibly a couple of thousand dollars. Such political perk behaviour was common under Smallwood and still goes on today, as evidenced in the 2007 spending scandal in the Newfoundland legislature; Frank Moores simply wasn't as discreet as Joey Smallwood.

The criticism was fierce. Everyone around the premier knew when it was salmon fishing season and partridge hunting season. That he was "gone upstream to spawn" was a common joke. Operating as the premier's assistant from an office next door, Vic Young knew better than most about Moores's absences. There was no doubt that they were frustrating and made for bad press, but as someone who had also worked under Smallwood, Young's perspective is a noteworthy contrast to the popular perception of the way Moores approached his job.

> "Frank was a businessman. He took on setting up organized democratic government, but I wouldn't say he loved

the job of premier. I think it was a burden to him, but he did it very well as a CEO, which most people, including me, didn't recognize at the time. Everyone knew what their job was and everyone did their job. When Joey wasn't there, nothing happened. When Frank wasn't there, everything happened, because people had their jobs to do. There's no doubt he put together the most talented cabinet in our history and he put them to work.

If someone could say that there was an urgent situation that had to be dealt within the next forty-eight hours, and Frank Moores was nowhere to be seen or contacted, that would be a very serious criticism, but that was just never the case. Even if he was on the river, we could reach him. No one could ever point to a decision that should have been made that wasn't because the premier wasn't around, and when he got at it, he got at it. The budget process is very intense, with meetings that last all day and all night and all next day, and at that time Frank was there. This was a job that had to be done, he dug in and got it done. He might say he wanted it done faster, he wasn't one for lingering around, but no one ever said Frank Moores didn't have a strong work ethic."

As well as provoking criticism from those in government, Moores was also alienating some of his grass roots supporters. He had decided to appoint Tom Farrell, who was having health problems, as President of Council, a position attached to the premier's office and not as arduous as a minister's post. Farrell hoped it might give him an opportunity to keep Moores more connected with the party troops around the province, but it wasn't easy. "I used to get mad at him regularly, because he was sloppy. I'd say, 'Ring somebody up, keep them happy, they're asking about you,' and he'd say, 'Oh yes, yes,' and then he'd forget it. If he was involved in a problem, he'd work twenty-four hours, but otherwise, ringing up and doing small things which are great for a leader to do, he had no time for that at all. He'd handle that when the time came, and he did, he loved the common touch, but he was lazy, bone lazy about keeping in touch with people."

One day around six o'clock a few of Moores's friends had joined him in his office for a drink. Farrell went into the office carrying a clipboard and said, "Are you going to do something about these calls?" Moores said, "Tom, you worry too much," whereupon Farrell "took the clipboard and threw it at him, right over his head, and hit the wall on the other side." Then he asked, "Jesus, what's the point?" and sat down and had a drink with them. "Whenever you were mad," Farrell said, "he'd just look at you, you know, and he'd smile, flash his teeth at you, and the next thing you'd forget it all. Like a Svengali, he hypnotized us all."

Away from the famous smile, people found that the charm wore off quickly. They weren't expecting a CEO and they didn't want a Svengali. In the middle of a national recession, with no money for development, the Moores government was not delivering on promises, and the premier was out fishing with big shots.

Well-known political and industry figures from around the world were introduced to Newfoundland's magnificent outdoors as the guests of Premier Moores. The government lodge on the Gander River, which pre-dated Moores, was sometimes used to entertain people, but Moores preferred shacks, tents, and a trailer on the river owned by him, Harry Steele, and Craig and Bas Dobbin. There they just sat on the bunks and ate their breakfasts from a linoleum-covered table; Craig Dobbin later expanded the property into a much more elaborate lodge.

His love of fishing and hunting endeared Moores to the common man in one way, but in the face of high unemployment and a stagnant economy, the way he enjoyed himself by entertaining important men on the rivers smacked of 'big ways' and didn't impress people who had to go to work or, if they had no work, thought they might be able to get some if only the premier stayed home and did his job. Moores admitted that, in the short term, possibly some of his entertaining was a waste of money, but he maintained that Newfoundland needed friends in high places. "Opening doors and access to money and credibility," he said, "was well worth the investment in paying for helicopter time or taking someone out on a boat and could reap benefits a hundred times over."

And of course he enjoyed himself, and he got a big thrill out of the reactions of powerful people to his beloved Newfoundland rivers. One of his favourite stories was about the American industrialist Bob Craft, the owner of International Forest Products, a trader in paper commodities, and later the owner of the New England Patriots. Craft came to Newfoundland to look into the paper industry, accompanied by his lawyer, Ted Sorenson, the former special council and speechwriter for John F. Kennedy. Sorenson and his wife weren't fishermen, but Moores took them in to enjoy a day on the Long Harbour river. Drinks in hand, they sat on the flat rocks at the river's edge watching the salmon jumping over the huge falls, four or five of them in the air at a time. Then a duckling came down over the falls and into the pool, head first and tossed around, followed by its mother and the whole family. The mother walked ashore, and they watched the ducklings follow her in single file to a place where the river was safe and she could lead them back in again. Craft and the Sorensons had never seen nature like this before. When Craft and Moores had to leave the next morning, the Sorensons asked if they could stay another day; they ended up staying for six days, falling utterly in love with Newfoundland.

Thirty years later Moores told me he had no regrets about that part of his life "because that's what I am. You have to be what you are if you're going to be genuine. I was premier and there were things I had to do. I was also a person who did his own thing, too, and I guess that was unusual for premiers. I knew there were people who got upset, but that was their problem, not mine."

CHAPTER 29

The Downhill Slope

FREEDOM OF SPEECH WAS INTOXICATING. In the first nine months of 1974 the province had had sixty-eight labour strikes, fifty-eight of them illegal. Missing the irony, Joey Smallwood announced he was returning to politics to save Newfoundland. The fact that the Liberals already had a leader, Ed Roberts, was no impediment to Joey, and he mounted a leadership challenge. The campaign and leadership convention was bitter and divisive, with Roberts winning by only 55 per cent. Moores had two years left in a five-year term and no intention of calling an election when, in the spring of 1975, Smallwood announced the formation of the Reform Liberal Party.

Moores was anxious to increase his majority. He was quietly polling, with positive results; Smallwood had had little time to organize, and the Liberal party was split. He was fresh from hosting a successful First Ministers' Conference in St. John's in July, where he had pushed through a resolution for a 200-mile fishing limit. With nine new seats possible due to redistribution, Moores called an election for September.

This campaign felt very different from the 1972 campaign. The Smallwood dragon had been slain once, and Moores didn't have the same enthusiasm about having to do it again. He made a few tactical errors, the first of which was overlooking the fact that opinion polls taken when there is no talk of an election often contrast sharply with those taken once the election has been called and the campaign begun. Smarting from what he considered sensationalist and irresponsible attacks in the House of Assembly, he decided that the government should not give the opposition credibility by responding to unfounded criticism during the campaign. Let them claim that roads in Newfoundland were in terrible condition; the government wouldn't dignify the claim by pointing out the three years of massive road improvements. Let them accuse the government of having done nothing for the common man; the government would not condescend to point out that collective bargaining and legal reform were crucial to the common man. It was an odd political strategy, to say the least.

Moores also believed that he didn't need the organizing services of George McLean in the 1975 election, and thus the control over publicity and campaign strategies was far less than in the 1971 and 1972 elections. On the other side, this was Ed Roberts's first campaign as Liberal leader. He had been preparing for more than three years, and despite the spoiler, Smallwood, Roberts was ready, running an organized and aggressive campaign.

This time Moores's opponent in his own district was media mogul Geoff Stirling, a great friend of Joey's who ran under Joey's Reform banner. If possible Stirling was even more colourful than Smallwood. He had just opened a television studio in Corner Brook, and at one point he campaigned on his television station for two hours, naked from the waist up.

The euphoric wave of hope that swept Moores into government had crashed on the shore of reality and receded, but as John Crosbie puts it, from the very beginning there was never any real recognition of the government's efforts.

"The first term involved a tremendous amount of work. I was working fifteen-hour days, with Come By Chance and the fantastic mess we had with the linerboard mill, wrestling that from Doyle, trying to save it. None of this impressed the public because they didn't know what was involved. The mess we discovered in Labrador, stopping Brinco from going on with the Lower Churchill on the same terms as the Upper, wasn't particularly impressive to the public because the public wants you to announce you're going to build this and that. Their background was Joey announcing things every day. So the government lost popularity during its first term. We never got any credit out in Stephenville for the linerboard mill. They went on strike. We're pouring money in, costing us a fortune to bring wood from Labrador and the sons of bitches went on strike. Three hundred people out there working didn't appreciate what we'd done."

Smallwood had had Newfoundland's pre-Confederation treasury surplus to fund almost every harebrained scheme that he dreamed up or outsiders proposed. In his book *I Chose Canada*, Smallwood listed under 'dreams that didn't come true' a replica of a German town, peopled by Germans, that would attract German tourists from Canada and the States; the longest Lover's Lane in the world; and tankers of orange juice being brought into Holyrood. When his chocolate and glove and hockey stick factories didn't pan out, he took to the range; dressed as a cowboy, he drove a herd of cattle down the Burin Peninsula highway with the idea of raising beef on the bleak terrain.

When Moores introduced his resource-based development policy, the province's surplus was long gone. Smallwood had squandered Newfoundland's money, and few protested because people were afraid to protest. The opposition didn't question him about it in the House because the opposition wasn't allowed to question anything. He was flamboyant and gave people hope. With unemployment rising, Moores gave them the truth: the country was in a recession and the government had no money to spend. The fact that few of Smallwood's schemes had worked in spite of the money he'd had to spend quickly got lost in the general economic dissatisfaction.

At rallies three miles apart, Smallwood outdrew Moores 850 to 450. All over the province Tory hands were not being shaken with the same enthusiasm as before, and when the lacklustre campaign was over the Tories had won thirty seats in the newly enlarged fifty-one seat House, lost five cabinet members, and polled less than half the popular vote. Once again, Joey Smallwood's ego got in the way of political astuteness. Instead of stopping Frank Moores, his Reform Liberal Party split the Liberal vote and prevented Ed Roberts from becoming Newfoundland's second Liberal premier.

Moores knew that PC popularity had faded somewhat, but the election results were a personal blow for the man who liked to be liked. In spite of the general rumblings, the size of the loss came as a surprise to him.

His second term was plagued with disillusionment and controversy. The freedom of speech and government reform issues that had been the priority of the first term were child's play compared to salvaging the Newfoundland economy. The government was constantly releasing figures about the number of jobs it had created and other economic improvements, but in 1975 unemployment figures hit a record high, the linerboard mill lost another $40 million, and a bitter trawlermen's strike split the province just as Moores ended a longstanding policy that gave welfare to strikers. Legislative sessions often deteriorated into unruly shouting matches and even fisticuffs.

In early 1975, Moores and Bill Marshall finally came to a parting of the ways. Towards the end of the previous spring's House Session, Tom Farrell showed Marshall a proposed contract that Farrell was uneasy about; a planned extension to Confederation Building, which had not gone through the proper tendering channels. The plans called for a long-term lease of up to 400,000 square feet of much-needed government office space at a rental of some

$800,000 per year; in a building that would be constructed by Craig Dobbin and financed by the rent payments. It was the final straw for Marshall. The contract could not be signed unless it was passed by cabinet, and the situation turned into what Marshall described as something like a dance: through the fall session and into the new year, they were waiting for him to be just five minutes late for a cabinet meeting to put it through, so he was always early. When the subject came up at a heated meeting, Marshall held his ground, supported by Gerry Ottenheimer and a couple of others.

Around 10 o'clock at night on February 23, Moores had a letter delivered to Marshall at his home. The letter said that if Marshall was not willing to take on a full cabinet portfolio with departmental responsibilities, Moores would call a press conference and announce that Marshall was resigning to pay more attention to his law practice; he requested Marshall's answer that night. Marshall told the nervous messenger that he would give Mr. Moores his answer in the morning. Moores called a cabinet meeting for the morning without notifying Marshall. Moores's press secretary informed Marshall that they were waiting for his answer. Marshall refused to budge, saying that he would give the premier the courtesy of issuing his statement first, and then he'd call his own press conference to tell the public his version of the story. Moores had underestimated Marshall, but even though Gerry Ottenheimer had warned Moores privately that he, too, would resign if the deal went ahead, the duelling press conferences were held. Marshall was later told that the late-night ultimatum had been Janis's idea.

Prior to this controversy, members who resigned had crossed the floor, but Marshall had no intention of doing that. In the House that day, Tom Farrell asked for a standing vote of confidence in the premier. Marshall, who had been moved to the back benches, would not stand up. He remembers thinking that at times he had been as close to Moores as anyone in the cabinet. He looked at Moores, he said, and told him that he would leave neither the party nor the caucus; he was there long before a lot of them and would be there long after they had gone. The public regarded Bill Marshall as straight as a die, completely ethical about government operations. It was an unnecessary and very public black eye, because Moores bowed to pressure and the deal was quashed within a week.

Moores believed in the concept and the spirit of public tendering, but total and strict compliance was too much of a stretch, intellectually and politically, for most people in the free-wheeling environment of the times. Comparing the smaller and fewer transgressions of his administration with what had gone on under Smallwood was pointless. Moores was the white knight who had campaigned on the importance of fair public tendering, and the public wasn't cynical enough yet to accept that he would bend the new law himself, let alone break it. This was, without a doubt, the issue that most tarnished the image of the Moores administration. Thirty years later Tom Farrell desicribed Bill Marshall as the conscience of the Moores government, and for his part, Marshall remained a keen observer of how the public tendering act was followed. "They observed it in the breach," he told me, "because they didn't want it, but it was observed even more so in the breach in the days when Clyde Wells and his troop came in. It's unfortunate nobody has gone into that."

In November of 1975 the province had had a mini-budget, which had never occurred before and has not occurred since. Although the world was in a recession, with inflation and interest rates out of control, and Canada had introduced an anti-inflation policy, the last of any belief in Frank Moores as a champion of the people disappeared when he went on province-wide TV to say that Newfoundland was broke; there was nothing the government could do but introduce a freeze on wages and hiring in the public service, hospitals, and schools. What people refused to recognize or acknowledge was that such action was long overdue in Newfoundland, even without the recession, because the province could not overcome its past. Perhaps the most realistic thing Frank Moores did as premier was to begin the Newfoundland restraint

Suspend formalities

Premier Moores and other guests at a civic luncheon in Bishop's Falls suspended formalities Saturday night and doffed jackets and ties as temperatures and humidity soared. The premier was in the central Newfoundland town to officially open the new fire hall. The dinner, held at the Lions Den, was tendered by the town to commemorate the opening of the new hall which houses two fire trucks and the fire department offices.

July 1975, in the heat of the campaign, Harold Collins in background.

Moores with Don Jamieson and Queen Elizabeth.

First Minister's Conference.

Congenial times in later years with John Crosbie.

ABOVE: The honorary Doctor of Law with his daughter Jill and Charlie White, Chair of Memorial University Boards of Regents.

BELOW: Moores's two closest friends, post politics, were Newfoundland entrepreneurs Harry Steele (middle) and Craig Dobbin (right).

LEFT: When Moores saw Beth Diamond it was the end of his rocky marriage to Janis Johnson.

BELOW: His marriage to Diamond in 1982 was a happy one and lasted until his death.

LEFT: A prolonged standing ovation brought the retiring premier to tears.

Telegram photo—Bill Sulley

An emotional moment

Premier Frank Moores rubbed tears from his eyes Friday night after he took the stage at the Mary Queen of Peace Parish Hall on MacDonald Drive for a tribute in his honor. The retiring premier couldn't be blamed for showing emotion following the reception he received from members of the Progressive Conservative Party. When he and his wife, Janis, entered the hall they were greeted by thundering applause and a standing ovation that continued long after the premier had taken his seat on stage.

ABOVE: The team that helped Brian Mulroney to become Prime Minister, inscribed "Frank, friend, advisor and key player, with gratitude, Brian. Moores is third from left back row.

BELOW: Moores with Brian Mulroney and Ronald Reagan.

TOP: A fishing trip with Jack Nicholas.

MIDDLE: In 1991 a chartered plane took strange bedfellows to Joey Smallwood's funeral. *Left to right*: Sergio Marchi, Ross Reid, Bill Doody, Bill Romkey, John Fraser, Jean Chrétien, Jack Pickersgill, Moores, Brian Tobin, Jack Mc-Carthy.

BOTTOM: Moores with the Mulroneys and Barbara Bush.

RIGHT: Moores with son
Stuart at a family wedding.

BELOW: Moores at Chaffey's
Lock on Beth's 60th birthday.
STUPHOTO

TOP LEFT: Granddad, the cook.

TOP RIGHT: The early fishing camp on the Cascapedia.

LEFT: With his son, Stefan, on Moores's last birthday.

BOTTOM: On the river ... the quintessential Moores.

program that would continue in some form for over thirty years, until the realization of income from the oil and gas resources, but at the time the program had a big impact on his reputation and how people felt about his administration. In April of 1976 the oil refinery at Come By Chance closed in the biggest bankruptcy in Canadian history.

Even though everything seemed to be going to hell in a handbasket, John Crosbie believed that Moores was in for the long haul. In response to a rumour that Crosbie was considering jumping to federal politics, Moores said, "I'd be upset if he left, but he'd certainly have my blessing." Nobody really believed him then, and when I asked him about it years later he laughed and said, "I probably would have encouraged John to run federally even before he did. I thought Ottawa was the perfect place for John and he was the perfect person for Ottawa, a bigger stage which suited him down to the ground. He was strongly encouraged. I think we did a favour to the federal party, John did anyway, by leaving. I suppose in one way I was relieved from the pressure of John's aggressiveness."

The pressure of his aggressiveness most certainly kept John Crosbie from being premier of Newfoundland. On May 13, 1970, before becoming party leader, Moores had told the *Evening Telegram* emphatically that if he was elected premier, he would resign after eight years, regardless of success at the polls, saying, "After that I sincerely believe that a party must refresh itself, and that includes bringing in new leadership with new ideas." Moores had not changed his mind about leaving office and obviously made a conscious decision to keep that information from Crosbie, who acknowledges that his career might have been quite different had Moores told him of his plans. "Frank didn't make it clear to me when I was going federal that he was planning to leave. I had no idea. If I'd known I might have chosen to stay and try to succeed him. Normally they never want to go. Very few political leaders leave voluntarily. I figured, having won the second election, Frank would try again." Crosbie was elected easily in a federal by-election in St. John's West in the fall of 1976.

Moores also found some diversion from the dismal provincial scene that year in the national Tory leadership race. He decided to back Brian Mulroney and discounted Mulroney's lack of elected political experience, believing him to be an attractive candidate, very articulate and very bright. Moores delivered over half of the Newfoundland votes to Mulroney and came close to securing a win. With westerner Claude Wagner leading, Clark second, and Mulroney third, Moores convinced Jack Horner, Wagner's lieutenant, that if Mulroney had to drop out his people would go to Clark, and therefore the only way to beat Clark was for Wagner's supporters to go to Mulroney; then Mulroney would beat Clark. It didn't happen. Moores later said, "The deal was made, but Diefenbaker got wind of it and hit the roof, which was probably a good thing because Brian wasn't ready to be leader of the party at that time." Despite the gloomy economic situation, Moores was more successful at home in 1976, winning two out of three by-elections.

Moores decided that one possible way for the government to help the economy would be to encourage Newfoundlanders to spend more of their vacation money at home. He had travelled for pleasure enough to recognize the huge tourism potential in Newfoundland and Labrador, and he created a new government department to develop it. Given the transportation obstacles of the time, even most Newfoundlanders had seen little of their own province, and the inferiority complex imposed by British colonialism and ingrained by Smallwood and Canadianism made many of them think there was nothing much in Newfoundland worth seeing anyway. Moores believed that if Newfoundlanders had a better sense of their own and their province's value, they could then be persuaded to travel within the province themselves. A common marketing strategy today, it was met with scepticism at a time when paved roads were just becoming the norm and everything 'from away' was thought to be better.

Moores commissioned the McConnell Agency from Montreal to design a campaign to promote Newfoundland's colourful history and develop tourism both at home and elsewhere. Part of the at-home strategy was aimed at school children. With enthusiastic advisors such as well-known educators Hudson Davis and Ged Blackmore, a Spirit of Newfoundland campaign was developed, using a board game and comic books to tell some of Newfoundland's myriad colourful events and adventures.

On the agency team that developed the campaign was a tall, beautiful senior executive named Beth Diamond. Beth Diamond saw Frank Moores for the first time when the team came to Newfoundland to present the campaign to cabinet. The first time she spoke to him personally was a few days later, when the team was invited to Craig Dobbin's house for a party in honour of country singer Charlie Pride. Dobbin recalled the meeting: "The minute she walked through the door, wearing that red dress, Frank took one look at her, and I knew we were in trouble."

CHAPTER 30

Time to Leave

IN 1977 THE GOVERNMENT could only be described as
under siege. In what he called the hardest decision he had made as
premier, Moores announced the closure of the linerboard mill. A
strike by hospital workers stretched into almost two months, and
Moores had to apologize to the province's nurses over a cover-up
by Tom Hickey, Acting Minister of Recreation and Rehabilitation, of
charges of neglect and abuse at Exon House, the provincial home
for developmentally delayed children. Government hiring practices
came into question and charges were levelled including bribery,
cover-ups, pay-offs, and patronage in relation to hospital and nurs-
ing home construction in the province. Allegations by Liberal
leader Ed Roberts that Moores had accepted an expensive television set from A.B. Walsh Electrical, a firm doing considerable business with the government, led Moores to call a judicial inquiry to
clear his name. Walsh eventually went to jail for fraud in relation to
other dealings with the government, and Moores was exonerated in
the TV deal.

The auditor general's report for the previous year, 1976, drew
attention to numerous public tender violations and cost overruns,
particularly in relation to the multi-million-dollar Health Science
Complex and Scrivener Projects (Nfld) Ltd., the project manager.

The opposition began probing into donations made to the Tory party by Scrivener and other contractors, and the public accounts committee began a series of investigations which eventually led Moores to ask Supreme Court Justice John Mahoney to conduct a public inquiry of the spending practices of the Department of Public Works from 1974 to 1977. Ongoing revelations from testimony at the Mahoney inquiry alleged a preferred list of contractors drawn up by Moores's closest friend, Tom Farrell, who was quoted by a witness as having said, "Don't worry about it, the civil servants will take the fall."

A new deal with Craig Dobbin to construct an office building adjacent to the existing Confederation Building dominated the headlines. Moores initially told the House there was no agreement at all with Dobbin, but in a fiery debate that lasted eighteen hours, Moores maintained that the government had negotiated with seven developers and that Dobbin's proposal was the best one. Then it was revealed that Dobbin had a letter of approval in principle signed by Moores and Tom Farrell, Minister of Public Works. Moores explained that it was only a directive of cabinet and not a legally binding minute in council and therefore could not be called a final agreement, but Dobbin had used the letter with Moores's signature to obtain bank financing. The distinction between a directive of cabinet and a legally binding minute in council was actually at the discretion of the cabinet secretary, Jim Channing. After the fiasco with Marshall about the office building and rental agreement, what Moores had actually done this time was to convene a cabinet meeting with only himself, Farrell, and one or two others, approve Dobbin's proposal, and send it down to Jim Channing, who had not yet done anything with it. Moores knew he was in real trouble, and around dawn he took a break, sending a message to Dobbin, who was in the gallery, to meet him in his office. There he asked Dobbin to write a letter informing the House that he had never been under the impression that he had a legal agreement with the government for the construction of an office building.

As far as Craig Dobbin was concerned, the bureaucrats had approved his plan and, based on Moores's letter, the banks were ready to lend him millions of dollars "to do what I want with after expenses." He said that he had already spent $400,000 for the design of the extension, and that he had gone to see John Crosbie, who, he claimed was astounded that Moores hadn't run the letter through the cabinet. Even so, Dobbin admitted that Moores might have had to resign over the issue because the pressure was so intense, but he added that Moores just "didn't have the guts at that time to face the adversaries within the party or outside the party."

In contrast Tom Farrell's memory of events makes John Crosbie the main adversary to the deal. "Crosbie was not going to stand for it, no matter what goddamned thing was signed, and one person that Frank was worried about all the time was Crosbie. Crosbie was on his back from day one, so Frank buckled on that, he had to, he had no way out of it. Dobbin was tough and had a brilliant mind when it came to making money and taking chances. He used to say, 'They can't close me down, the banks would go broke.' That's the attitude he had. Frank wasn't like that. Frank didn't have the balls Dobbin had, hard as nails. Frank was a country boy when it came to Craig."

The year ended with Moores taking personal responsibility for the widespread abuse uncovered in the fisheries gear replacement program, which had been initiated in 1974. The program, designed to help fishermen whose equipment had been destroyed by ice, had such loose guidelines that a man who had suffered an accident involving the severing of his penis and been sent to a specialist in the US was said to have had his expenses paid under the gear replacement program. While Moores was not Minister of Fisheries, he said it was easier to take the blame himself than to blame other people. The truth was that he had little fight left in him.

In January of 1978 Moores mounted an international campaign to support the seal hunt and to counter attacks on the industry by the Greenpeace organization. The hostility towards the seal hunt in the late seventies was at a pitch it has never attained since because the pro-hunt facts had never been presented to the European press. It was a subject Moores was passionate about, but the tour was seen by skeptics as an attempt to garner some favourable press and probably an excuse to get out of town for a while.

Moores engaged McConnell Advertising, and Beth Diamond was assigned to design and coordinate a campaign to explain to the European and American press "what the seal hunt was all about, why it was done the way it was done, how it looked to the public, but in fact how humane it was." The delegation was comprised of Moores, MHA John Lundrigan, pre-eminent marine biologist Joe McGuiness, veteran sealer Captain Morrissey Johnson, Tom Hughes, head of the Ontario Humane Society, and Beth Diamond.

Prior to leaving for Europe, Moores was slapped with a law suit by anti-sealing activist Brigitte Bardot. On American television, he remarked that Miss Bardot certainly knew a lot about the sealing, but she spelled it c-e-i-l-i-n-g instead of s-e-a-l-i-n-g. The actress did not pursue the suit.

The tour encountered major incidents in Germany and France, security was extreme, and Moores was the prime target. He received so many death threats in Germany that Interpol put the group on the top floor of a hotel, with an empty floor below them and Interpol agents guarding both floors. Moores recalled how the seriousness of the situation was driven home to him. "I wasn't allowed out of the room. There was a knock on the door and in comes this very slickly uniformed gentleman, very military top, knee-length leather boots, all that. He clicked his heels in front of me, took out a clipboard and said, 'Name.' I gave him my name. 'Address.' I gave him my address. He slammed his clipboard shut, stepped back, and went out the door. I said to the guy from Interpol, who was always in the room, 'What the hell is that all about?' He said, 'That's the information for your toe tag if they have to send your body back home.'"

The chemistry between Moores and Beth Diamond was obvious,

but even Frank Moores's mating instincts were no match for Interpol. The group was always together, but one night he and Diamond decided to slip away for dinner alone. They went down the back stairs of the hotel and ended up in an intimate little cave of a restaurant complete with violins. Moores couldn't understand why the waiter he beckoned over to the table didn't seem to know much about the menu until he took a good look and recognized one of the Interpol agents assigned to protect him.

The press conference in Germany was becoming abrasive when Second World War veteran Tom Hughes asked to speak and passionately contrasted the Germans' reaction to the killing of seals with their passivity towards the concentration camps. Standing in the back of the hall, PR person Beth Diamond died a thousand deaths, but from that time on the German press reported the Newfoundland as well as the Greenpeace perspective. The pro-sealing campaign of 1978 was successful in garnering balanced press in both Europe and the United States, but Moores resigned before the next season, and the momentum was lost. The model has not been followed by any other premier since, much to the detriment of the Newfoundland sealing industry.

By the time the tour was over, Moores and Beth Diamond were involved, but Diamond, already in a relationship that was falling apart and knowing Moores's reputation, decided she was better off forgetting the whole thing. One vivid scene changed her mind.

"I was still doing the youth project and was in Newfoundland on business again in the fall. Frank asked me if I would stay for the weekend, and I thought about it and decided I would. He was off somewhere, Corner Brook I think, and said he would pick me up at the hotel on Saturday morning about nine o'clock. I cancelled my flight. Nine-thirty came and went, ten o'clock came and went, ten-thirty, and I thought, I'm going home. I called the airport and got back on my original flight, going at twelve-thirty, and went to the airport. I was sitting in the old terminal in the departure lounge with the glass partition, reading, and I heard bang, bang on the glass, and there he was, motioning for me to come, and I said, 'No,' and he banged again. So I went out and he said, 'Where are your bags?' I said, 'They're aboard.' He said, 'We'll get them off,' and I said, 'No we won't. I'm going home.'

His chopper had been in trouble and they had to land, and that's why he was late. I didn't stay, I went home, but that's when I realized that maybe some of the things he had said to me were true, because there he was, the premier, knocking on the glass in the middle of the airport, not caring who saw him. It actually shocked me. I thought, He's not fooling around here, he's serious. I truly believe we were meant to be, and I think the last twenty-five years proved that."

The 1978 Speech from the Throne saw the continuation of spending restraints and promises to keep trying to jump-start the economy, emphasizing the potential for hydroelectric development of the Lower Churchill. Moores was looking forward to the announcement with René Lévesque planned for the following week that he believed would turn the public mood and generate optimism and faith in the future.

The "Vive le Terre-Neuve libre" at the end of Alex Hickman's budget was a tongue-in-cheek comment on the province's heavy economic chains, and Hickman hadn't intended it to stay in the final copy. It was appropriate, however, as budget highlights included increases in sales tax, tobacco tax, liquor tax, and electrical rates and a three-dollar daily charge for hospital ward care. Following the tabling of the budget, one of Moores's closest confidants and personal friends, cabinet minister John Lundrigan resigned with his entire district association because a promised hospital for their district wasn't included.

Faced with proposed cutbacks in their numbers as part of the restraint program, the teachers union to which Moores had given a 40 per cent raise were threatening action. Steelworkers in Baie Verte went on strike, followed by mine and mill workers at IOC, carpenters, and the province's more than six thousand civil servants.

On April 25 documents were tabled in the House by Steve Neary alleging that Tom Farrell, then Minister of Industrial Development, had been involved in corruption during his time as Minister of Public Works. In the early morning of the next day a fire broke out in the bedroom of Farrell's Elizabeth Towers apartment, almost gutting it. The confidential first and second police reports which implicated Farrell in deliberately setting the fire were deemed incomplete by the Director of Public Prosecutions, and a third report was ordered. Prior to the third report, the contents of the first two were leaked to the media, resulting in Farrell's being tried and convicted in the court of public opinion. The leak was later found to have been carried out by one Brian Tobin, executive assistant to Liberal leader Bill Rowe. The incident damaged Rowe's political career but was a portent of the slickness of the man who would become known as Teflon Tobin. Opposition members reported wire taps and files rifled, and one minister reported threats on his life.

In his ongoing efforts to make corruption charges stick, Steve Neary claimed to have proof that the premier, a party of his close government friends, and their wives had enjoyed a two-week holiday on a Greek yacht in the Aegean Sea, paid for by Scrivener. The truth—that Moores actually owned the yacht—was more interesting but less scandalous.

In July, under tremendous public pressure, Industrial Relations Minister Farrell and Labour Minister Joe Rousseau resigned to await the results of the Mahoney inquiry. Farrell was formally charged with having set fire to his Elizabeth Towers apartment, but a preliminary hearing determined that there were no grounds for the charge and the case was dismissed.

A CBC national radio broadcast reported that a poll taken that year showed that two-thirds of the decided voters in the province favoured the Liberals, while Moores's personal support was down to less than 25 percent. Federal leader Joe Clark was considered to be distancing himself from Moores; when he visited Newfoundland that year, Moores was out of the province, and it was reported that he had been asked not to be present.

For the man who liked being liked, liked to be shown affection, and did genuinely care about people, it wasn't much fun to feel unpopular for the first time in his life. Moores began making more frequent 'business trips' to Montreal, where Beth Diamond had ended her relationship and taken an apartment on her own. In October at the PC annual general meeting Moores told the delegates that this might be the last time he spoke to them as their premier. Emotions were running high, and a motion for leadership review was soundly defeated 342 to eight. He then said he'd be around to lead them into the next election, but on January 19, 1979, just into his eighth year, Moores announced his resignation, calling for a leadership convention in mid-March.

CHAPTER 31

What Do You Do for an Encore?

THE DAY AFTER he announced his resignation, in the kindest editorial towards Moores in some time, the *Telegram* said, "Time will reveal if the fact that he was so personable and persuasive on the hustings also made him too much of the nice guy when it came to making tough decisions in caucus and cabinet, to the end that his colleagues at times seemed to be riding off in all directions." Moores described to me what he was feeling at the time.

"I was quiet for a premier, and some people thought I had lost interest. I wasn't bored, but I didn't have the enthusiasm I did on day one, and we had done what we set out to do. We replaced Smallwood—that was a dictatorship—but what do you do for an encore? The biggest frustration we had was not having any money to do anything; my whole time there was, what can we cut that doesn't hurt, how do we try to make ends meet, which we could never do and still try to develop and help people. It was a tough time to be premier of the province. We could bring in democracy; that didn't cost anything. We could bring in a lack of fear. We could bring in the public tendering act; we could bring in all these sorts of things. But anything that cost any real dough, we couldn't. It was very frustrating. It was awful.

There were two reasons why I resigned. One was uncertainty about the leadership. The leader has a lot to do with which way an election goes. Could I pull it off again? I had severe doubts about that. A lot of the cabinet were saying yes when I knew damned well some of them should have been saying no. There was too much yes, yes, yes. Rumours were starting to stick about the corruption, which was totally untrue. I wasn't going to invent a new issue or a new person, so I was thinking that the only way the party could remain was a change in leadership."

Moores's second reason for resigning was that, when he was elected, he had announced that he would not serve for any more than eight years. Politics was a commitment for him but not a vocation. Aggressive as he was on the campaign trail, he had no interest in burnishing his own image once he was elected. "Some people said I was lazy, I've said it myself," he told me, "but I'm not a lazy person. There are lots of things that I don't think are important until they get to a stage that they have to be dealt with. It was a flaw for a premier and a flaw for anybody. But the ability of being able to sort out the problem quicker than most people would be able to is a plus, and you wouldn't be able to do that if you were working all the time."

Moores remained in his seat until the new leader was elected. On the day he walked out of Confederation Building, no longer premier, Craig Dobbin was by his side. They were on their way to a celebratory lunch. Moores excused himself early because he had to drive Janis to the airport. She was taking their son Stefan to her home in Winnipeg. Her outgoing flight left just in time for Frank to meet the incoming flight carrying Beth Diamond.

Brian Peckford's public statements once he assumed office seemed calculated to distance himself from and embarrass Moores. It was speculated that making Moores persona non grata was one of the conditions of Peckford's getting Bill Marshall and John Carter's support for his leadership bid, a rumour still denied vehemently by both Marshall and Peckford. Peckford denies any deliberate vendetta against Moores, but he does recall that even though Moores had assured him he would not publicly support any candidate to succeed him, he then supported Bill Doody.

Peckford himself may have been partly responsible for Moores's change of heart. Moores recalled that immediately after he resigned, Peckford came up to him and said that, if Moores hadn't announced he was getting out, Peckford was ready to lead the group on his own. "Not only was that unnecessary," Moores said, "it was a form of egotism and judgment that I began to worry about. It was just his nature to dwell on something and then be very aggressive with what he had to say." He believed that Brian Peckford became a very different man after winning the leadership.

Peckford publicly announced a review of policies and "certain decisions made during the latter stages of Frank Moores's premiership." Some of his actions were the routine changes of a new premier with new ideas; some were justified, such as rescinding Moores's lifting of a freeze on the development of fishing camps on Labrador salmon rivers; but others seemed to have no rationale except that Frank Moores had been involved. A *Maclean's* article quoted Peckford's calling himself the only honest man, because Moores and Smallwood had "bombed out" by letting themselves become trapped in deals that permitted outside interests to siphon off Newfoundland's share. When I reminded Brian Peckford of this statement, he seemed surprised and said, without hesitation, that the statement was wrong.

One of the victims of the "review of certain decisions" was the $600,000 Spirit of Newfoundland program. It had taken some time to develop the concept, gather all the potential material, design the games, comic books, heritage films, and teachers' manuals, and have it all produced. The finished products were delivered to the Department of Education in late 1978. Moores knew he'd be resigning in a couple of months and was pleased that everything was ready to be rolled out across the province. The rollout never happened. Moores deeply regretted the cancellation, and it contributed to his disappointment in Brian Peckford. "There was never one game played because Peckford said it was childish and a waste of money. Peckford was a very different man than I was, very different. We had had ranting from Joey for twenty-three years, and that's the last thing you wanted to emulate. Peckford came close when he became premier. He was a first-class cabinet minister, and there was no sign of the born-again until after he became premier." Today Brian Peckford doesn't recall the program and denies there was ever any attempt to discredit or embarrass Moores.

But Moores was embarrassed. He was charged with building an illegal fishing cabin in Labrador, even though he had gone through the necessary application process and had been given approval. He was acquitted, but the smear remained. He was also "hauled up" before the Public Accounts Committee and successfully defended accusations of using government funds to pay $56,000 for party polling. In a twenty-three page statement, he documented the three phases of this public opinion survey. It had been commissioned after numerous discussions with his new executive assistant, Rex Murphy, about the concern that the government had good programs but did not communicate them well to the public. Emphasizing that an uninformed public was a public not well served, he expressed his regret that the PAC, which he had initiated, was "being used for personal political advancement." He described the committee as McCarthy-like, noting that committee members who had been ministers in his government when the survey was approved were suffering from selective amnesia.

Peckford also questioned the Moores government's decision to make Mt. Scio House the premier's official residence at a nominal sum. He then decided to move in himself, at a cost of $100,000 to the treasury for renovations, furniture, and accessories, whereas Moores had paid rent for the house and provided his own furniture, drapes, and carpets.

Moores said that once he was out of politics, he didn't think it was his job to criticize his successors. All the same, he remarked about Peckford, "I think he thought that our government was corrupt, and he was almost disappointed when he found out we were not."

Moores still wanted to make Newfoundland his home base. He had bought a house in Hughes Pond on the outskirts of St. John's and set up a consulting firm in the city with former colleagues Bill Doody and John Lundrigan, but there was little need in New-foundland and Labrador for the kind of services Moores could pro-vide, and the business folded after a year. Moores also became involved in business with his friend Craig Dobbin. One day when they were sitting on a rock in Long Harbour, Moores told Dobbin that he intended to resign from politics. Dobbin said, "How the hell are we going to get in here to go fishing if you resign as premier?"

Moores answered, "The only way we're going to do it is if you buy a helicopter because we sure as hell won't have the use of the government helicopter."

"I don't have enough money to buy a helicopter. How about you putting up half?"

Moores and Dobbin shared the cost of a helicopter, but soon their pilot pointed out that they needed an engineer, and the engi-neer pointed out that he might as well service three helicopters as one. Thus began Sealand Helicopters, now CHC, which, Moores said, is the biggest helicopter company in the world; Moores sat on its board of directors and took stock options as remuneration.

Moores retained his great faith in the potential of Newfound-land port development, exchanging his vision of a super port for the fisheries for a huge one-stop service centre in Conception Bay for the oil and gas industry. Eric Dawe promoted the project, and he helped Moores find 110 acres of land on the north side of Bay Roberts and 200 acres at Shearstown that could be purchased for the site of a fully integrated offshore oil and gas service base called Port Atlantis. Over $3.5 million was spent on the engineering study, the plans, and meetings with potential customers and financiers. Key players were Petro-Canada, Great West Life, and Lavalin Engineering, of Montreal, the engineers of the James Bay hydro project and Expo 67. Another investor attracted to Port Atlantis was a company called NBM Land Holdings, the principals of which were a German businessman called Karlheinz Schreiber and the Bavarian politician Franz Josef Strauss, who was chairman of Airbus Industrie.

Eric Dawe's elegant nineteenth-century family home in Bay Roberts was the scene of many meetings and much of the entertainment involved in wooing the oil companies and financiers. Prospective investors and customers from places including Jamaica, Bermuda, Texas, and Calgary nibbled hors d'oeuvres and sipped cocktails around a cozy fire; they showed considerable interest, but they balked at the final commitment. Port Atlantis would have offered all the warehousing, offices, storage, wharves, equipment, and services needed by the offshore industry in one place, but in the end the oil companies elected to procure what they needed in various locations around St. John's. The Port Atlantis concept was arguably much smarter, and as far as Moores and Dawe were concerned, the failure simply came down to the fact that the oil wives and families preferred the social and cultural life in St. John's. The project quietly died, and Moores accepted the fact that he had to become a mainlander. In our last conversation he talked about how much it bothered him that people thought he had turned his back on Newfoundland. "After you have been premier, where the hell do you apply for a job? Where does a premier apply for a job in a small province like Newfoundland? I was relatively well off, but politics had drained me more than most people think. It cost me a lot of my own money every single year I was in politics. I was well off, but not so well off that I could retire, so I ended up in Ottawa."

CHAPTER 32

Reinventing Himself

IN THE FALL OF 1982, a simple invitation handwritten in sepia on cream deckle-edged stationary invited family and a few close friends to the marriage of Grace Elizabeth Diamond to Frank Duff Moores at Elgin United Church, with a reception to follow at Dorothy's Fishing Lodge, Chaffey's Lock. The Moores had a newly renovated house in Westmount, and the new Mrs. Moores was working with her husband trying to generate offshore activity and government consulting work. Brian and Mila Mulroney lived ten minutes away.

The Moores and the Mulroneys socialized and attended the same galas and events. By Moores's account he and Brian Mulroney were "never close friends, but we were friends and developed a respect for each other when IOC was the biggest employer in the province." Moores had joined Mulroney on many occasions at the Iron Ore Company of Canada's Labrador fishing camp. Beth Moores, describing both Mulroneys as very kind, lovely people, was very fond of Mila Mulroney from the minute she met her and remained fiercely loyal to her through the years of criticism to come.

But before Mila's husband could become prime minister, Tory leader Joe Clark, struggling to rebuild a weakened party, had to go. Moores says he became more and more convinced that Mulroney's biculturalism was the key to beating Trudeau. Shored up by a lucrative personal contract with IOC, Moores quietly started organizing a campaign to oust Clark in favour of Mulroney. "I was up to my ears in it; some people say that I headed it. I've always believed if you can't get elected there is no point being there. That's why I acted like I did against Joe Clark's leadership. I had never met a finer man than Joe Clark. I found him to be a gentleman and everything that is good. The only thing with Joe was that he couldn't get elected. If you can't get elected, politics is not where you should be."

For a year he had confidential meetings with Tory MPs and provincial presidents across the country. It was a hard secret to keep, and at least once it nearly got out. Elmer MacKay's office in Ottawa was across the hall from the office of Jeff Scott, from Hamilton, who was a Joe Clark man. Heading for a meeting in MacKay's office, someone went into Scott's office by mistake and asked if that was where the meeting was, to the horror of the other conspirators waiting behind MacKay's door a few feet away. Moores's attention to detail this time was concentrated on lining up delegates and getting the defeated candidates on side. Judging by what he knew of the provincial associations and information gleaned from the people he talked to, he was convinced Mulroney had a majority.

When John Crosbie announced his contention for the leadership, Moores was in an awkward situation, but he remained a political realist. "Crosbie lacked the national support that Mulroney had, and he had no support whatsoever in Quebec, especially after his remark that he didn't speak Chinese, either, but "I couldn't not support John," Moores said. "Being a fellow Newfoundlander, I had to give that impression. I didn't vote for him, but I didn't do one thing to damage him, either. I didn't say a word about him. I worked for Brian, and he knew that. It was never discussed, but he certainly knew." Beth Moores anchored their base in the convention stands with the Crosbie group while Moores worked the convention floor with his ex-wife Janis Johnson, Mulroney's Manitoba organizer, leaving several times to confer with her and other Mulroney strategists. Once Crosbie was off the ballot, Moores was the key player in moving most of his supporters to Mulroney, ensuring his election.

Moores denied charges by Dalton Camp that offshore money had financed the campaign, but he was splitting hairs. Austrian multi-millionaire Walter Wolf, former owner of Canada's Formula One racing team, later revealed that he had paid Moores's director's fees from one of his companies in order to contribute income while Moores worked to get rid of Clark, and Moores himself admitted that Karlheinz Schreiber "might have put a few dollars in the pot to help the cause." Wolf's Montreal home was one of several burgled in 1984, causing possibly incriminating records to disappear. According to German tax law, a middleman could facilitate the sale of German products to foreigners with such grease money, but in Canada, accepting it is a very different matter. Nonetheless Karlheinz Schreiber had quietly begun to make himself and his *schmiergelder* useful to Frank Moores and the man who would be prime minister.

With Tory power on the horizon, Moores purchased a small Ottawa lobbying firm named Alta Nova and renamed it Government Consulting International, GCI. He recruited Mulroney loyalists Gerald Doucet and Gary Ouellet and former Liberal cabinet ministers Francis Fox and Jean Marchand. The Moores were still living in Montreal, but they rented a furnished apartment in Ottawa, a very nice one that belonged to an Arabian princess. They would arrive early on Monday morning and go back to Montreal most Friday nights, unless of course there was an event in Ottawa that shouldn't be missed. Moores's secretary from Newfoundland moved to Ottawa with her husband so she could continue working with Moores, and his daughter Debbie worked there for some time. Debbie's description of the firm's work offers a bit of balance to the glitzy image GCI quickly developed.

"Lobbying was sort of new then, more like government relations. Companies, especially American or foreign, would want to know about all the regulations that would impact on their business. There was no e-mail. We went through all the legislation and put together a monthly bulletin. We had people who had worked in many different departments. They understood the legislation and the priorities of government and could help deal with the government. There weren't any other firms who put things together the way we did. We did research as well. If Federal Express wanted to clarify all the regulations that would affect their operations or someone wanted to make a presentation to CIDA, what's the best way to make it attractive to them, what would they be most interested in, what won't they be? It sounds so elementary, but it was standard stuff. Now the government has people who do that, but back then they didn't."

When Mulroney became prime minister the following year with the largest majority in Canadian history, GCI quickly became the most powerful lobbying firm in Ottawa and earned Moores a reputation as one of the most powerful men in the country. Moores scoffed at that suggestion and also at suggestions that there was anything improper in the way GCI did business.

"Total bullshit. I ran a business and I had good personal relationships. I could phone them, probably easier than anyone else because I had been in caucus with most of them and I had worked with some of them to help to get Joe retired. My power extended as far as the cabinet minister concerned wanted to come out and join me for a drink. I understood how the political system worked and the first thing I did was hire senior bureaucrats, some high-powered ones.

We had good clients, big clients like Budweiser and Mercedes etc., heavy duty, with good retainers, and you had to have good people to service them. The clients would tell us what their objective was and what they were trying to do, and we would advise them the best way to do it. We would take them to the bureaucrats who were going to be responsible for the file so they could get all the facts and figures established, and then we would keep on the bureaucrats to push it up the line. There's no point doing anything unless you maximize what you can do, and we sure as hell did that. We had people walking in the door representing some of the biggest firms in the world, asking if we would take them on. We would never take two people from the same area; if you had Budweiser you couldn't take Labatt.

GCI became controversial because it was so successful. We operated totally above board. Because of my association with politics and with Mulroney in particular, we became known as political lobbyists. I had no input into the government structure. I was not an advisor to anyone, including Mulroney, contrary to reports. I never mentioned one client we had to Brian Mulroney. If he knew, what could he do about it? The one thing that never worked was to go to the minister. Ministers never dictated to the bureaucrats in Ottawa, there were too many of them. We could tell people who they had to see, we could tell them how to approach them and what would work and what wouldn't, and we would follow through for them so it was pushed up so they got a yes or no.

They said we introduced contingency fees. That's probably true. I still believe in it. The other way, you have your money coming in and can draw it out for as long as you can without doing the job you were paid to do. I would rather have a situation where we worked like hell, and if we were successful we got rewarded for it. You take any salesman who gets a commission, that's what you're talking about. I'm a big believer in rewarding people who do a good job, and not rewarding people who don't. I know there are people who say you shouldn't have contingencies; those are people who are too damn lazy to get off their arses and work and earn any money other than through a base salary.

The consultants that were there in Ottawa at the time, and ones who saw an opportunity and came after, would float rumours about us because we turned Ottawa upside down as far as consulting was concerned. It was a great way to make a living, a great way to do a lot for industry, and good for the government because they got the proper proposals presented to them in the proper way. I couldn't see a down side until the rumours started to fly. The Air Canada resignation was a classic example. I was on the board of Air Canada, and the reason I resigned was simple: we represented Ward Air. Max Ward was in the charter business, and he decided he wanted to get into regular scheduling, worst thing he ever did. When he applied to be a scheduled airline in Canada, I had to get off the Air Canada board because I had a conflict. I had to represent him, and I could not do that as an Air Canada director. The Air Canada board was not a normal board like a business board. They were all appointees, this was a board of privilege. Our job was to go and see what the CEO had to say and then rubber-stamp it. There was no input by the directors of any consequence. In those days it was a political reward. I hated like hell to get off that board. If it hadn't been for the firm, I would have given up Ward Air instead of Air Canada, but the firm had an income from the Ward Air account and no income from my director's fees at Air Canada. I had no choice. Pierre Jeanniot (the CEO of Air Canada) got screwed up when he said Airbus was the reason I resigned. He had so much press pressure he had to say some damn thing. I was gone before that subject even raised its head!"

For a few heady years the Moores's social calendar featured names such as Queen Elizabeth, Queen Beatrice of the Netherlands, and

Queen Noor of Jordan; places like 24 Sussex Drive, the White House, foreign embassies, the American State Department, and the Knickerbocker Club; and events including Ronald Reagan's inauguration festivities and the Shamrock Summit. They watched the Super Bowl with CIA director William Casey, and Beth Moores enjoyed Academy Awards night with the girls at Harrington Lake. Frank Moores hosted and fished with industry CEOs and people such as President George H.W. Bush, Norman Schwarzkopf, and Dick Cheney at his fishing lodge on the Grand Cascapedia River or at Tree Top cabin in Labrador, the cabin which had caused the controversy when he resigned as premier and which he eventually sold to Harry Steele.

Fans of American television journalist Paula Zahn, watching a feature she did on President Bush, saw shots of the president sitting around a campfire with Frank Moores; the two might have been chatting about the day's fishing at Moores's camp and how Moores taught Jeb Bush's son to fish. On their last day on the river, the fog came in suddenly. Bush had to speak in Boston that night, so a helicopter picked up him and Moores from the river, still in their hip waders and fishing clothes. The secret service men, unable to get to that chopper, followed behind, bringing Bush's briefcase containing his speech, his clothes for the night, and the rest of his gear. Because the president wasn't allowed to travel without secret service protection, Moores was sworn in, quipping to Bush, "If you think I'm going to take a bullet for you, you have another thing coming."

Then in 1988 Frank and Beth Moores were not only dropped from the Prime Minister's guest list and inner circle without explanation but were actually "uninvited" to the New Year's celebrations at Sussex Drive. Moores chose nonchalance. "Beth was a bit upset because she and Mila were close. I wasn't the least bit upset. If he didn't want to talk to me, that was fine. There are people that I'm friends with; if that happened I would pick up the phone and say, what the hell is wrong with you? I wasn't close enough to Brian for that."

That was exactly the point Mulroney appeared to be trying to make. The official story was that Moores had said in an interview to the *Evening Telegram* that Mulroney wasn't likely to get re-elected. Asked what he thought about the Prime Minister's chances for re-election, what Moores actually said was, "If the election was held today, I think he would be defeated, but there is a long time between today and the day of the election. Who knows what the issues will be." Moores and Mulroney's relationship recovered somewhat from that incident, but not for long. It next got back to Mulroney that Moores said he was turning himself into a rock star and that, at a meeting held in GCI's board room with the CEOs of all GCI's client companies, Moores said that it was time for Mulroney to resign because he was hurting the party and hurting himself. The story was far-fetched at best, as there would never be a reason for Moores to have all his top clients together for anything other than perhaps a Christmas party, but Mulroney bought it. It would be ten years before he spoke to Frank Moores again.

Some say the estrangement with Mulroney was why Moores left GCI. It may have been a factor, but true to character, once the objective of building GCI into a successful business was accomplished, Moores lost the fire in his belly. He began to delegate more and more of the work, and by 1990 he decided to semi-retire for the third and last time. For a few years he enjoyed his new status in relative peace and quiet.

CHAPTER 33

Retirement

IN 1989 THE COTTAGE AT BIRCH POINT had been razed down to the original fireplace and rebuilt as a permanent residence. Beth Moores is originally from Toronto, and six of Moores's eight children and their children are in striking distance; only two remain in Newfoundland. Moores described Birch Point as tranquil and peaceful, surrounded by water like a miniature Avalon. "The climate is good here," he said, "and as you get older climate becomes important, but I'm always tempted to get salt and heave it in the bay to make me feel more at home."

The closest town, Elgin, a ten-minute drive away, has a grocery store, a drugstore, and a hardware store, and Westport, a picturesque town of about a thousand, with charming restaurants, art and antique festivals, is less than half an hour away. "In the Ottawa sense of social life," he said, "you could almost say we are hermits, very happy hermits. Craig Dobbin and Harry Steele are still my best friends, and we have some very close friends here that we see once a week, and of course when the kids are around socializing is an understatement. We are very happy here, living alone."

The rifts caused within Moores's first family by his affair with and marriage to Janis had eventually healed, and he had a friendly relationship with Dodie and a close relationship with his children and grandchildren. Because there was no antagonism between Dodie and Beth, family visits and get-togethers were easy, relaxed affairs and often included his and Janis's son, Stefan. He treated his sons and sons-in-law to an annual getaway at the fishing camp and pursued his interests in salmon fishing, bird hunting, golfing, and gourmet cooking.

Although Moores maintained that his favourite place in the world would always be the barrens of Newfoundland in the fall, he and Beth usually spent from the end of October to close to Christmas in Florida, and then they would return to Chaffey's for several weeks of family time—skating parties and big meals with children and grandchildren. The middle of January saw them back in Florida until April, golfing and playing bridge. During the spring and summer Frank would take several fishing trips to the Cascapedia River, Newfoundland, and Labrador. This was the usual schedule, but it by no means defined how he liked to spend his time.

Beth Moores gives an intimate portrait of the man most knew only as a public figure and few knew privately.

"I think the reason Frank lived so vivaciously was not for entertainment, but it was just his curiosity about life and people, who they were and where they came from, and about periods in history and how they related to present day. As much as he loved home, he loved travel and meticulously planned every trip, making copious notes about the history and culture, the best places to eat. He always asked questions, and he read voraciously. Our home was filled with huge tomes of history, wars, biographies, poetry, classics, and modern fiction, too. He had several books going at the same time, always, and he'd read about four newspapers a day, and magazines. He read it all, and he was a wonderful raconteur himself and could entertain with an endless trove of stories. I think if I had to pick what I loved most about him, it would be his keen wit and sense of humour. A day never went by, even at the height of Airbus, that he didn't make me laugh with a one-liner or acute observation.

He had so many interests that after living with him for twenty-five years there was still stuff that would come out of his mouth that I had no idea he had an interest in. He loved sports and he knew the stats of them all. He loved art and could quote poetry. He was an incredible seaman. He loved the theatre—drama, musicals, and especially British comedy—and music was huge in his life. We had drawers full of CDs, tapes, and old records. He loved classical music and Buddy Wasisname. Sometimes you'd hear the bagpipes playing in the car before you saw him coming, and he spent the last summer of his life on the deck listening to Il Divo and making tapes of his favourite music for the kids.

He made wonderful meals, roast beef and Yorkshire pudding, goose, wonderful sauces, gravy. His lamb was extraordinary. He made a lot of Newfoundland desserts and dishes—great pea soup, dumplings, game, partridge. He worked out of a Carbonear cookbook and his mother's cookbook. When it came to a special occasion, or if we had house guests, Frank would do up menus, breakfast, lunch, and dinner, on little cards. He loved it. He'd get right into the peeling of grapes, etcetera, and hand-wrote a hundred menus for his granddaughter Becky's wedding in a calligraphy-like script, and he always wrote with pen and ink. The grandchildren, except for the older ones, didn't know Granddad as anything but a cook. They didn't know he was a well-known man, premier, and so on. They knew that it was Granddad and he cooked the best meals, and when they found out they were coming here they would get really excited. I remember a housekeeper we had in Montreal, an older woman, who said, 'I have never been in

such an upside down house. Frank does the cooking and
you carry the logs up to the fireplace.' I could fix an electrical
switch; Frank would have blown the place up."

Moores stayed active on some boards, both for income and to keep
involved in the business world; he chaired some local community
college boards, got involved with the Canadian Legion, and headed
up a committee to save the local doctor when he was falsely accused. For a few years semi-retirement was good. Then in 1994 journalist Stevie Cameron released her book *On The Take: Crime,
Corruption and Greed in the Mulroney Years*. Cameron's hatred of
Brian Mulroney was well known in journalistic and political circles. Her book spun threads of innuendo, speculation, and un-
named sources into a case showing that the former prime minister
took huge kickbacks for influencing Air Canada to purchase thirty-
four airplanes valued at $1.8 billion from the European supplier
Airbus, instead of from the American company, Boeing. Karlheinz
Schreiber was the German connection, and Frank Moores was
named as the liaison.

He was contacted by the CBC program *the fifth estate* for an in-
terview. With the politician's wariness about selective editing,
Moores agreed, on the condition that the interview would be live.
The fifth estate declined his offer and went ahead in March of 1995,
without Moores but with an informant who was in the shadows.
Moores still wasn't taking the issue too seriously when, in early
November, he received a notice from his bank in Switzerland that
his accounts had been frozen.

An offshore account wasn't a big deal in the days before Internet
banking and transfers became common. Si Moores had one, and to
Frank, who never did own or use a computer, it would have seemed
like a reasonable way to collect his fees. He said he always had every
intention of bringing the money back to Canada and paying the
appropriate taxes, but they were overdue when he made voluntary
disclosure to Revenue Canada in November of 1995, after learning

that, based partly on the existence of these accounts, a Department of Justice lawyer had sent a letter to Swiss bank authorities requesting assistance in investigating alleged corrupt activities by Brian Mulroney, Frank Moores, and Karlheinz Schreiber. He later regretted his voluntary disclosure as one of the biggest mistakes he ever made. Coupled with the Department of Justice investigation, the disclosure provoked an investigation by Revenue Canada, and for twelve years, his accounts were frozen while they accumulated interest compounding at 12 per cent a year. When the investigation showed that there was nothing untoward about the accounts, the tax bill, Moores said, was 400 per cent more than the whole account was worth.

Much was made of one of these accounts. Moores had named it Devon, with the initials B.M.; Cameron's theory was that the account was named after a street that "B.M.," the former prime minister, had lived on. She didn't know that Moores had a strong sentimental family connection with Devon, England, and she apparently didn't notice that there was another person in his life, much closer to him than Brian Mulroney, with the initials B.M. The only way Moores could derail Cameron's argument was to make the records of that account public, and the only way to do that was to hire a Swiss lawyer, at a cost of approximately US $35,000, to procure those records. They showed that the account was in the name of Beth Moores and that it had never held more than $500. Frank had opened it for her as much for the novelty as anything else.

But from then on life changed. Beth Moores described what they endured as "absolute horror, this speculation and accusation, and we never knew where it was coming from or who was saying it or what it was based on. The worst part was not knowing, truly not knowing what it was all about." The media parked themselves outside the Moores's condo in a gated Florida community. Beth was accosted on her way to a building improvement committee meeting; Frank found a group surrounding his car and gave a terse statement denying any knowledge or involvement.

Everything they said or did was irrelevant. For almost three weeks, Brian Mulroney and/or Frank Moores and/or Karlheinz Schreiber were on the front page of every national newspaper. Reporters breached the security of Beth and Frank Moores's Florida condo building and got tossed out. High-powered cameras were set up on the public beach and trained on the apartment. Having not hung drapes so as to take advantage of the view, Beth Moores took to going around on her hands and knees. She describes what it was like:

"That whole time was so dark and so awful. Our life was getting up in the morning to the sound of the fax machine going, and I would put the coffee on—we lived on coffee and cigarettes. For days sometimes we didn't get out of our PJs. We had all the papers monitored, and they were sending us the clippings from that morning, and you'd start pulling out reams of stuff from the fax machine. I would spend an hour trying to flatten it all to the wall, and then we would read them, and then the lawyers would be on the phone, and that was how our life went. I was devastated by it and didn't have the tough skin that Frank had to have through his political days in Newfoundland. He saw it very quickly for what it was, he knew it was political. To say that he was devastated would be true, but nothing like I was. I could not believe that these people on the other side of the House could do this. That was my naivety.

Frank had a very interesting way of handling any problem that is thrown at him: he would go into a little bit of a depression and get very quiet and very focused. He would often pace, and if you spoke to him he wouldn't have heard you; he was just terribly focused in on the problem at hand. He would sort it in his mind and decide how he was going to handle it. Once he came to those decisions there wasn't a hint of depression. It was getting on with it, fixing it, and not crying about the fact that he was in this situation. I think his biggest upset about it was the effect it would have on the kids and on me and his family and friends."

At the end of November *the fifth estate* rebroadcast the March show, with the informant no longer in shadows. The mysterious informant who was given such credence and who was presented to the public with such drama because he feared for his safety was Giorgio Pelossi, a former associate of Karlheinz Schreiber. Claiming Schreiber had reneged on a promised 20 per cent cut, Pelossi had helped himself to some of Schreiber's earnings, over $1.3 million by Schreiber's account, been fired by Schreiber, and was being investigated for money laundering. However, information that tended to discredit Pelossi or any other source received little press attention. From the beginning, between Cameron's speculations and *the fifth estate*'s sensationalism, the story fed on itself.

At first, before I talked with Frank Moores, *On the Take* and Cameron's next book, *The Last Amigo*, seemed pretty damning to me. I hadn't paid close attention to the Airbus scandal as it unfolded. Like most Canadians I got my information from the media; I didn't believe the extent of the wrong-doing, but also, like most Canadians, I believed there must be something to the story or the media wouldn't be pursuing and reporting it for so long and with such determination. I should have known better, having made most of my living in the media and knowing full well what ambiguity and editing can do for reporters trying to make audiences believe what they want them to believe. Yet in my more than thirty years of media experience I had seen it done only with self-righteous fervour by journalists convinced that, in the interest of exposing wrongdoing, the end justified the means. I'd never seen speculating, implying, and manipulating information and misinformation done with malice.

I didn't think Frank Moores was above bending the rules, and I didn't know him well enough and wasn't naive enough to categorically dismiss all the allegations against him. To try to clarify the chain of events and evidence in the Airbus affair and be prepared to question him, I downloaded dozens of transcripts of interviews and testimony, national news reports, articles and analysis. Reading Cameron's *On the Take* and *The Last Amigo,* I gradually came to think that proof was not on her agenda. Even so, I read on, still believing there had to be something here and I was determined to understand.

To say that I arrived at Frank Moore's Birch Point house with any clear sense of his involvement would be a bit of a stretch, but I was as well informed as I could be, and I still had the where-there's-smoke-there's-fire mindset. Oddly enough, it was arriving at his house that put the story into perspective for me. The Moores had offered their hospitality, and I was to stay there for three days. Beth Moores met me at the Ottawa airport. During the drive to the house in Chaffey's Lock she apologized for not putting me in the main floor guest room with the ensuite bathroom because Frank was sleeping there. Battling cancer, he found the stairs to their bedroom difficult and wasn't sleeping well, and as his caregiver, Beth needed her sleep.

I was taken aback. Stevie Cameron had written that one of the things Frank Moores had done with the first of his ill-gotten gains was build a two-bedroom guest house at Birch Point. It was December, and I had packed winter boots in case I had to walk to the main house from the guest house after a snowfall. There was no guest house, and immediately I realized that a journalist who hadn't verified something as tangible as a house might not deserve any credence about the unverified and perhaps unverifiable material in her books. Beth Moores laughed and apologized again when I told her I had been expecting my own quarters, but the laughter was humourless, as it was when she talked of Cameron's story about how Frank had taken a prospective buyer through their house in Montreal, lifted the carpet to expose a safe in a snazzy basement entertainment room, and said, "That's where we kept the millions."

"It never ever happened," she said. "In the basement next to the apartment that we had put in for the housekeeper was cement flooring with two big laundry tubs and lots of cupboards, and set into the floor was a safe where we kept our important papers and my jewellery. The house went on the market on a Thursday or Friday, and there were two different couples that came through the door. I was there and Frank wasn't. I didn't show them the house, the real estate agent did. The first couple bought it. The room she talked about didn't exist. The only thing true was that there was a safe."

Stevie Cameron also says that Moores owned a lodge and fishing rights on the Cascapedia River worth at least two million dollars. There was certainly a lot of money tied up in the Grand Cascapedia camps, but camp owners, however wealthy, do not own fishing rights, and not every camp had the same luxuries. Third Island, the camp in which Moores had a part-ownership with Brian Jones, was one of the most modest, though still expensive by ordinary standards. Jones and Moores upgraded Third Island over the years, and Moores eventually sold his share to Jones for approximately $750,000 to offset the expenses and loss of income resulting from the Airbus affair.

CHAPTER 34

The Saga of Airbus

MOORES REACTED TO THE AIRBUS SCANDAL the same way he had to the Newfoundland opposition in the 1975 provincial campaign: he refused to dignify what he called groundless accusations by responding. Some of his close friends thought that was a mistake. Craig Dobbin was horrified. "I went to him a dozen times and said, 'Frank, you have got to start fighting back.' He didn't want to get into the public arena, he didn't have the dough, and he thought it would go away. It didn't go away for all these years, and it's not gone away yet. Jean Chrétien is a very vindictive man, an evil bastard, and they tried a lot of filth on Frank. He was smeared badly by that slut, and you can quote me, Stevie Cameron, and Linden MacIntyre and *the fifth estate*, not a very nice combination." Others had similar opinions.

Moores himself said little publicly but talked to me in recorded conversation.

"At the very beginning of the Airbus thing, I said, there's absolutely no truth to it. I had two conversations with people at Airbus. The reason I had them was because we represented MBB, which is Messerschmidt-Bölkow-Blohm, in Germany, and they produced the twelve helicopters that eventually the Coast Guard in Canada bought. That was our project with them.

In Germany they have a system where a politician is the chairman of some of these merged companies. Franz Josef Strauss, who was premier of Bavaria, was chairman of MBB. He also happened to be, on a revolving basis, chairman of Aérospatiale, who produced Airbus, and MBB was a German shareholder in Airbus. He got in touch with me and said they were trying in any way in the world to try to get a North American to buy their aircraft—anyone in North America, but Max Ward was his target because Max had a big operation. They wanted to get their plane at the gates in North American airports. That was the big objective. Strauss asked what they should do to influence Mr. Ward to buy an Airbus. I said you can do whatever you want, but first of all, your product has to be competitive in quality, and the price has to be lower because they're used to dealing with Boeing, McDonnell Douglas, whatever, North American suppliers, and in order for a European supplier to get in, you've got to come in with a very, very low price—a loss leader if you like. You've got to lose money on it if you want to get in. That was my advice to him. That was one conversation with Airbus.

Conversation number two was a couple of years later. A chap named Stuart Iddles, who was their sales president I think, phoned the office and said that Premier Strauss had asked him to call me on his behalf, that he thought he needed lobbyists in Ottawa. We already represented Ward Air, so he knew we couldn't be lobbyists for them, but who would we recommend? I gave him a couple of names and said these people would know the industry, know the Department of Transport, know the aviation business, if you insist on lobbying, and I also told him I didn't think having lobbyists would have any effect in God's world on what Air Canada would decide because Air Canada's decisions were totally autonomous. Air Canada never asked the government for approval. They had their financial studies; they had their commercial studies; they had their operating plans. And they weighed up every aircraft in the world, and when they made a decision to go with Airbus, it was based totally on qualifications, not on any political influence. There was no way any government could influence Air Canada to go against their own recommendations—I don't care who they were. I said, 'You don't need lobbyists. It is decided on merit, so what you should be working on is making sure you get the best plan in to the customer.' That was my second conversation about Airbus, my two contributions to the success of Airbus."

GCI was also engaged by Thyssen AG to help with a proposed project to manufacture a light armoured vehicle in Bear Head, on the Canso Strait in Cape Breton. Thyssen's Bear Head representative in Canada was Karlheinz Schreiber. Moores welcomed Schreiber and the Bear Head project with open arms.

"He needed help for these great plans for Canada, all of which, by the way, were good. The big thing about coming to Canada was free trade. There is a list of countries that are acceptable to NATO to sell armaments to, and the reason they wanted to be in Canada was to be under the umbrella. They would manufacture the same sort of thing as General Motors was doing, but they could supply the Marine Corps with a superior vehicle, which they did.

They had a vehicle called a Fuchs, fox in English, and it was totally self contained. Biological weapons wouldn't affect it at all; they could steam right through because it was sealed off. Their technology in engineering and armaments was superior. They had a big industry in Germany, but here they had much better access to the US potential than they could ever get out of Germany. They wanted to build a presence in Canada, and they needed a kick-start. People said the project was going to cost the government $250 million. Well, that's exactly what it was going to cost because there were 250 vehicles involved. The Department of Defence needed 250 light armoured vehicles, and they were $1 million each. It still cost the government $250 million, because they had to turn around to General Motors and order the same damn thing. The Thyssen project for Cape Breton, I still think, was one of the biggest opportunities missed by the federal government. They were guaranteeing five thousand jobs for a minimum of ten years in a depressed area, and all they were asking for was the right to bid on a tender.

The only thing they were looking for from the government was to put in the harbour facility at the wharf, because that was a federal responsibility, and nothing else except for the right to tender. We spent a lot of time and money, but we couldn't get it for them. So much for my influence. It seemed a lot of the senior bureaucrats—I'm not talking about the military, I'm talking about the bureaucrats—didn't know if they were working for the Department of Defence or if they were working for General Motors. A hell of a lot of them went to work for General Motors when they retired from defence, I know that. But we couldn't crack it at all, at all. It was a crime because it was a good opportunity.

Schreiber had that project, which everyone who was involved in thought was a good idea. Greg Alford, who was working for me, even went to work for him. Schreiber introduced me to the MBB contract, which was a mistake for me because the money that was made on that—the commissions from that is what I banked offshore, plus the fees that I got from Thyssen I banked offshore. That's where they were doing their banking, that's the way they operated.

This was the norm for them. We split the commissions, there's no question about it, as I understood it. He was the one that brought the customer. I was the one to follow through on it. Any commissions that we got for success, which is what it was all based on—and MBB paid a retainer to GCI as well—any success we had, the commissions would be split fifty-fifty. We had a partnership, for want of a better expression, without it being formalized.

The offshore bank account was mistake, but if every Canadian with an offshore account had to stand to attention, you'd have half of Bay Street on their feet. The crazy thing about it all is that if Airbus had paid these huge commissions, I could have taken them at GCI. I mean, this is what we did: represented people. But Airbus was never a client. Thyssen and MBB were, and they were registered as such. And if we had Airbus, we'd obviously register them. Why not? This huge amount of money which was supposed to have changed hands, it just never existed. And the idea that I was paid—Airbus paid Schreiber, Schreiber paid me, and I paid Mulroney—there's not a syllable of truth in it. How do you deny it? Say, 'That's not true,' that's all you can say."

The fact that Moores did not engage in any legal or public defence of himself added to the presumption of guilt. In the beginning he considered it. He started a lawsuit against the CBC but dropped it, and the presumption was that he felt he couldn't win. That he might have been concerned about the cost and also a bit intimidated by the legal process occurred to no one except people close to him. The Airbus affair had very quickly affected Moores financially. He was on the Canadian Helicopter and Vector boards and was due to go on others when Airbus struck. The expected directorships dried up. When the allegations didn't go away but instead started to expand, Moores called Craig Dobbin and offered his resignation. Dobbin refused to consider the issue.

Moores told his St. Andrew's schoolmate Chris Wansbrough, then chairman of Rogers Cable, that once when he was in Toronto on other business, he had dropped by the offices of the law firm he had engaged to advise him, just to see if there was anything new. Before he knew it he was in the office of his "big name lawyer," surrounded by a number of others, all of them taking notes. Adding up the billable hours that drive law firms, Moores estimated that that little impromptu visit cost him thousands. He sought advice from Roy McMurtry, who became Ontario's Attorney General, about dealing with a big Toronto law firm. McMurtry agreed with his strategy: to be on the record and have the law suit started, but not to be in a big hurry to spend hundreds of thousands of dollars or more, noting that libel suits at best are a double-edged sword for the plaintiff. Eventually the house in Montreal and the Florida condo were sold to offset the financial effect of Airbus. The last asset to go was Frank's share in the fishing camp on the Grand Cascapedia because selling it meant the end of an annual trip there with his sons and sons-in-law.

Moores's decision not to take on the press made him an easier target once Mulroney gained some semblance of protection with the success of his own lawsuit. In 2001 Stevie Cameron and *fifth estate* producer Harvey Cashore published *The Last Amigo*, billed as the culmination of ten years of exhaustive studies into the mysterious Karlheinz Schreiber. In Newfoundland Frank Moores's name had more resonance than Karlheinz Schreiber's, and Cameron announced in a St. John's television interview, "What we've been able to prove is that Frank Moores lied about his role in Airbus." She went on to say that he was a big player in the story and had received money from Airbus, and that she and Cashore had the documents, including Moores's bank records, to prove it. Cashore rounded off the interview by speculating that it was only a matter of time before charges were laid. In fact, while Karlheinz Schreiber had fought the disclosure of the records of his Swiss bank account, Frank Moores had had no such objections, and the RCMP had received all of his banking records in July of 1996, five years before Cameron and Cashore's book. No charges had been laid or were ever laid because Moores's accounts revealed nothing criminal.

On the one occasion when Moores agreed to talk to the press, he was bitterly disappointed. In 2003, when the RCMP announced they were closing the investigation, Deanne Fleet from CBC television in Newfoundland called Birch Point to get his reaction. Moores was in Ottawa at the time, and Beth thought she should get the message to him because "when you're dealing with the press from Newfoundland, you feel that they know him better and that they don't have an axe to grind. Plus we knew who she was." Moores went to the Ottawa studio for a taped interview. When the show aired, in the studio in St. John's with Fleet was Harvey Cashore. The program used little of what Moores said, and Cashore responded to or refuted what they did use with disdain or sarcasm, while Moores had no opportunity to respond to Cashore. Typical of Moores, he was more distressed that the reporter was from Newfoundland than he was about being "totally set up."

CBC wasn't alone in the selective presentation of the case. The RCMP were equally selective about what they chose to ignore and what they gathered as evidence. John Lundrigan was the lobbyist acting for Boeing when all this was supposed to have happened and thus had a vested interest in Boeing's getting the Airbus contract. His client had lost, and the RCMP expected that Lundrigan might give them something they wanted to hear. They were wrong. Lundrigan said, "I spent two hours with the RCMP in an interview, and I told them there was nothing there; if there had been I would have known because Boeing was not shy. The US Ambassador to Canada and the Boeing people and I used to meet regularly on this issue. There was always a big cry from Boeing and the Americans generally that Airbus was heavily subsidized. If Boeing had gotten the contract you wouldn't have heard a sound, but as far as Frank doing something illegal, it was total bullshit, and I told them it was a total disgrace, the worst kind of injustice that could ever befall anyone, to give that impression based on speculation, innuendo, suggestion, no evidence for anything."

One of the most astonishing aspects of the RCMP's handling of this case is who they didn't talk to. They didn't talk to the Minister of Transportation, John Crosbie, about a potential major scandal involving the prime minister and air transport, and they didn't talk to the accused, Frank Moores. In fact, once Moores realized that the Airbus affair wasn't going to go away, he contacted the RCMP through his lawyer and asked to make a statement; they put him off, more than once. Seven years after the investigation began, around ten o'clock one night, Moores received a phone call at home from someone at the RCMP asking to sit down with him and talk. Moores replied, "I have to check with my lawyer and my wife and not necessarily in that order." Beth Moores could see no reason for Frank to accommodate the RCMP at that point, after all that had happened, and his lawyer, Mark Gelowitz, agreed. Gelowitz then got a phone call from the RCMP suggesting that maybe Mr. Moores would like to unburden himself, to which he replied, and followed up in writing, "If Mr. Moores feels the need to unburden himself, he can talk to me or I will get him a priest."

John Crosbie doesn't mince words about Frank Moores and the so-called Airbus scandal.

"Never once did Frank come to me when I was a minister to ask me to do something about anything, but there were these rumours going around, so I got the CEO of Air Canada (Pierre Jeanniot) in and asked him about it. They had set up three committees: their directors, their technical, and their economic people. All three had recommended that the Airbus was better than the Boeing. Everything was on the up and up, purely a decision by Air Canada, and they had never been contacted by Mulroney or anyone from his office. Boeing and the American ambassador were creating a lot of trouble; Boeing and Airbus were savage rivals. Boeing, there was nothing they wouldn't do, bribery and everything. They've done everything under the sun. The whole thing was engineered by Chrétien, Allan Rock, and Herb Gray. All these years I have never been approached by the RCMP. I was the goddamn Minister of Transportation to whom Air Canada reported. The RCMP never once asked me if I had been approached or knew anything about it."

No member of the Air Canada board ever claimed to have been lobbied by Frank Moores or anyone else. In refuting the allegations that Air Canada was vulnerable to political interference, board member Milton Harris informed *The Globe and Mail* and its readers in a letter to the editor that during the first competition between Boeing and Airbus over sales to Air Canada in 1978, the Trudeau government favoured Airbus, but the twelve Liberal-appointed board members unanimously accepted Air Canada management's recommendation and purchased the Boeing 767. The letter was printed, but its contents didn't interest any of the press reporting on the Airbus scandal. I went through numerous newspaper reports written after the RCMP dropped the charges against Brian Mulroney for lack of evidence in April 2003, and in only one, by *National Post* Ottawa bureau chief Robert Fife, did I find any mention of the fact that the RCMP had apologized to Frank Moores. *The Globe and Mail* reported that Mr. Mulroney and Mr. Schreiber had each received letters telling them the investigation was closed. No mention was made of Frank Moores. He, too, had received a letter, but not the public apology he asked for. He just wanted to get on with his life, but some bitterness stayed with him.

"It didn't matter. I'm owed several apologies—it was the Department of Justice who wrote that crap, so the government should have apologized—but by politicians primarily. The Airbus thing was totally politically inspired. It had to be. Norm Inkster, who'd been the commissioner of the RCMP, had given public speeches to the effect that they'd investigated it for two to three weeks and knew there was nothing to it. And all of a sudden, it was resurrected again to keep Mulroney's name front and centre and remind people of what they themselves had made up, the corrupt Mulroney years. They didn't care who they hurt. They didn't care who was innocent or guilty—it was a strict political play. Someone had to keep stirring it, and in my view, it had to be that trio, Chrétien, Allan Rock, Herb Gray, because they were the ones in the departments responsible. Equally I think the RCMP was a guilty party to it, or Murray, the commissioner of the RCMP, was. I often wondered if it would be possible to record his confession if he ever had one, because if he hadn't had political influence on him, he was incredibly stupid. I mean, it just didn't make any sense whatsoever.

The press loved it because it sold newspapers. The more they could beat the drum, the better it would be. It was a vicious circle I got caught up in. Stevie Cameron became a celebrity for her best-selling books about a case that was actually conjured up by her obsessive determination to try and find something that would stick to Brian Mulroney. You read the allegations in her books and they almost become facts unless you examine them closely. There's no point in responding to them; she would just write another one. It is unadulterated crap and to give it serious thought is a total waste of time. Then we find out she was the informant. Her credibility in the literary profession has sure as hell been shot, if not totally, clearly a lot of it. There is no wonder she's writing about the pig farmer in British Columbia. She should be totally at ease."

Roy McMurtry, who started to read one of Cameron's books but was so offended by her journalistic style that he didn't finish it, said "I never believed for a moment that Frank would be involved in anything illegal and I still don't, him or Brian. I know Frank could be aggressive when it came to lobbying but there was a line that Frank would not cross that would bring his integrity into question.

Moores wasn't alone in his estimation of the political involvement. Bill Marshall, now a supreme court judge, while conceding that he thought Moores had gotten in way over his head, as he felt he had a tendency to do, observed, "There were two people who had to answer to how it is that the criminal justice system could be used for that purpose. It was obvious the Prime Minister of Canada and the Justice Minister of Canada were trying to use the criminal code in order to settle old political scores." Marshall went on to note that he knew Moores had an aversion for court, saying, "He had to be protected against himself because if anyone had sued him he would pay almost anything so he wouldn't have to go to court." Nevertheless, the constant accusations wore on him, and sometimes Moores thought that he "probably should have slapped a law suit on her right away." He was then sixty-six years old. "To take it to its end—and I would have taken it to its very end—it would have cost me millions of dollars, which I didn't have. It would have taken years out of my life, which would take me up to where I am now, with cancer, and life in retirement. Spending time with my children and grandchildren and enjoying the countryside and being able to read when I want to and relax when I want to or fish when I want to—it was a damn sight more important to me than vengeance against the government or Stevie Cameron."

CHAPTER 35

The Master Puppeteer

KARLHEINZ SCHREIBER SEEMED to be the common element in the various ways in which the universe began to fall apart around Frank Moores, and in this aspect, Moores, with his attraction to high rollers, was partly the master of his own fate. Just as he hadn't been put off years before by John Shaheen, he didn't seem to be put off in the least by anything about Karlheinz Schreiber, although he knew that many others were. In the relatively small-time Newfoundland power circles, Tom Farrell had described Frank Moores as a country boy when it came to Craig Dobbin. Dobbin would have been a country boy compared to Karlheinz Schreiber.

On one trip to Europe the Moores were invited to dinner at the Schreibers' Bavarian home. The residence was surrounded by high walls and contained a heavily armed room encased in steel from which Schreiber could monitor movement all over his property. A little unusual, but not unusual enough to convince Frank Moores to join the growing number of people who wanted to keep their distance from the outwardly affable German. Like most generous people Moores was particularly appreciative of generosity in others, and Schreiber catered to his tastes, on another occasion inviting the Moores to Vienna as his guests for the Opera Ball.

Schreiber's early professional life was spent with the Bundesnachrichtendienst or BND, the West German intelligence service. The BND's mandate was to uncover and inform the German government about potential threats to German interests from other countries, threats such as weapons and drug proliferation and trafficking, money laundering, organized crime, illegal migration, illegal transfer of technology, and information warfare. Because it was Germany's only overseas intelligence service, it is not unreasonable to assume that the BND also concerned itself with industrial and corporate matters.

Karlheinz Schreiber next emerged as an international arms dealer, lobbyist, deal maker, and a major fundraiser for the Christian Democratic Union under Chancellor Helmut Kohl. Kohl was credited with bringing about German reunification and was a key figure in creating the European Union, but the world-wide reputation he enjoyed during his sixteen-year chancellorship was destroyed by a massive party financing scandal when it was discovered that the CDU had received and maintained illegal funding under his leadership. Key elements in the scandal were the sale of army tanks to Saudi Arabia by Thyssen AG, secret code-named Swiss bank accounts, and a cash donation in excess of 1.3 million Deutschmarks from Karlheinz Schreiber in 1991.

Schreiber made people nervous when he was active on the Canadian business scene and behind the political scenes, and he still does as he fights his extradition to Germany. His influence is fascinating in its diversity. A former Tory cabinet minister, Elmer MacKay, and a former Liberal cabinet minister, Marc Lalonde, each offered a $100,000 surety to have him released on bail. A person very close to Frank and Beth Moores described to me the feeling that Schreiber was the puppeteer who pulled the strings that they all danced to. Not a particularly incriminating thing to say about Schreiber, except that the person was also adamant about not being identified because "quite frankly I'm afraid of him."

When I asked Moores to describe Karlheinz Schreiber, he told me it was difficult. "As a person I quite liked him, he was good company. He was generous, but having said that, Schreiber never spent a single cent on a physical asset for me ever, none whatsoever. I was independently able myself. Ambitious and, as the British would say, too clever by half; business was much more politically driven to him than it really was here. Whether he was dishonest by Canadian standards I don't know. As far as I was concerned everything was above board." He didn't tell me, but had told others, that he considered Karlheinz Schreiber to be a person you would not want to get on the wrong side of.

Moores leased his Florida condo through a company belonging to Schreiber, and Stevie Cameron implied that this had to be proof of something fishy. According to Moores, "There was nothing wrong with that condo business except in her imagination, to make her book sexier." Moores maintained he rented the condo from a company in Lichtenstein set up through Schreiber, paid all of the expenses, and furnished it; a portion of the rent could be included in an option to purchase it, which he eventually did. Moores may have chosen to see nothing fishy about the arrangement, but there's little doubt that Schreiber saw it as bait.

Key to the whole foundation of the Airbus affair was the close relationship between Frank Moores and Brian Mulroney. Canadians believed that Moores and Mulroney were in cahoots, getting their stories straight, whereas in fact the two had not been on speaking terms for years. My information, obtained after Moores passed away from a source close to Mulroney, is that it was the master puppeteer Karlheinz Schreiber who passed tales of Moores's supposed disloyalty on to Brian Mulroney. It was Karlheinz Schreiber who did not want the two men talking to each other.

Despite all the resources put into digging, all the testimony, and all the time that has passed, it is still not clear where the corruption surrounding Karlheinz Schreiber's activities in Canada began or ends. That there was corruption is obvious, and it may not have ended at all. It's quite possible that the only way he corrupted Brian

Mulroney was by offering him money after he left the prime minister's office and that Mulroney seemed to have to do little, if anything, to earn. Mulroney may well have felt he was entitled to it
simply because, in his own words, "If you accumulated all the sor-
row over my life, it does not compare to the agony and anguish I
have gone through since I met Schreiber." He may have corrupted
Frank Moores by offering him a good deal on a Florida condo, by
telling him that accepting commissions was not illegal in Europe,
and that a Swiss bank account was the way to go. Moores may have
been too willing to dance to that tune, but it was Karlheinz Schreiber
who played it. Schreiber's machinations certainly corrupted the objectivity of prominent Canadian journalists, the ethics of Canadian
parliamentarians, and the integrity of the Royal Canadian Mounted
Police. The true story of the Airbus scandal might better be called
The Master Puppeteer. Viewed away from the intricate plots conceived
by Cameron, MacIntyre, and others, a scenario presents itself that is
no less devious in its simplicity. It may in fact have been enacted another time, against Schreiber instead of by him.

In Germany in 2005 a former deputy defence minister named
Holger Pfahls admitted under oath to taking $2.4 million from Karl-
heinz Schreiber, who was hoping Pfahls could influence the German
government's decision about selling Thyssen tanks to Saudi Arabia
in 1991; Pfahls said that Schreiber had paid him by transferring the
money into a Swiss bank account. More serious corruption charges
were dropped after Pfahls admitted that he had, in reality, done no
lobbying of the government, and former Chancellor Helmut Kohl,
himself compromised by Schreiber, testified that Pfahls had not
attempted to influence the government's decision on the Saudi
deal. Pfahls was sentenced to two years and three months in jail for
accepting illegal payments from Schreiber. The fact that he hadn't
actually done what Schreiber thought he was paying for was not relevant.

Karlheinz Schreiber may have known this scam very well. In
1995 he had convinced Airbus that he could influence Air Canada

to purchase its aircraft. He stood to make a lot of money, perhaps the elusive $20 million, but his involvement was actually unnecessary and superfluous. Air Canada made the purchase from Airbus based on the merits of the aircraft and the deal. Perhaps Schreiber, not about to admit that he had nothing to do with the decision, accepted the commission and began to create the impression that he had earned it. Setting the stage with his generosity and building the scenes with wisps of rumour and innuendo, he may have been the producer of a puppet show starring Brian Mulroney and Frank Moores, with an ever-increasing supporting cast of politicians, law enforcement officers, and media, many with their own interpretations of their roles.

And everybody danced.

CHAPTER 36

Reflections

IN 2004 MOORES WAS DIAGNOSED with liver cancer and told to go home and get his affairs in order. A friend suggested a doctor at the world famous Sloan-Kettering Cancer Institute in New York who was having success with a treatment considered cutting edge in the US but still experimental in Canada. Getting in was not easy and time was of the essence. It was a Monday. Wednesday was the day new patients were seen at Sloan-Kettering. While a desperate Beth Moores was racking her brains over how to get Frank accepted, she answered the phone to hear a voice from the past.

Brian Mulroney wanted to know if there was anything he and Mila could do. After a few phone calls from the Mulroneys, to whom Moores still hadn't spoken to in years, and the help of the Montreal Canadiens team doctor, David Mulder, with whom he had fished, Moores had an appointment for nine a.m. Wednesday; thus he began a series of expensive visits to New York for treatment. For a few months the results were amazing. Some of his tumours almost disappeared, and this reprieve gave him hope for a few months and ultimately an extra year of life. He and Brian Mulroney finally began talking on the phone, picking up where they had left off, discussing the old days, the present situation, and all the good things.

In early 2005 Moores was once again contacted by a journalist from CBC Newfoundland. Doug Letto, host of the television evening news package *Here and Now*, was in Ottawa and asked if he could bring a cameraman and tape an interview with Moores at Chaffeys Lock. Frank was nervous again but decided to trust Letto when he said he just wanted to do a piece to let people catch up with him and see how he was doing. It was a good decision. Letto's half-hour special showed a thin, tired Frank Moores, talking candidly about his time as premier and emotionally about his children, who were with him constantly throughout his illness, tickling his back to make him feel better, cooking his favourite foods to tempt his appetite. Newfoundlanders were shocked to see how ill he looked, and an outburst of good wishes and affection followed. Moores got phone calls from people he hadn't heard from in years who couldn't possibly have guessed how much hearing from them meant to him.

Around the same time, Beth and Frank bought tickets for themselves and eight others to see Buddy Wasisname and the Other Fellers in Kingston. Moores, a big fan, had introduced their music and humour to many of his friends. When it came time to go, he was not feeling well but was determined to make the hour-long drive to Kingston for the show. After they came back for their encore, Kevin Blackmore, "Buddy," stepped to the microphone and said, "There is a very special person in the audience tonight who did a great deal for our province of Newfoundland, former premier Frank Moores." Buddy would have been amazed to know how much it meant to the modest ex-premier and his wife, who sat with tears in their eyes and then were surrounded by dozens of well-wishers. It was one of his last public appearances.

When Moores got sick, the old helicopter connection between him and Craig Dobbin took a turn neither could have anticipated. When he had to go back and forth to Toronto General Hospital, Dobbin sent a helicopter to transport him, and through Dobbin, Frank was able to keep a promise to his grandson. Moores had helped his son Stuart catch his first salmon on the Long Harbour River in Newfoundland, and he had promised the same experience to Stuart's son, Cam Duff Moores. Frank planned fishing trips well in advance. "Around March he'd start to set up for going fishing," Beth told me. "He'd be checking his lines; they'd be strung along, and he'd make his list, several pages long. One year I filed it, and the next year when he started to make his list, I hauled out this list I had kept. I have never seen anyone look so deflated in my life. That was part of the tradition, making a list."

Beth had been helping Frank dress for months and had her doubts about whether he'd be able to make the Long Harbour trip. She underestimated his determination. On June 26 Dobbin sent a private plane to pick up Frank, Stuart, and Cam in Kingston. "That morning I heard him bumping around downstairs," she told me, "and he was almost fully dressed by himself." Frank Moores returned to his beloved Long Harbour River for the last time. He was too weak to make it down to the river, but he had already taught Cam the art of fly fishing, and on the first day ten-year-old Cam caught his first salmon off his granddad's favourite rock. Two weeks later, surrounded by his family, Moores smiled that famous smile and passed away peacefully.

I had three days with Frank and Beth Moores in December of 2004 and another couple of days with Beth following the St. Andrew's memorial service for Frank in October of 2005. During the first visit, Frank and I spent a couple of hours each morning and afternoon recording.

Moores was keenly aware of the things his government failed to do, of his direct role in some of the failures, and ultimate responsibility for everything that happened on his watch. More in-depth reflections on "the negatives," as he called them, was to be the topic of another session that didn't happen. We did get into "the positives" because, he joked, "that won't take nearly as much time."

He was right about that for two reasons: As a society we give great importance to the process of analyzing mistakes and failures, to each theory, factor, and detail; if we are positive people, we do it in the name of learning and not repeating; if we are negative people, we do it in the name of criticizing, chastising, and even punishing. Achievements and successes do not inspire in-depth examination.

The other reason is that Frank Moores had no interest in listing and expounding on the hundreds of significant ways government and daily life in Newfoundland and Labrador was improved under his leadership. He thought of his contribution to Newfoundland in very simple terms.

> "I was proud of being premier, of course, but I can honestly say that at no time did I take it as anything other then being a representative of the people. I was very intolerant of cabinet ministers and backbenchers that I had who didn't realize what their responsibilities really were. I have always had one strength, really: I have always enjoyed people. I basically respect people a lot, a lot. I always have and, please God, I always will."

Frank and I discussed current politics in the place he still called home. Danny Williams was struggling with Ottawa for Newfoundland's rights to its oil resources, a struggle that Moores had begun thirty years before. Given the size of Newfoundland's population compared with the value of its resources, he felt that Newfoundland should have become the richest province in Canada long ago. In colonial days, he pointed out, the profits from the fishery and the pulp and paper companies were taken back to England, and nothing was ever reinvested in Newfoundland. The same thing happened with the Churchill Falls project: Newfoundland reaped nothing but the benefits of the construction. The offshore oil and gas, he believed, could provide the force to turn Newfoundland in the right direction; knowing I was going to see Williams shortly after I returned to Newfoundland, he said, "Tell him what he's doing is right on and to keep it up."

Although Moores chose to live on the mainland, there was no doubt about where his heart was.

> "I consider myself a Newfoundlander before a Canadian. Newfoundland's place in Canada has always been very tenuous. The attitude towards Newfoundland is almost like we're a mascot to Canada; tourists love it, but it's always been a place that no one takes very seriously. Newfoundlanders are much more independent about their heritage and their province than any province in Canada, with the possible exception of Quebec. If Newfoundland had fair return on its resources, I would say the likelihood of separation from Canada in Newfoundland would be much greater than it is in Quebec. Don't forget, Newfoundland joined Confederation by less than 1 per cent of the popular vote, and the terms of union were bad.
>
> The spirit of Newfoundland is still very much alive. I would love to live there, but I'm here and the kids are all around, so there's mixed emotions. Newfoundland has never left me, and I have never left Newfoundland in my mind and my heart, my memories and my thoughts. I could never be prouder of being anything than I am of being a Newfoundlander."

Moores said he'd never had "any great ambitions" about a legacy. "People are going to think of me what they do, but I would rather they thought of me as a decent person than someone who did a lot of harm. I guess I'd like to be remembered as a decent guy, somebody who cared about people, someone who had done his best, someone who was a good father and a good husband." He laughed and added, "To several people." Reflecting on his time as premier, he said that he had made mistakes, but he couldn't think of anything he had done that he was ashamed of. He paused for a moment, and then said:

"The affairs would be something I would be ashamed of in hindsight, not because I had them and not because I was premier, but because it would affect my children and people who were close to me who meant a hell of lot more than the affair. Politics had a lot to do with it. If I had never entered politics and stayed in Harbour Grace, I would still be married to Dodie, no question. The thing I regret the most in my life is hurting Dodie.

What I am most thankful for is having the luck of being born in Newfoundland, and I'm proudest of bringing democracy back to it, without question. There are three major events in recent Newfoundland history: one was when the Commission of Government was established, one was when Confederation came, and the third was when democracy was restored in the province.

The defeat of Smallwood sounds simplistic. Freedom of speech, which everyone takes for granted now, was not in existence when I came into power. The extremes that Smallwood went to in the end to silence criticism were absolutely mind-boggling. People of the age will remember, but people of this age wouldn't have a clue what it was like. You look at places in the world today with the same problem and you can't imagine that we broke though it, the same principles, the same situation, but we didn't have an army, thank god. Well, we had an army, but they didn't have guns. I hope history remembers that election that brought democracy to Newfoundland."

Epilogue

I LIKED FRANK MOORES. I believe that he lacked the toughness necessary to be a political leader, that his hedonistic side adversely affected his judgement and performance, and that, as Tom Farrell put it, "when it came to women he was terrible altogether." Even so, as I heard over and over from every quarter, "You couldn't help but like him."

I began researching this book with the expectation that I would learn some new unsavoury things about him. I didn't. I will be accused by some of not dwelling enough on Moores's weaknesses. In my opinion, that has been done for years, if not unfairly, then certainly disproportionately, and it is past time to bring his reputation into clearer focus. He died without seeing any of the contents of this book. When I realized how quickly he was weakening, I decided to send him transcripts of how some of his associates assess his legacy as premier. I was too late. I think it appropriate, particularly in light of the negativity attached to his name in recent years, to include a cross-section of those assessments here. The speakers are Charlie White, QC, a senior partner in a St. John's law firm, who was with him at the beginning of his political career; Bill Marshall, QC, retired supreme court judge, who became estranged from him; John Crosbie, his colleague and challenger, now lieutenant-governor of Newfoundland and Labrador; Vic Young, a senior civil servant,

now retired; and Bill Rowe, a former political foe who became a political commentator and is now an open-line radio host. Following
Moores's death, Rowe wrote an editorial for the St John's *Telegram*
entitled "Who Has Been Our Greatest Premier?"; the assessment
below comes from that editorial.

> I'd have to go with the man who was my political enemy,
> who reduced my colleagues and me to an opposition rump
> of nine MHAS, who deflected our ferocious criticism with
> humour and gentlemanliness as easily as he emptied a bot-
> tle of vintage Burgundy. He created a modern epoch of po-
> litical thinking and participation, a quantum leap from our
> immature political pubescence to near-adult maturity.
> Frank Moores is a true historic figure.
>
> — Bill Rowe

> Smallwood's lack of interest in anything that was not
> grandiose basically sowed the seeds for destroying our cul-
> ture. And a guy stepped forward who, at thirty-five, could
> have retired to the Bahamas or decided for the rest of his life
> to collect directorships, because he had the style and busi-
> ness smarts. He chose instead to go out and beat Jimmy
> Tucker in Bonavista and start a chain of events that led to
> Smallwood's fall. I don't believe he has gotten the recogni-
> tion that he should have. Frank was a great politician with-
> out the killer instinct, a very poor self-promoter. He changed
> everything. He took us from a third-world state into a mod-
> ern Canadian democracy. He did it. He spent his own money
> because we certainly couldn't raise any. He wrote the cheque
> himself.
>
> — Charlie White

The most prominent success that comes to the minds of
most when asked to address the positive aspects of Frank

Moores's legacy is the re-establishing of freedom of speech. That people were afraid to speak their minds in those days is completely beyond the comprehension of the new generation. I can remember when we were in Opposition and I was getting some information with respect to government guarantees. A person who I had great respect for had given me a tip and met with me in a hotel room. Before he would speak he opened the shower curtain to make sure that there was no one behind it. That reflected the sentiment of an awful lot of people. As the new style of governance became apparent to the general public, fear of speaking out on the conduct of government subsided. Soon criticisms and opinions were freely voiced as never before. To his credit, although he must have smarted at times from attacks directed his way from the genies he had let out of the box, Frank never attempted to stifle them. He maintained this aspect of open government to the end. That and his emphasis on rural development were his biggest accomplishments.

— Bill Marshall

Considering the environment he came into, what he had to deal with, the expectations of people, I think he did well as a premier. Because of the things that were initiated with Frank and his government, we have the offshore oil, for example. Smallwood had given Doyle and Shaheen control over the offshore, and we had to get in and put in a decent regime for the offshore and so on. Frank's government was best at things that improved the government, although they were not things the public was interested in. There were major accomplishments but not things the public thinks are glamorous, like establishing a plant with two hundred jobs. He had his foibles, but when it came to dealing with people, he had very positive virtues. He was the opposite of Harper, he was interested in people and people knew it. He was honest and pleasant. Overall, he should get high marks.

— John Crosbie

He was a visionary. He came in with big expectations, beyond, here is the lion killer, and Joey is gone. He was supposed to perform miracles and he didn't. It's as simple as that. The whole offshore oil jurisdiction issue started with Frank. By the time Frank left it was well under way, something he handed on to Peckford. He was not egotistical, he had a job to do and tried for eight years, and some of it worked and some of it didn't. He didn't like it, didn't get anything out of it. All the people who worked around him have a lot of good things to say about Frank. I often hear people say one of the best premiers we had was Frank Moores, and then when I question them on it they can't give me any details. I ask why, and they say, 'Because he was; he just was.'"

— Vic Young

The last word goes to Frank's daughter Debbie. "He knew in his own mind what he had accomplished, and we knew, and they couldn't change that, and to my father, unlike many politicians, what his family and friends thought was the most important thing. He didn't define himself as a politician or by his public image, so it (the Airbus scandal) affected him but didn't destroy him. He didn't have an ounce of self pity, even when he had cancer. Everyone says he was a child of privilege, which is true, but when he went to St. Andrew's he was probably one of the poorer ones. His family made money, but a lot of the others inherited money. He was the guy who talked funny and even looked funny, and I think it gave him perspective: you might think you're the top of the heap, but you can just as easily be at the bottom of the heap. It helped shape him in a way, gave him a perspective about not judging people. He never felt superior to anyone."

Selected Bibliography

Baker, Melvin. *Falling into the Canadian Lap: The Confederation of Newfoundland and Canada, 1945-1949.* Presentation to the Royal Commission on Renewing and Strengthening Our Place in Canada, 2003.

Cameron, Stevie. *On the Take: Crime, Corruption and Greed in the Mulroney Years.* Toronto: Macfarlane Walter and Ross, 1994.

Cameron, Stevie, and Harvey Cashore. *The Last Amigo: Karlheinz Schreiber and the Anatomy of a Scandal.* Toronto: Macfarlane Walter and Ross, 2001.

Collins, Harold. *Always A Straight Shooter.* St. John's: DRC Publishing, 2004.

Crosbie, John C. *No Holds Barred: My Life in Politics.* Toronto: McClelland and Stewart, 1997.

Feehan, Jim, and Melvin Baker. *Report into Churchill Falls Renewal Clause.* Division of University Relations, Memorial University of Newfoundland. 2006.

Fitzgerald, John. *Newfoundland at the Crossroads: Documents on Confederation with Canada.* St. John's: Terra Nova Publishing, 2002.

Gwyn, Richard. *Smallwood: The Unlikely Revolutionary.* Toronto: McClelland and Stewart, 1999.

Kaplan, William. *A Secret Trial: Brian Mulroney, Stevie Cameron and the Public Trust.* Montrèal: McGill-Queens University Press, 2004.

Kaplan, William. *Presumed Guilty: Brian Mulroney, the Airbus Affair and the Government of Canada.* Toronto: McClelland and Stewart, 1998.

Matthews, Ralph. The Outport Breakup, Horizon Canada Vol. 9. 1987. Quebec Laval University.

Report of Royal Commission to Enquire into the Leasing of Premises for the Use of the Newfoundland Liquor Commission. Government of Newfoundland, June 1973.

Smallwood, Joseph R. *I Chose Canada: Memoirs of the Honourable Joseph R. "Joey" Smallwood.* Toronto: Macmillan, 1973.

Smith, Philip. *Brinco: The Story of Churchill Falls.* Toronto: McClelland and Stewart, 1975.

Tobin, Brian. Address on Churchill Falls to Montreal Rotary Club (October 1996), and to Empire Club of Canada, Toronto (November 1996).

Wells, Janice. "Stephenville Theatre Festival Marketing Report." 1996.

Index